# HOUGHTON MIFFLIN

## WORLD REGIONAL STUDIES

Unless we know about the traditions and ways of life of people in other nations, we cannot develop an adequate understanding of the present-day world. The goal of the World Regional Studies series is to provide a well-rounded picture of human experience in these major areas of the world:

The Middle East

Africa

China

India

Japan

Russia

Using history as the organizing principle, the books in this series incorporate concepts and skills from the social sciences and from the humanities. Political and economic systems, geography, social organization and human values, the fine arts, and religion are all discussed in depth.

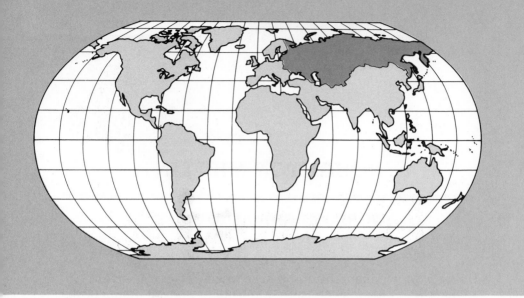

# WORLD REGIONAL STUDIES

# Russia

## Third Edition

### Michael Kublin
### Hyman Kublin

**HOUGHTON MIFFLIN COMPANY / Boston**

Atlanta / Dallas / Geneva, Illinois / Palo Alto / Princeton / Toronto

## Michael Kublin

Dr. Kublin received his Ph.D in History from New York University. He also has an MBA from Pace University. His area of specialization is Russian history. He is currently Assistant Professor of International Business at the University of New Haven and taught history previously at Kingsborough Community College in Brooklyn, New York. Dr. Kublin is also general editor for the Houghton Mifflin World Regional Studies series.

## Hyman Kublin

A specialist in non-Western history, the elder Dr. Kublin received his Ph.D from Harvard University. Formerly Associate Dean of Graduate Studies of the City University of New York, he taught history at Brooklyn College, the University of California (Berkeley), the University of Delaware, and the University of Hawaii. He was a Fulbright Research Professor at Waseda University in Japan.

## Howard R. Anderson

Dr. Anderson, consulting editor, taught social studies in Michigan, Iowa, and New York. He also taught at the University of Iowa and at Cornell University, and served as President of the National Council for the Social Studies.

Special thanks to Alison Lipski and Christine Walnycky, reference librarians at the University of New Haven Library, who were extremely helpful; and to Janet Blaustein Kublin, who did extensive research and editing. For valuable advice and assistance, the authors and publisher are indebted to Sydney Rosenburh, former Assistant Professor of History at Kingsborough Community College, Brooklyn, New York.

Cover photo: St. Basil's Church in Moscow's Red Square

The chapter opener art on the first page of every chapter symbolizes the onion domes that are characteristic of Russian architecture.

# CONTENTS

# MAPS

# CHARTS, GRAPHS, AND TABLES

# PHOTO ESSAYS

# INTRODUCTION

The year 1988 marked the one thousandth anniversary of the introduction of Christianity into Russia. In 1987 the Soviet Union celebrated the seventieth anniversary of the Communist takeover of the government. The Communists had come to power in 1917 on the ruins of the 400-year-old monarchy. The Soviet Union today is a blend of the old and the new. Certainly communism has had an enormous impact on every aspect of Russian life, but much about the Soviet Union of today derives from the country's pre-Communist past.

In the years since 1917 the Soviet Union has become, along with the United States, one of the world's two superpowers. What the future holds for this giant is a matter for speculation. Whatever happens, the emergence of Soviet Russia as a 20th-century superpower is a fascinating story.

## The Soviet Landmass

It is difficult to convey an impression of land as vast and varied as the Soviet Union, which occupies a large part of both Europe and Asia. A journey across the country from west to east would take a traveler more than a quarter of the distance around the globe. The continental United States has four time zones; the Soviet Union has eleven. Climate and vegetation vary greatly from one part of the Soviet Union to another.

As Russia expanded over the centuries, it came to govern many different ethnic groups. Today there are over 280 million people in the Soviet Union, speaking more than a hundred languages. No country is larger than the Soviet Union in area or contains more nationalities. Only China and India have more people.

## A Young Nation

Soviet Russia is a comparatively young country. A little more than a thousand years ago, most of what we call Russia was inhabited by nomadic groups. At that time the Slavs, the largest language group in modern Russia, lived in the eastern central region of the broad European plain.

From that plain they expanded in all directions across European Russia and into what is now Eastern Europe.

For hundreds of years the Russians focused their attention on the Byzantine Empire, which provided opportunities for trade and cultural borrowings. It was from Byzantium that the Russians learned about the Eastern Orthodox Church. After the Turks captured the Byzantine capital of Constantinople in 1453, the Russians increasingly shifted their focus to central and Western Europe. Later, in the 1500's, the Russians became interested in Siberia.

## The Problems of Frontier

Since ancient times, the European plain has been a broad well-traveled highway for invasions into Russia. As a result, security has been an age-old and elusive goal for the Russians. When they, in turn, began to expand, their goal in part was to find more easily defensible frontiers, or at least to create buffer states that would make penetration of the Russian heartland more difficult. Another reason for Russian expansion was the czars' desire for warm-water ports and access to the oceans.

## Czarist Regime

Almost 200 years ago Czar Paul (1796–1801) stated matter-of-factly: "No one in Russia is great except the person to whom I am speaking and only so long as I am speaking to him." Although Paul may have been exaggerating, he did exercise enormous control over his subjects.

By the mid-1400's the Russians were ruled by czars who held absolute power. The czarist system rested on the institution of serfdom, which tied millions of peasants to the land. This institution, which had declined in Western Europe several centuries before, ensured that Russian peasants remained poor, uneducated, and oppressed. Czarist power was supported by a privileged class of landholding nobles and a large inefficient bureaucracy.

The political development of Western Europe and Russia was very different. In most of Western Europe three groups in particular challenged the power of the monarchy: the aristocracy, the Church, and the merchant class. The nobles banded together and demanded that the monarch share power with them. The clergy and then the merchants also insisted on limits to monarchial power. Monarchs rarely relinquished their power without a struggle, but the nature of the struggle and the amount of power surrendered varied in each country. Throughout most of Western Europe, however, the eventual result was a decline in monarchial power and the rise of constitutional and representative government. The constitution defined the extent of government authority and the rights of the people. The representative assembly, based on ever-widening suffrage, became the ultimate seat of political power.

The Russian czars were unwilling to give up any part of their power to anyone. Others, such as nobles, bureaucrats, and church officials, might act in the czar's name, but they had no independent authority of their own. It is true that some individual czars were weak and sometimes groups of nobles' or even peasants' armies sought power, but these struggles were usually concerned with who would be the autocrat and not whether Russia should be an autocracy.

After the emancipation of the serfs in the 1860's, increased industrialization and the resulting social changes led to the rise of reformers and revolutionaries. In 1905 in the midst of revolution, the czar granted his subjects a constitution. A parliament was created, and the people were guaranteed certain basic civil rights. Actually the czar had given up little of his authority, but in time, the Russian people might have developed a democratic government. In 1914, however, Russia entered World War I. Two and a half years later, under the pressures of war and the accumulated repression of centuries, the czarist regime fell.

## The Communists in Power

For Russia 1917 was a year of two revolutions. In March the czarist regime was replaced by a provisional government. This was intended to be a temporary arrangement until the Russian people could elect a constitutional convention. In November, however, the Bolsheviks—Russian Communists— suddenly seized power. They disbanded the constitutional convention by force and imposed their own rule on the country.

The Communists created a new government structure called the Union of Soviet Socialist Republics. The government was controlled by the Communist Party, which, in turn, was controlled by a small number of people. The vast majority of Soviet citizens had no political power. They were allowed to vote, but only for candidates chosen by the Party. In theory the Soviet people were constitutionally guaranteed a wide number of freedoms. In practice the Party decided what was permissible and what was not. The argument offered to justify this state of affairs was new. While the czars had claimed that they had a divine right to rule, the Communists contended that they were merely acting on behalf of the people.

The successive leaders of the Soviet Union concentrated the nation's resources on achieving industrialization and military strength. Despite many setbacks, by the second half of the twentieth century the Soviet Union had transformed itself into one of the world's two superpowers. This achievement came at the expense of the people, however. Despite never-ending promises, the Communist regime has been unable to provide its citizens with a decent standard of living.

## Soviet-American Rivalry

After the close of World War II, only the United States was prepared to challenge the Soviet drive for expansion. Dedicated to different and often conflicting goals, these two superpowers contended against each other throughout much of the world for power and influence. Although their quarrels have never led to open warfare, they have backed third parties in local wars and made menacing statements to each other.

The possibility of a conflict between the superpowers has caused people great fear. The rivalry of the Soviet Union and the United States will continue, at least for the foreseeable future. On the other hand, there is much evidence that each side is becoming more willing to re-examine problems that divide them and to consider ways to scale back the arms race. Leaders in both countries realize that excessive competition in weapons production limits their ability to solve domestic problems.

## Democratization

Beginning in the mid-1980's with this lessening of world tensions, the Soviet Union began to "democratize" its political system and society. People became freer to do and say as they pleased, but this was democracy Soviet-style, not American-style. Ultimate power still resided in the Communist Party and the Party indicated no intention of sharing its power. No one can predict how long democratization will last or how far it will go. Just as the Party has allowed the people greater freedom, so, too, it may decide one day to restrict that freedom.

# 1

# Russia and the Russians

Two themes have dominated the course of Russian history over the last several hundred years: autocracy and geographic expansion. An **autocracy** is a government that has unlimited power over its people. For more than 400 years every important change in Russia came about through the dictates of the czar. In 1917 the czar was overthrown by a revolution and soon afterwards the Communist party came to power. The Communists still rule Russia. Like the czar before them, the Communists have been unwilling to share their power with other groups.

Today, Russia, now called the Union of Soviet Socialist Republics, is a territorial giant more than twice the size of the United States, Canada, or China. Since the USSR occupies a large part of both Asia and Europe, a trip across the country from west to east would take a traveler more than a quarter of the distance around the globe. However, Russia was not always a large country. During much of its history, it was a relatively small country in eastern Europe. But in the 1500's czarist Russia began to expand. Since then tremendous tracts of land have been absorbed in every direction, with the most sizable but not the most valuable gains being made in the east.

As Russia expanded over the centuries, it came to govern many different ethnic groups. Today there are more than 280 million people in the Soviet Union and they speak more than a hundred languages. No country is larger than the Soviet Union or contains more nationalities, and only China and India have more people.

# 1. A History of Expansion

The Soviet Union has been compared to an amoeba: expanding, always expanding. The country we now call the Soviet Union began as a tiny principality, the Duchy of Muscovy (Moscow) in European Russia. Over the centuries, land was added in every direction. Sometimes the Princes of Muscovy and their successors, the czars, had to fight long and bloody wars against powerful neighbors to gain new lands. At other times, there was little foreign opposition to Russian expansion. By the 1800's, Russia spanned large parts of both Europe and Asia.

Until 500 years ago, however, most peoples in Europe and Asia had never heard of the Russians. Sailors could not reach Russia because the region lacked access to the open sea. Moreover, strong and frequently aggressive states and kingdoms along Russia's western border made it difficult for the Russians to establish close contacts with the lands and peoples of central and western Europe. Great distances, vast deserts, and high mountains separated the Russians from Asia. It was only in the mid-1500's that daring English and Dutch explorers and merchant adventurers opened the northern sea route around Scandinavia to "mysterious Muscovy," as Russia was then called.

## Access to the Sea

For more than a thousand years the Russians were cut off from the various seas that enclose the continental landmass of Eurasia—Europe and Asia. Many Russian rulers were eager to have political and commercial relations with distant lands, but their hopes were frustrated by their inability to reach the sea. In time the expanding Russian state gained ports facing the White, Baltic, and Black seas. Long stretches of land facing the Arctic and Pacific oceans were brought under czarist control. Yet most of these territorial annexations were useless for the purposes the Russians had in mind.

Why were the czars less than satisfied with their acquisitions? Mainly because Russia did not gain its much-needed free access to the sea. (See map, pages 6–7.) Russia's usable coastline is small, since most of it borders the frozen Arctic Ocean. Good harbors are scarce. Leningrad on the Baltic, Murmansk and Archangel on the White Sea, and Vladivostok on the Pacific are icebound for many months of the year. Odessa on the Black Sea is one of the few major warm-water ports open the year round. But even from Odessa, Russians could not reach the open sea. For centuries access to the Mediterranean from the

Black Sea was limited for Russians because the Bosporus and the Dardanelles were controlled by other nations. By the twentieth century, Russia had acquired several thousand miles of coastline, but the country was still essentially locked in the interior of Eurasia.

### The World's Largest Plain

Northern Eurasia consists of several thousand miles of flat terrain. (See map, pages 6–7.) This enormous plain extends with scarcely a break from the shores of the Atlantic, into eastern Europe, and across Siberia. Called the Northern European Plain until it reaches Russia, it then becomes, in succession, the Central European Lowlands, the Central Russian Lowlands, and the West Siberian Plain.

An occasional line of hills breaks the endless monotony of the wide-open spaces. In the Soviet Union these include ranges in the Central Russian Uplands as well as the Ural Mountains, the traditional dividing line between Europe and Asia. But few of these hills represent a noticeable change in the terrain. For instance, the slopes on either side of the Urals rise and descend so gently that travelers can cross them without being aware that they have been on a mountain range.

For the most part, Russian history unfolded in the Central European Lowlands and the Central Russian Lowlands, the re-

With more than twice the area of any other nation, the USSR has 33 people per square mile, compared with over 288 people in China and nearly 68 in the United States.

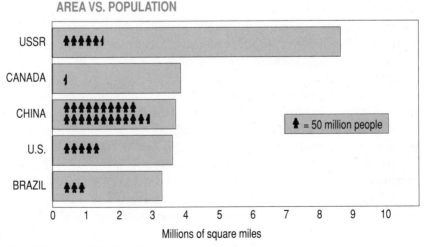

AREA VS. POPULATION

♣ = 50 million people

Millions of square miles

Source: *World Almanac and Book of Facts*, 1989

gion commonly known as European Russia. Only in the last century or two, have large numbers of Russians moved into the areas to the east. In the western part of Siberia, Russian peasants settled on the land as early as the seventeenth century and developed it into a prime agricultural region. In other parts of these eastern territories Russian settlers exploited the resources of the forest, opened mines, and engaged in fur trapping. But until the early years of the twentieth century Soviet Asia was a vast, underdeveloped land known mainly for its penal colonies and salt mines. Desperate as their plight may have been, few Russian peasants were ready to migrate into these frontier territories.

Since the Communists have been in power, they have made great efforts to develop Siberia. Thousands of miles of railways and highways have been built and communications facilities have been greatly improved. Industrial centers have risen where once only forests grew. Huge dams and hydroelectric plants, some of the largest in the world, have been constructed to harness the power of Siberia's rivers. The new cities of the region are so young that their names are not found on pre-World War II maps. By one means or another the Soviet government has seen to it that the flow of settlers from European Russia to Siberia has been maintained.

## Mountain Boundaries

Russians have come face to face with mountain barriers only during the past few centuries. For hundreds of years, the Russians were able to scatter in all directions without encountering these obstacles. It was only during the 1800's that Russian armies pressing into the regions south of Siberia met the many mountain ranges that now mark Russia's long southern land frontier. The highest mountains of European Russia are the rugged Great Caucasus, sandwiched between the Black and Caspian seas.

Stretching eastward from the Great Caucasus along the borders of Iran, Afghanistan, Pakistan, and India and then northward along the borders of Tibet and western China, are many of the loftiest mountain ranges in the world. The main bodies of these mountain belts, however, generally lie in non-Russian territory. These mountain barriers have checked Russian expansion, but they have not prevented the government of the czars, and later the Soviet government, from meddling in the affairs of the countries that lay beyond.

## Size as an Asset

Throughout its history Russia has lacked natural frontiers along some of its borders. Consequently it has been exposed to invasions from the southeast, the west, and to a lesser extent, the southwest. The Russians felt secure only along their long northern frontier and in the southern border region separating their land from the Middle East and South Asia. Several times the Russians were attacked by invaders who brought havoc and destruction. The most important invasions, discussed later in this book, were those of the Mongols in the 1200's, of Napoleon in the 1800's, and of Nazi Germany in World War II.

The Russians escaped complete disaster from the invasions because of their country's vast size. The great distances in Russia enabled the Russian armies to sacrifice land to the invader in order to gain time to gather their strength. Thus when Napoleon pushed back the Russian forces and captured Moscow, he found no government officials with whom to discuss peace. A shortage of food and the onset of winter compelled Napoleon to retreat. Winter weather and continuous Russian attacks destroyed his army. In World War II Hitler's armies reached the Black Sea and the Volga River. Once again the invaders found themselves short of supplies and faced with a severe Russian winter. Forced to choose between surrender and retreat, some German armies surrendered. Those that retreated were pursued by Russian armies all the way back to Berlin, where they, too, were forced to surrender.

## The Last Phase of Russian Expansion

The Soviet Union reached its present territorial limits immediately after World War II. When Germany was defeated, Soviet Russia retained much of the land in eastern Europe that it had occupied during the war. This included the countries of Estonia, Latvia, and Lithuania, as well as parts of Poland, Hungary, and Rumania. The Soviet Union also annexed scattered holdings along its southern border and in Asia. The most important of the latter were the southern half of Sakhalin (SAH-kah-LEEN), a strategic island off the coast of Siberia, and the Kurile (kyoo-REEL) Islands. Both had belonged to Japan before the war, and the USSR's continued occupation of them has aroused deep resentment among the Japanese. (See map, page 152–153.)

Although the USSR has apparently reached its geographic limits, it continues to exert enormous influence beyond its borders. The Communist nations in Eastern Europe, although tech-

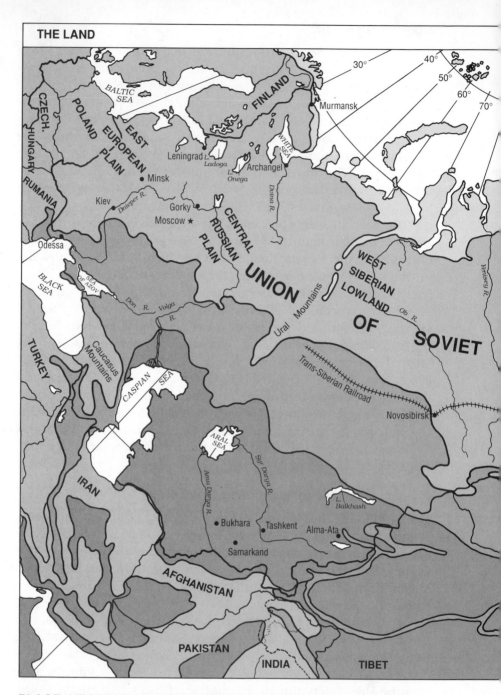

**PLACE: VEGETATION BELTS OF THE SOVIET UNION.** Three fourths of all Soviet people live west of the Ural Mountains, on the plains where the Russian state began. From this area the forests of the taiga region extend eastward,

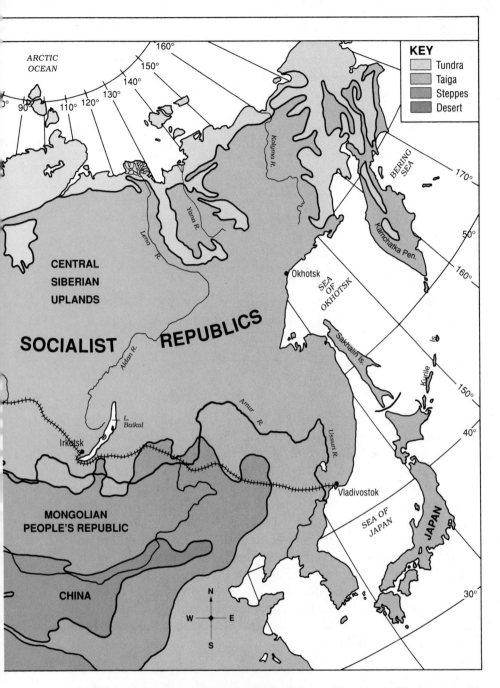

paralleling the fertile steppes to the south. Extreme climatic conditions make habitation difficult in the frozen tundra that forms the nation's northern rim, and in the arid deserts of the southwest.

nically independent, must be careful not to offend their powerful neighbor. In 1980 and 1981 the threat of a Soviet invasion convinced the Communist government in Poland to resist demands from the people for **democratization** of the political system. A stream of foreign aid to such nations as Cuba, Syria, and Vietnam has given the Soviet Union considerable influence in other parts of the world as well.

## Check Your Understanding

1. How did Russia's geographic location encourage expansion?
2. Where did most of Russian history take place?
3. In what two areas are there mountain barriers to Russian expansion?
4. How did the Soviet Union expand after World War II?
5. *Thinking Critically:* How has Russia's geographic location been a defensive asset?

## 2. Climate and Geography

From east to west the Soviet Union equals the distance from London to San Francisco, while north to south it covers as much territory as lies between Winnipeg and Mexico City. But since most of the Soviet Union falls in latitudes north of the U.S.–Canada border, the country does not enjoy the temperate climate of the United States. Moscow, the USSR's largest city, is farther north than Quebec. Leningrad, the hub of one of the Soviet Union's main industrial complexes, is in the same general latitude as Anchorage, Alaska. Even the "warm" section of European Russia, the Black Sea area, is no farther north than our Great Lakes. Most Russians have had to adapt to long, hard winters, a short growing season, and the need to develop fully every usable bit of land. The handicap of a northerly location has not been easy to overcome.

### The Coldest Winters

The Soviet Union experiences the coldest winters in the populated world. A classic description of winter weather in Russia has been provided by George Kennan, a famous American jour-

Winter in Siberia is a constant battle against the snow. The landscape is transformed when the frozen snow forms a second crust above the earth's surface. Although winter means great complications in most cases, the job of repairing telephone lines appears to be easier when the snow brings them within reach.

nalist of the nineteenth century. He recorded his impressions on a long journey through European Russia and Siberia in 1885–1886:

> Between Kuskunskaya and Krasneyarsk [towns in south central Siberia] we experienced the lowest temperature of the winter,—forty-five degrees below zero,—and had an opportunity to observe again the phenomenon of extreme cold. Clouds of vapor rose all the time from the bodies of our horses; the freight-wagon caravans were constantly enshrouded in mist, and frequently, after passing one of them, we would find the road foggy with frozen moisture for a distance of a quarter of a mile. When we opened the door of a station-house, a great volume of steam seemed to rush into it ahead of us; little jets of vapor played around the holes and crevices of the windows and doors; and in a warm room white frost accumulated to a thickness of nearly half an inch upon the inner ends of iron bolts that went through the window casings to the outside air. Throughout Friday and Saturday, January 15th and 16th, we stopped to drink tea at most every post-station we passed, and even then we were constantly cold. [George Kennan, *Siberia and the Exile System.*]

Kennan's route, it should be stressed, led through *southern* Siberia, in a latitude approximately the same as Moscow's. Had he traveled farther north, he would have been exposed to even more severe winter weather. The average January temperature at Verkhoyansk in north Siberia is about –59°F. The lowest recorded natural temperature on earth, –92°F, was registered in this locale.

Northern location alone is not responsible for the below-zero temperatures that prevail in large parts of the Soviet Union during the long winter. The British Isles are in the same latitude as Moscow, but they experience much milder winters. The difference is that the USSR has a continental climate, which is found only in regions that are situated at great distances from the sea. Unlike most of those countries along the eastern and western fringes of Eurasia, Russia is not significantly affected by the warm winds from the Atlantic and Pacific oceans. Long before reaching Russian population centers, these breezes have lost their force over neighboring countries. The warm tropical air currents from the Indian Ocean are prevented from penetrating the Russian landmass by mountain barriers along its southern frontiers. In addition, from the early fall until late spring all of northern Eurasia is exposed to freezing blasts and gusts of air from the Arctic. Snowfalls are so frequent and heavy that the sight of bare earth is rare for weeks and even months at a time.

During the late spring the snow and ice melt and disappear over large areas of northern Russia. For a few months warm and comfortable weather prevails. In the central and southern regions the summer season lasts longer. These areas, particularly the Ukraine and western Siberia, are the heartlands of the country's agriculture.

### Vegetation Belts

The vegetation in the USSR shows marked contrasts from north to south. Four belts of trees and plant life stand out sharply, although they overlap considerably as they approach one another. In studying the history of Russia, it is necessary to keep the characteristics of vegetation and climate constantly in mind. There is no doubt that the patterns of settlement, living, and the economy in Russia have been affected by these features of nature.

The bands are described below as they appear from north to south. (See map, pages 6–7.) The nearly treeless belt of **tundra** in the north is sparsely settled, and probably will remain so. The **taiga,** or forest land of Russia, has been the center of Russian history. Below the taiga is a fertile belt, known as the **steppes.** For centuries these grasslands were the homeland of fierce nomadic horsemen who repeatedly invaded the Russian centers of population to the west. South of the steppes is the broad belt of desert and semi-desert area. Together with mountain barriers, this band has effectively barred Russia from close contact with the Middle East and Asia. Advanced technology and modern means of transportation and communication have made these four belts less significant today than in earlier times, but their historical and cultural importance cannot be overlooked.

## The Tundra

The northern rim of the Soviet Union, including the offshore islands and the lands bordering the Arctic Circle, constitutes the tundra region. About 10 percent of the country lies within this zone. A geographic feature that makes the tundra almost uninhabitable is **permafrost**, a layer of permanently frozen ground hundreds of feet thick. Since this frozen soil can absorb no moisture, water from the summer thaw creates swamps all over northern Russia. The scanty vegetation of the tundra is largely made up of mosses and low grasses, although a few stunted trees are found here and there. The major animals in the tundra are reindeer, which are able to survive on the limited forage.

The dismal tundra wasteland is completely unsuitable for agriculture. Of the few people living there, most are nomadic hunters and fishermen whose people have occupied the region since prehistoric times. Parts of the tundra are rich in mineral deposits, particularly phosphate rock, iron, and nickel. The many lakes and rapids have made possible the development of hydroelectric power. But, in general, the tundra has limited economic value.

## The Taiga

Nearly half of the Soviet Union lies within the broad forest land called the taiga. From north to south evergreen trees—spruce and pine—and birch gradually give way to deciduous varieties. Until the 1500's, the ancestors of the Russians dwelled in the European sector of the taiga. Unable to cope with the warlike peoples who held the steppes farther south, they found a measure of safety within the deep forests that could not easily be penetrated by mounted soldiers. Today, as in centuries gone by, many homes in this area are constructed of wood, which is also an important source of fuel. Even now log cabins, similar to those built by American pioneers, may be seen here and there.

**A VAST LAND.** Spreading over two continents, the Soviet Union varies greatly in its climate and vegetation. The taiga's forests (above, left) provide a contrast to the deserts from the Caspian Sea to Mongolia (above, right). Herders tend cattle on the rolling steppes (right) and reindeer on the vast tundra (below).

It is little wonder that for many centuries the chief tool and weapon of the Russian was the axe.

Until the 1500's, the population of even the European portion of the taiga was small and scattered. The soil is rather poor, and the weather permits only a short growing season. When the Russians of early medieval times began trading with merchants of the Byzantine Empire, they had little more to offer than forest products. Today the inhabitants of the area grow rye, barley, and oats, which are suited to the cold climate and limited growing season. However, they cannot grow wheat, the staple of the Russian diet. Limited resources have always handicapped the development of the region.

## The Steppes

The superior soil of the steppes has always been coveted by peoples from the taiga. But these fertile grasslands have also attracted nomadic horsemen. For hundreds of years the steppe lands of Eurasia were fought over by farmers and graziers, with the more aggressive cattlemen, sheepherders, and horse raiders usually having the upper hand.

Free of mountains, forests, and other natural barriers, the steppes served for centuries as an invasion route for peoples from East and Central Asia. Mounted warriors from as far away as Mongolia were able to move rapidly across the flat grasslands in search of plunder and new homes. From time to time Huns, Avars, Khazars, Magyars, Mongols, and other warring peoples galloped westward across the steppes, not halting until they had plunged into central Europe. The Magyars remained to found the kingdom of Hungary.

The steppes were also sought after by states to the west and south. The medieval kingdoms of eastern and southeastern Europe sought to expand into the Russian steppe lands. So too did the Ottoman Turks. After several centuries of struggle the Russians, edging into the region from the north, finally succeeded in ousting their rivals. With this triumph the foundation was laid for the mighty czarist empire of the eighteenth and nineteenth centuries. In bringing the steppes under Russian control the Cossacks, hard-riding frontiersmen, made a notable contribution.

Southern Russia, especially the region in the southwest known as the Ukraine, has been an important agricultural area for hundreds of years. Since the early 1800's, the farmer's plough has steadily brought more of the lush grassland under cultivation. The Ukraine has been transformed into the "bread

## The Cossacks

The Cossacks were originally runaway peasants, fugitives, and adventurers. During the 1400's, these people began to form independent military communities in the steppe region along the Don and Dnieper rivers. Although most Cossacks were Russian, the word *Cossack* does not identify a specific ethnic or racial group.

Cossack frontier communities formed a **buffer** between Moscow and the Turks and the Mongols of the Middle East and Asia. The Cossacks were encouraged to seize and colonize new territory, which eventually came under Russian control. These reckless horsemen played a major role in the conquest of Siberia.

Each village was a military democracy where every man gave 20 years of military service. Men could vote in the village assembly and elect village officials. All villagers shared ownership of land and possessions. The Cossacks were fiercely proud of their communal governments and their rough military life.

In one respect the Cossacks were a constant threat to Moscow. Beyond the czar's reach, the steppes became a gathering place for revolutionaries, many of whom were poor peasants who had fled there to escape serfdom. Both the seventeenth-century uprising of Razin and a century later, Pugachev's revolt had Cossack support. (See page 78.)

By 1700 the Cossacks had come under Russian control. The czars allowed the Cossacks many privileges in return for military service. In 1869 a decree awarding land to all army officers undermined the communal land system of the Cossacks and introduced social classes within the villages. As experienced military men, Cossack soldiers enjoyed far greater status and wealth than the peasants. Anxious to maintain their favored position, many Cossacks actively opposed the 1917 Revolution. Afterwards the new Soviet government revoked the privileges the czars had granted the Cossacks, but they remained a distinct group within the country. The Cossacks are usually remembered as instruments of czarist oppression. Unfortunately their heroic exploits along the steppe and their major role in the conquest of Siberia are usually forgotten.

basket" of Russia. As late as World War I much of the country's grain supply was grown in this area, leaving an ample surplus that made Russia one of the major food exporting nations in Europe. Except when drought strikes, and this is a fairly frequent occurrence, southern Russia still produces abundant crops.

Wheat is the principal agricultural product of the Ukraine, although rye and barley are also raised. Sugar beets, cabbage, and potatoes are other major crops. Efforts have also been made to raise corn and cotton in this area, but cotton does better in the Caucasus and in Soviet Central Asia. In the Caucasus region such subtropical fruits as oranges and grapes have long been raised, and the tea of that area is famed throughout Russia.

### The Desert Region

During the 1800's, large territories lying between the steppes and the mountain ranges marking the northern frontiers of countries in the Middle East and South Asia were annexed by the Russian Empire. Much of this area was uninhabited desert or semi-desert. Here and there, however, where an adequate supply of water existed, old cities were to be found. Some, such as Tashkent, Bukhara, and Samarkand, were centers of kingdoms and empires of bygone days.

These desert regions have posed a challenge to successive Russian governments. In some areas sources of water for irrigation have been found, and these lands have been turned into cotton producing areas. For the most part, however, the barren lands have little economic value.

## Check Your Understanding

1. List and describe the four vegetation belts in the Soviet Union.
2. How has each region affected Russian history?
3. **Thinking Critically:** In what ways has Russia's climate been a handicap to its development?

## 3. The Problem of Transportation

In a country as huge as Russia, a transportation problem is to be expected. The Communists have made some progress in solving the problem, but transportation facilities are still inadequate.

Soviet leaders have had greater success in linking their country to others than in joining the various regions of the Soviet Union itself. Only one railroad crosses the breadth of the land, roads in many areas are in poor shape, and air service to many parts of the Soviet Union is infrequent and unreliable. River transportation is good in European Russia, poor in Soviet Asia. Despite great efforts on the part of Soviet leaders, there is little possibility that the problem of transportation will be solved in the foreseeable future.

## Soviet Railroads

Far more so than the United States, the Soviet Union relies on railroads to transport goods and people. In the Soviet Union about 70 percent of all freight goes by rail. For the United States the figure is about 37 percent. The Soviet Union has the longest continuous railroad in the world, the Trans-Siberian Railroad. Running from the Polish frontier to Vladivostok, it is 6,284 miles long and requires 9.5 days to travel. Railroads connect all major cities and industrial centers in the Soviet Union.

A good part of Russia's railway system was built before the Russian Revolution of 1917. In its attempt to catch up with the West, the Soviet government began stressing rapid **industrialization,** but the pre-1917 railway system was inadequate for the country's economic needs. Although the Communists have tried to enlarge and improve the railway system, much work still needs to be done. Schedules are unreliable, warehousing facilities are inadequate, and, most of all, the system itself is in much need of repair. Indeed, by the late 1980's, Soviet railroads actually carried less freight than they had in the previous decade. Factories often have to hold up production because parts fail to arrive on time. Agricultural produce rots because the railroads are old and slow.

## A Network of Poor Roads

In many parts of the Soviet Union land travel is nearly as difficult today as it was before the 1917 Revolution. Even the large cities have been connected by highways only in recent decades. Farm roads are often little more than dirt tracks that become impassable during spring thaws. In winter, many roads are blocked by snowdrifts, while others can be traveled only in a horsedrawn sleigh. Since World War II the Soviet government has made a determined effort to expand and improve the country's system of roads. But construction problems caused by a

## The Trans-Siberian Railroad

During the reign of Czar Alexander I Russia was, for a time, the most important power in Europe. Such a status brought with it opportunities for international trade that were unknown before. But Russia was in a weak position to exploit world markets, since it was cut off from open, ice-free seas by vast expanses of foreign territory.

Visionaries began to imagine Siberia as Russia's avenue to the Pacific. At the same time, Russian leaders were awakening to the great potential of Siberia for its gold, silver, timber, and fertile soil. The czarist government decided to develop Siberia and to link European Russia with the Pacific by building a railroad across the great land.

The start of construction on the line in 1891 brought on Siberia's only land rush. The government encouraged settlers to move east by offering low fares on the railroad, inexpensive land, and even free land in some districts. In 1892, some 100,000 Russians set out for Siberia. By 1896 the annual figure had risen to a quarter million. But the eastward movement was ill-conceived and poorly managed. Families who lived through the difficult trip found their new lands bare and unsuited for farming. Food was scarce, and thousands of immigrants died. After this experience, Russians could not be convinced that Siberia was the land of hope.

Construction of the railroad proved in itself to be one of the most difficult tasks in Russian history. Numerous engineering problems were encountered, and the forced labor of convicts was anything but satisfactory. But by 1904 the line was nearly completed. When the final stretch was finished in 1917, the railroad stretched 4,607 miles from the Ural Mountains to Vladivostok—the longest railroad in the world. If the track from the terminus in the Urals northeastward to Leningrad is added, the distance is 5,973 miles, while the line from Leningrad to the Polish frontier adds more than 300 miles. The railroad was expensive in terms of both money and lives, but this cost was shrugged off by the czars. At last their huge empire was linked from east to west and they had their outlet on the sea.

harsh climate, a shortage of building materials, and the vast distances to be covered have seriously handicapped the program. With all the new construction, the Soviet Union still has only about 15 percent as many miles of hard-surfaced roads as the United States.

Even if Russia had the roads, there would be few vehicles to use them. Most Russians cannot afford automobiles, and those who have the money receive them only after being on a waiting list for several years. The government-owned automobile factories simply cannot keep up with the demand. The largest cities have splendid systems of streets and boulevards. But most people depend on streetcars or buses for transportation. Leningrad and Moscow boast magnificent subway systems, with clean, handsomely decorated stations and excellent service.

## Rivers as a Transportation Network

The rivers of the Soviet Union can be divided into two networks, European and Asian. Those in European Russia have great value for transportation, although railroads and airlines make them less essential than in earlier days. Meandering across the flat plains of European Russia, these rivers are easily navigable by boats and barges. Rivers in the northern part of European Russia and Siberia, when frozen, become nature's own highways. Centuries ago Mongols penetrated far into Russia by advancing over icebound rivers. Today pedestrians and drivers sometimes use these frozen rivers as shortcuts.

Long before the 1500's, the rivers of European Russia were important for internal trade, but some were more important than others for trade with the rest of the world. The Dvina (dvih-NAH) River runs northward and empties into the White Sea. The Volga, the longest river in Europe, has somewhat limited use because it flows into the landlocked Caspian Sea. The Dnieper (DNYEH-per) flows into the Black Sea and the Don River into the Sea of Azov, an extension of the Black Sea. However, to reach the Mediterranean from the Black Sea, Russian ships must pass through the Bosporous and the Dardanelles. For centuries this narrow opening was controlled by countries unfriendly to Russia.

The major rivers in Soviet Asia have more value for power than for transportation. Most of them flow northward into the Arctic Ocean through land that is sparsely settled. Thus such rivers as the Ob (OHP-yih), Yenisey (YEH-nih-SEY), and Lena (LYEH-nuh) are among the largest in the world, but until recently

**TRANSPORTATION.** Heavy trucks (top) move supplies over snow-covered roads in Siberia. Nuclear-powered ice-breakers open Soviet harbors for trade (left). In which ports would these ships be needed? Sign on a Trans-Siberian Railroad car (above) shows it bound from Irkutsk to Moscow. How far is this? In Moscow a sub-way system with ornate stations (below) provides fast service.

have been of limited value. The Soviet government has built a number of dams on these rivers and their tributaries, thereby generating hydroelectric power for Siberian industry.

Another well-known waterway in Soviet Asia that provides hydroelectricity is the Amur (uh-MOOR). Called the Heilongjiang, or "Black Dragon," by the Chinese, this river provides part of the boundary between the Soviet Union and the People's Republic of China. The Amu Darya (uh-MOO DUHR-yuh) and the Syr (SIHR) Darya pass through desert land. They dry up during the hot summers, but during the cooler months they empty into the landlocked Aral Sea.

## Inland Bodies of Water

The Soviet Union has many lakes, inland seas, and rivers. The largest of these is the Caspian Sea, located between Europe and Asia. This sea is also the largest inland body of water in the world. Several hundred miles east of the Caspian is the Aral Sea. The Black Sea, to the southwest of Russia, has for centuries been one of the most important bodies of water in the world. All of these seas are salt water. Russia's great freshwater expanses include Lake Baikal (buy-KOWL), the deepest lake in the world, and Lake Ladoga (LAH-duh-guh), the largest inland body of water in Europe.

These lakes and seas have great importance for Russia. The Caspian Sea, famed for its sturgeon, the source of caviar, has been used for commerce since ancient times. Lake Ladoga, joined to the Gulf of Finland and the Baltic Sea by the Neva (nyeh-VAH) River, is an important link between the industrial region of Leningrad and the Soviet Union's world markets. A series of rivers and canals also links this lake with the White Sea in the north and the Caspian Sea, which is several thousand miles to the southeast. The Soviet government has also developed several other interlocking systems of rivers, lakes, and canals.

## Ocean Shipping

The Soviet Union has overcome great geographic handicaps to become one of the world's leading maritime nations. To cope with the barrier of frozen seas, the Soviets have developed nuclear-powered icebreakers. In the process the Soviets have become pioneers in Arctic exploration. The USSR has also built several million tons of ocean going ships. Operating primarily from harbors on the Black Sea and in friendly countries, these ships sail to every major port on the globe.

## Air Travel

Air travel has bridged the great expanses of the Soviet Union. Service is provided by Aeroflot, the government-owned airline. It is the Soviet Union's only civilian airline and the world's largest. Regularly scheduled flights connect the major cities of the Soviet Union and link the nation with almost 100 countries. In 1967 flights were inaugurated between Moscow and Tokyo, and in 1968 passenger service to New York was begun. Besides carrying passengers and freight within the Soviet Union, Aeroflot performs a wide variety of other services such as crop dusting. Recently criticisms have surfaced about Aeroflot's poor passenger service. Some critics contend that if Aeroflot had competition the service would be better.

## Check Your Understanding

1. Why are railroads the principal means of transportation in the Soviet Union?
2. Why are there few cars and trucks in the USSR?
3. Why are the Soviet Union's rivers and inland waterways important?
4. **Thinking Critically:** How do you explain the difference in the transportation situation in the USSR and the United States? Consider geography as well as economic goals.

## 4. The People of the Soviet Union

**"Ethnic group"** is a rather indefinite term used by social scientists to describe a large group of people who share a common **culture**. The Soviet Union has many ethnic groups. According to Soviet estimates, the total population in the late 1980's was 282 million. Represented among these people were over a hundred ethnic groups, of which only 23 had as many as a million members. About half of the Soviet people are Great Russians and another quarter belong to ethnic groups closely related to the Great Russians. Thus, though the Soviet Union has a great variety of nationalities, three quarters of its people have similar languages, customs, and cultural heritages.

### The Indo-European Language Family

Those Soviet citizens classified as Great Russians, or related to the Great Russians, belong to the large group of eastern Europeans who speak Slavic languages. These languages form a branch of the Indo-European language family, which includes most of the languages of western and eastern Europe, the northern Mediterranean region, and also the Indian subcontinent.

Customarily, the Slavic peoples are divided into three branches. The western Slavs include the Poles of Poland, the Czechs and Slovaks of Czechoslovakia, and the Wends of eastern Germany. The principal southern Slavic groups are the Serbs, Croats, and Slovenes of Yugoslavia and the Bulgarians and related peoples of the Balkan states—Yugoslavia, Rumania, Bulgaria, Albania, Greece, and the European parts of Turkey. Many of the western and southern Slavs living in the Soviet Union occupy areas that formerly were parts of other countries. Great Russians, Byelorussians, Ukrainians, and several smaller nationalities in the Soviet Union are eastern Slavs. Only scattered groupings of eastern Slavs are found outside the boundaries of the USSR. Taken together, Slavic-speaking peoples constitute one of the largest branches of the great Indo-European language family.

### The Great Russians

The core of the Soviet state is the Great Russian people. Their ancestral homeland is the Russian Soviet Federated Republic, the largest by far of the 15 republics that make up the USSR. Their ethnic center is Moscow, the capital of the Soviet Union. Their language, Russian, is the national language. Russian is also the second language of most other ethnic groups in the Soviet Union. Until **communism** began to take the place of organized religion in the USSR, the **Russian Orthodox Church**, the denomination to which most Great Russians belonged, was the state church. For centuries this church formed a force in Russian life that was second only to the power of the czar. The Great Russians have had the greatest role in forming the national culture.

### Ukrainians and Byelorussians

Next to the Great Russians, the Ukrainians and Byelorussians are the major ethnic groups in the USSR. About 16 percent of the population is Ukrainian. Living in the rich agricultural region that bears their name, the Ukrainians are similar to other eastern Slavs. Because they are a proud people, they have long resented the political domination of the Great Russians. For centuries, Ukrainians have kept alive their distinctive cultural

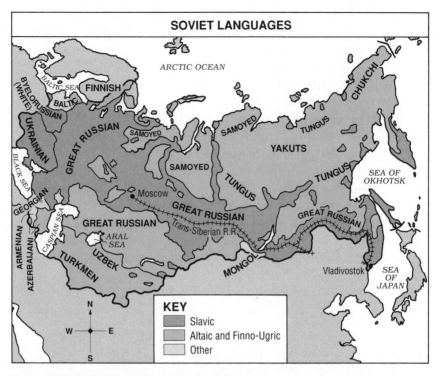

# SOVIET LANGUAGES

ARCTIC OCEAN

FINNISH

BYELORUSSIAN (WHITE)

BALTIC SEA

BALTIC

UKRAINIAN

GREAT RUSSIAN

SAMOYED

SAMOYED

SAMOYED

CHUKCHI

TUNGUS

YAKUTS

TUNGUS

TUNGUS

SEA OF OKHOTSK

BLACK SEA

GEORGIAN

Moscow

GREAT RUSSIAN

Trans-Siberian R.R.

GREAT RUSSIAN

ARMENIAN

AZERBAIJANI

CASPIAN SEA

GREAT RUSSIAN

ARAL SEA

UZBEK

TURKMEN

MONGOL

Vladivostok

SEA OF JAPAN

N W E S

**KEY**
- Slavic
- Altaic and Finno-Ugric
- Other

**SOVIET PEOPLES AND LANGUAGES.**  Where certain languages predominate can be seen in the map above. Note how Russian settlement followed the Trans-Siberian Railroad eastward. Though peoples speaking Altaic (Turkic) and Finno-Ugric languages are spread over a huge area, they are a minority in population. Uzbeks and Kazakhs, largest of the Turkic groups, together make up only 8 percent of the USSR's people. As is clear from the graph, which represents total Soviet population, Great Russians and their fellow Slavs—Ukrainians and Byelorussians—outnumber all others.

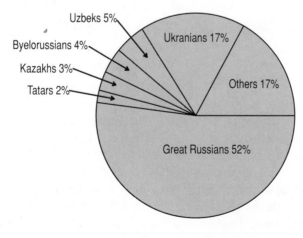

Uzbeks 5%
Byelorussians 4%
Kazakhs 3%
Tatars 2%
Ukranians 17%
Others 17%
Great Russians 52%

(Source: *The Information Please Almanac, 1989*)

traditions, including their language—Ukrainian. While most Ukrainians were once members of the Russian Orthodox Church, a substantial number were converted to Roman Catholicism during a period when their land often formed a part of the Polish or Lithuanian empires, which were both Roman Catholic lands.

The Byelorussians, also called White Russians, are the third largest Slavic group in the Soviet Union. They represent somewhat less than 4 percent of the population. Some scholars believe their name comes from the traditional white garments worn by their ancestors. ("Byelo" means "white.") The Byelorussians were ruled by other countries for 500 years and, like the Ukrainians, developed their own traditions. In language and religion the Byelorussians are similar to the Great Russians. These people have long made their home in the west central part of European Russia.

## Estonians

At the eastern end of the southern shore of the Baltic Sea are the formerly independent states of Estonia, Latvia, and Lithuania. Overrun many times in the past by Swedes, Poles, Germans, and Russians, they broke away from Russia after the Russian Revolution of 1917 only to be reannexed by the Soviet Union in 1940.

The Estonian people have lived in their present home for many centuries. They are one of the very few European people who do not speak an Indo-European language. Estonian, like Finnish and Hungarian, is distantly related to such Asian languages as Turkish, Mongol, and Manchu. Most Estonians changed from Catholicism to Lutheranism during the 1500's and 1600's.

## Latvians and Lithuanians

The Latvians and the Lithuanians have also inhabited the Baltic region for hundreds of years. The former never exerted much political or cultural influence in eastern Europe. But the Lithuanians, often in alliance with the Poles, were the founders of medieval kingdoms whose power extended far into the Ukraine. Both Latvian and Lithuanian are Indo-European languages. The Latvians were converts to Lutheranism during the Protestant Reformation, while most Lithuanians, like the Poles, remained Catholics.

(Continued on page 28)

PEOPLE.  The majority of Soviet citizens belong to the Slavic language group, which includes Great Russians as well as Ukranians and Byelorussians. The two women (bottom) reading about the Soviet-American summit meeting have the Slavic features usually considered Russian. Very "un-Russian" is the Uzbek girl picking cotton on a collective farm (top, right). The largest non-Slavic ethnic group, Uzbeks are Altaic (Turkic) peoples. Mongol peoples, such as the father and son (top, left), are descendants of Tatar chieftains who ruled Russia centuries ago.

## Nationalities in the Soviet Union

The czarist policy of **Russification**, or imposing the Great
Russian culture on the many other nationalities within
the empire, was denounced by the Bolsheviks before the
1917 Revolution. But when the Communists came to power, they inherited the same problems of trying to unite
the various peoples in the state. They knew that many of
the national groups, if given a choice, would set up their
own independent countries rather than remain part of
Russia.

To reconcile their insistence on keeping the empire
together with their stated views on self-determination, the
Bolsheviks created a union of republics in 1921 based
along national lines. Theoretically each nationality had a
degree of **autonomy** and identity in its republic, although
actually the Communist goal was complete centralization
of power.

The Soviets have used ethnic loyalties to advance the
Communist cause when possible and opposed them when
it was to their advantage. During the early years of the
Communist state there was little suppression of ethnic
traditions. By the 1930's, however, the need for increased
industrialization and centralization made it important that
all the people have the same language, philosophy, and
loyalties. Since the Russian Republic led the revolution, it
became the model for the other republics. Schools in each
republic taught the Russian language, culture, and history
as well as the traditions of the native culture. Promising
leaders of non-Russian groups were killed, and Russians
moved into all the republics, assuming powerful positions
in industry, the Communist Party, and the government.

The nationalities problem remains very much alive
today in the Soviet Union. Indeed there has been a resurgence of ethnic sentiment since the mid-1970's. During
the late 1980's various ethnic groups in Estonia, Armenia,
and Georgia began to call for greater local autonomy. A
few bold individuals have even suggested virtual independence from the Soviet Union. Dealing with ethnic demands
is one of the most difficult challenges facing the Soviet
government.

# The Soviet Republics

| Republic | Entry into Union | Major Ethnic Group (%) | Total Population (Millions) | Area (1000 sq. mi.) |
|---|---|---|---|---|
| Russian | Original member, 1922 | Russians, (83) | 145.3 | 6,593 |
| Byelorussian | Original member, 1922 | Byelorussian (79) | 10.1 | 80 |
| Ukranian | Original member, 1922 | Ukranians (74) | 51.2 | 232 |
| Turkmen | Formed from parts of Turkestan, Bokhara, and Khiva, 1925 | Turkmens (68) | 3.4 | 188 |
| Uzbek | Formed from parts of Khiva and Bokhara, 1925 | Uzbeks, (69) | 19.0 | 174 |
| Tadzhik | Formed from parts of Bokhara and Turkestan, 1929 | Tadzhiks (59) | 4.8 | 55 |
| Azerbaijanis | Formed from division of Transcaucasian Republic, 1936 | Azerbaijanis (78) | 6.8 | 33 |
| Armenian | | Armenians (88) | 3.4 | 12 |
| Georgian | | Georgians (69) | 5.3 | 27 |
| Kazakh | Formed from provinces within RSFSR, 1936 | Russians (41) | 16.2 | 1,048 |
| Kirghiz | Autonomous region in RSFSR until entry in 1936 | Kirghis (48) | 4.1 | 77 |
| Estonian | Annexed in World War II, 1940 | Estonians (65) | 1.6 | 17 |
| Latvian | Annexed in World War II, 1940 | Latvians (54) | 2.6 | 2.5 |
| Lithuanian | Annexed in World War II, 1940 | Lithuanians (80) | 3.6 | 25 |
| Moldavian | Formed from parts of Moldavian Autonomous Republic and Bessarabia (ceded from Rumania), 1940 | Moldavians (64) | 4.2 | 13 |

Source: USSR '88 © Novosti Press Agency, 1988.

## Turkic Peoples

Next to Indo-European, Turkic is the chief language group in the Soviet Union. Peoples speaking Turkic languages were among the new "national minorities" added to the Russian Empire when the czar began taking over huge territories south of Siberia during the 1800's. The most numerous of the Turkic-speaking peoples are the Uzbeks, who also form the largest non-Slavic ethnic group in the Soviet Union. They live in the Uzbek Soviet Socialist Republic, the wealthiest of the several Soviet republics in Central Asia. Because Uzbekistan has resources of coal, oil, and other minerals, the Soviet government has done much toward industrializing the republic. Uzbekistan also has been converted into a cotton-growing region.

On occasion the Turkic peoples of Central Asia would find themselves united under a single government, but for the most part they have been ruled by outsiders. Romans, Greeks, Persians, Mongols, Chinese, Arabs, and finally, Russians, in turn have dominated Central Asia. On the other hand, Turkic peoples did their share of invading. Frequently swarming into lands across the mountains, they founded empires in China, Afghanistan, India, and parts of the Middle East. It was Turkic peoples who founded the Ottoman Empire, a major power in the Middle East from the late 1400's into the 1800's.

Although considerable "Russification" has occurred in Central Asia under the Soviet regime, the ancestral culture of the Turks remains. Turkic languages, literature, music, dance, costume, and art are still very much a part of local patterns of life, as is Islam, the traditional religion for many centuries. Recognizing the artistic merit of Islamic architecture, the Soviet government has provided funds for the restoration and maintenance of many buildings, monuments, and mosques at Samarkand, Tashkent, and Bukhara, capitals of once brilliant Turkish empires.

## Armenians, Georgians, and Azerbaijanis

In the land south of the Caucasus Mountains, and between the Black and Caspian seas, lies the ancient region of Transcaucasia. According to legend, Noah's Ark came to rest on the slopes of Mt. Ararat, a high peak that towers above this region. From Biblical times on many independent states were founded in Transcaucasia by the ancestors of present-day Armenians, Georgians, and Azerbaijanis. Invariably, however, these states were overwhelmed by more powerful neighbors. After being ruled for several hundred years by the Ottoman Turks, Transcaucasia was incorporated into the czarist empire in the early 1800's.

Though living in the same region, the Armenians, Georgians, and Azerbaijanis are quite different from one another. The people of the Azerbaijan SSR are of Turkish descent, speak a Turkic language, and are followers of Islam. Both the Georgians and the Armenians were converted to Christianity many centuries ago. The Armenians speak an Indo-European language, but the Georgian language defies classification into any of the traditional language groups. It is quite unlike any other language heard in Russia. Joseph Stalin, the dictator who succeeded Lenin as head of the Soviet Union, was a Georgian. In his speeches he always showed his non-Russian origin by speaking Russian with a thick accent.

### Jews

Some of the world's oldest Jewish communities outside the Middle East are in Soviet Central Asia. Today more Jews live in the Soviet Union than in the state of Israel. Numbering about three million, they are the descendants of Jews who settled in Russia over the centuries. Under the czarist government Jews were restricted to specified areas in central and southern European Russia. Since the Russian Revolution of 1917 they have scattered throughout the country.

Czarist persecution of the Jews became increasingly severe in the late nineteenth and early twentieth centuries. Consequently, hundreds of thousands of Jews migrated to western Europe, the United States, and Palestine, now Israel. Later many others fled for their lives during the Communist Revolution. Over the years the Soviet government not only curbed the emigration of Jews but interfered with their rights, confiscated their property, subjected them to physical abuse, and imprisoned them. This anti-Semitism gave rise to worldwide protests, especially in recent decades. (See page 252.)

### Minor Ethnic Groups

In addition to the peoples already mentioned, the Soviet Union has representatives of nearly every major ethnic group in Eurasia. Some communities in the Soviet Union are composed of peoples separated, by either force or choice, from the lands of their origin. Thus, official Soviet censuses list Germans, Poles, Finns, Greeks, Bulgarians, Hungarians, Rumanians, Mongols, and Koreans. No country in the world, including the United States, is as ethnically diverse as the Soviet Union.

## Check Your Understanding

1. What languages of the Indo European language family do most peoples in the Soviet Union speak?
2. **a.** Into what three branches are the Slavs usually divided?
   **b.** List one representative group within each branch.
3. What are the three largest ethnic groups in the Soviet Union?
4. How did the Estonians, Latvians, and Lithuanians become part of the Soviet Union?
5. How do the Turkic peoples differ from other ethnic groups in the Soviet Union?
6. What are the principal ethnic groups in the Caucasus region?
7. Why did thousands of Jews leave Russia during the czarist period?
8. ***Thinking Critically:*** What alternatives to Russification might the Soviets have used in order to get people to work for the development of the state?

## CHAPTER REVIEW

### ■ Chapter Summary

***Section 1.*** Russia's history is one of expansionism. Only in 1945 did the country finally reach its current borders. Russia's early history unfolded in European Russia while Siberia was not settled by Russians until the 1600's. Even today much of it is undeveloped. Russian expansion to the south was checked by mountain ranges. One reason for Russian expansion was a need to gain access to sea routes that were not frozen for large parts of the year.

***Section 2.*** Climate and vegetation have greatly affected the course of Russia's development. Large parts of the USSR are barren and inhospitable wastelands. The northern tundra and most of the forest belt are unsuitable for agriculture. The fertile steppe lands farther south occasionally suffer from inadequate rainfall, and the southernmost territories are largely desert and semi-desert.

**Section 3.** The immense distances in Russia have posed problems for both the czars and for later Soviet leaders in their efforts to develop efficient transportation systems. Railroads carry the bulk of traffic because roads are poorly developed. From early times to the present, Russians have made good use of their European rivers and in recent times have linked them with canals. In this century, ocean-going commercial shipping has been expanded and air routes have been developed. Domestic transportation is still inadequate, however, to meet the nation's needs.

**Section 4.** More than 100 different ethnic groups are found in the Soviet Union but three fourths of the population is Slavic. Except for the Turkic peoples, all other ethnic groups in the nation are numerically small. Significant minority peoples include those around the Black Sea and in the region known as Transcaucasia.

### ■ Vocabulary Review

*Define:* democratization, tundra, taiga, steppe, permafrost, buffer, ethnic group, communism, Russian Orthodox Church, culture, Russification, autonomy

### ■ Places to Locate

*Locate:* Bosporous and Dardanelles, European Russia, East European Plain, Central Russian Plain, West Siberian Lowland, Central Siberian Uplands, Siberia, Trans-Siberian Railroad, tundra, taiga, steppes, Archangel, Murmansk, Dvina River, Volga River, Dnieper River, Don River, Ob River, Amur River, Caspian Sea, Black Sea, Lake Baikal

### ■ People to Know

*Identify:* Great Russians, Ukrainians, Byelorussians, Estonians, Latvians, Lithuanians, Turkic peoples, Armenians, Georgians, Azerbaijanis

### ■ Thinking Critically

1. Why was a warm-water port so important to the Russian czars? Based on what you know from studying history, what other reasons can you give for their desire to expand in all directions?
2. If you lived in Leningrad, what effects do you think the extreme cold might have on your everyday life?

## ■ Extending and Applying Your Knowledge

1. Siberia has been called "the Soviet Union's Alaska," although it is much larger than that state. Do research for a brief oral report on the efforts of either the czars or the Soviet government to develop the region's resources.

2. Using maps and accounts of the region you can find in the library, write a description of what you would see as a passenger on the Trans-Siberian Railroad bound from Moscow to Vladivostok.

3. Choose one of the ethnic groups listed on page 27 and research its history and present status in the Soviet Union. Along with several other students use this material to write articles for a magazine about the current status of nationalities in the Soviet Union.

# 2

# The Emergence of a United Russia

The Russians and their way of life have long puzzled peoples both in Europe and Asia. Europeans have often pointed to the strong "Asian" characteristics of the Russians. Asians have emphasized those that are Western. Even the Russians themselves, especially their nineteenth century writers and philosophers, were deeply concerned about this problem of **national identity.**

Part of the answer to this dilemma is found in Russian history. It is not only that the Russians were late arrivals on the stage of civilization. The fact that the Russian way of life evolved on the fringes of great European and Asian civilizations is also important. The Russians were scarcely touched by the influences of ancient Egypt, Mesopotamia, Persia, Greece, Rome, India, and China. When they finally began to break out of their isolation, they were simultaneously affected by ways of life prevailing in Europe, the Middle East, and Central Asia.

Once the process of **cultural diffusion** began in Russia, geography did much to shape that country's history. This was particularly true during the early periods. Time and again during these centuries the steppes of the south provided a pathway for conquerors and cultures from Central Asia, while the river network in western Russia formed a highway for similar influences from Europe. Both geographic features aided in the spread of Byzantine culture. This intermingling of peoples and cultures in Russia produced a civilization that cannot be defined as Asian or European, but as a combination of both.

# 1. The First Russian State

Eastern Europe was a wide open frontier as late as a thousand years ago. Long after brilliant civilizations had risen, flourished, and in some instances died out in other parts of the world, the broad plain of eastern Europe was inhabited only by wandering peoples. These roving groups surged back and forth through the forest and across the steppes, warring among themselves and struggling against the forces of nature to survive.

Within this region of eastern Europe two belts of vegetation existed—the forest and the steppe. The peoples who lived within these zones developed two very different types of culture. The forest peoples came to rely on agriculture for their livelihood. To the south, the steppe peoples developed cultures based on the raising of livestock. In neither area was one group able to establish control over its neighbors. It would take an outside force, the fierce Norsemen of the Scandinavian peninsula, to bring some order to the land that became Russia. We begin the study of Russian history with the steppe peoples simply because we know more about them than we do about the forest peoples.

## The Scythians

Some centuries before 500 B.C. a people known as the Scythians (SITH-ee-uhnz) made their appearance on the broad steppes of what is now southern Russia. In time they became known to the Greeks and later, to the Romans, both of whom had military posts on the Black Sea, which borders the Russian steppes. From Greek and Roman records we have learned something

Scenes from a Scythian vase of the fourth century B.C. provide information about the Central Asian nomads.

## Development of the Russian State

| 862 | Legendary founding of Russia by Rurik |
| 879–1240 | Kievan period |
| 987 or 988 | Conversion of Vladimir I |
| 1237–1450 | Mongol period |
| 1328 | Moscow named seat of Russian Orthodox Church |
| 1453 | Fall of Constantinople |
| 1462–1505 | Ivan III (the Great) |
| 1478 | Novgorod captured by Ivan III |
| 1533–1584 | Ivan IV (the Terrible) |
| 1598 | The end of the Muscovite dynasty |
| 1605–1613 | Time of Troubles |

about the Scythians. Herodotus (hih-RAHD-uh-tuhs), a Greek historian of the fifth century B.C., was particularly impressed by the warlike behavior and savage customs of the Scythians. Apparently they were sufficiently skillful in warfare to keep both the Greeks and Romans from conquering them.

The Scythians possessed impressive artistic talents. The works of Scythian goldsmiths and silversmiths, for example, were widely admired. Utensils and ornaments exhibiting Scythian influences were produced in both western Europe and China. Today fine collections of Scythian jewelry and other personal adornments are found in Leningrad's famed Hermitage Museum and in the Treasure Room of the Kremlin Museum in Moscow.

### Other Nomadic Peoples

Around 200 B.C., intruders from the east put an end to Scythian domination of the steppes. Between then and the A.D. 500's, the steppes were in a constant state of confusion. Such peoples as the Sarmations (sahr-MAY-shih-uhnz), Goths, Huns, Avars, and Khazars successively held the rich steppes under their control. In time most of these invaders from the interior of Asia moved westward against the sagging Roman Empire.

As each successive invader took over the steppes, the people already there would be scattered. About the time a group would begin to establish itself, new invaders from the east would take over. There was little progress toward a united state in the steppes during these early centuries.

## The Eastern Slavs

About 2,500 years ago, Slavic peoples inhabited the region north of the Carpathian Mountains in what is now Czechoslovakia, Poland, the Ukraine, and Rumania. Unfortunately the archaeological and historical records of these early times have little to say about these Slavic groups, the ancestors of the great majority of the Russian peoples. During the first several centuries A.D., these peoples began migrating in various directions. Shortly after the A.D. 500's, groups of eastern Slavs began edging eastward from the Carpathian region into the central portion of European Russia. Some of the more venturesome turned southward into the steppes, where presumably they intermarried with nomadic peoples already in that region. Most eastern Slavs, however, continued to move slowly eastward toward the forested lands.

By the 600's and 700's, groups of eastern Slavs had given up nomadic ways for a settled life in the forests and swamps of present-day western Russia. Since they found farming difficult and unprofitable, they engaged in trade. In the forests were animals they could kill for their furs, and there were also bees. Furs, beeswax, and honey were gathered for shipment to Constantinople, the great capital and trading center of the Byzantine Empire. The eastern Slavs also traded in slaves, whom they obtained as prisoners of war in their battles with neighboring peoples.

In time the small settlements of the eastern Slavs grew into towns. The most important of these were along the larger rivers lying between Lake Ladoga in the north and the Black Sea in the south. Some of the communities became important cities in later Russian history. Among these were Kiev (KEE-yeff), Smolensk (smuh-LYEHENSK), Novgorod (NOFF-guh-rut), and Rostov. Such settlements, each of which was a state within itself, became gathering points for goods used in the Byzantine trade.

## The Varangians

In the Scandinavian peninsula and in present-day Denmark lived peoples called Norsemen or Vikings. Fierce sea-rovers, they repeatedly invaded the British Isles, the coastal regions of western Europe, and even entered the Mediterranean. When their demands for **tribute** were not met, they would pillage and enslave inhabitants. Some decided, around the A.D. 700's, that an easier way to acquire wealth was through trade. The Varangians (vuh-RAN-jee-uhns), as the eastern Slavs called the Vikings, in time became an important element in early Russian life. They settled in towns along the rivers and provided troops to protect convoys bringing goods across the hostile steppes. (See map, page 41.) Gradually the Varangians took over the rich trade with Byzantium.

After a time the Varangians became the ruling class in the trading towns of early Russia. The popular version of how this came about is told in *The Russian Primary Chronicle*, the principal source of information about the eastern Slavs. The entry for the years 860–862 tells the story:

> The tributaries [peoples who paid tribute—in this case, the eastern Slavs] of the Varangians drove them back beyond the sea and refusing them further tribute, set out to govern themselves. There was no law among them, but tribe rose against tribe. Discord thus ensued among them, they began to war one against another. They said to themselves, "Let us seek a prince who may rule over us and judge according to the law." They accordingly went overseas to the Varangian Russes; these particular Varangians were known as Russes, just as some are called Swedes, and others Normans, English, and Gotlanders. . . . They then said to the people of Rus, "Our land is great and rich, but there is no order in it. Come to rule and reign over us." They thus selected three brothers, with their kinsfolk, who took with them all the Russes and migrated. The oldest, Rurik, located himself in Novogorod [sic]. [Samuel H. Cross and Olgord P Sherbowitz-Wetzer, trans. and eds., *The Russian Primary Chronicle; Laurentian Text*.]

Almost certainly the establishment of Varangian rule in Russia did not occur exactly as told in the *Chronicle*. Compiled, and frequently revised, by Christian monks over a period of several centuries, the book was not completed until the early 1100's. It seems to include as much myth as fact since the monks recorded **oral traditions** passed on from one generation to the next without analyzing their contents. We cannot be certain that such a person as Rurik even existed. However, Rurik is popularly credited with founding the first Russian state in 862. His capital was Novgorod, a town lying a short distance south of present-day Leningrad.

The Varangians were never numerous in Russia and, in time, they became culturally indistinguishable from the Slavs. The Varangians intermarried with the Slavs, used the Russian language, and adopted Slavic names and customs. Thus within a few generations their only link with the past was a fierce pride in their Varangian origins.

## Check Your Understanding

1. Why did the Scythian domination of the steppes end?
2. Why were the peoples of the steppes unable to unite from about 200 B.C. to the 500's A.D.?
3. What peoples moved into the forested areas of eastern Europe?
4. How did the Varangians provide leadership for the eastern Slavs?
5. **Thinking Critically:** According to *The Russian Primary Chronicle,* how did the Varangians come to rule over the eastern Slavs? Do you think this account is true? If it is not true, why might a ruling house want later generations to believe events happened this way?

## 2. Kievan Russia

Before the Varangians were assimilated, they had established themselves as the ruling upper class, expanded commerce, and founded a dynasty that ruled in Russia for over 700 years. Beginning in 879, Kiev became the center of the rapidly expanding Varangian state. Kiev was so powerful for a while that the years 879–1240 are termed the Kievan period. The political structure built by the Varangians did not last, and indeed, comparatively little is known about it. However, during the Kievan period, Russian trade was largely with the Byzantine Empire. The culture of that great state on the eastern Mediterranean came to be reflected in Russia's own religion, language, art, architecture, music, and literature. Today, many centuries after the close of the Kievan period, the USSR still shows the effects of those early contacts with the Byzantine Empire.

## A Loose Federation

During the Kievan period no single ruler exercised control over the Russian people. The state of Kiev was only one of many principalities that rose and fell over a span of three and a half centuries. For a long while the state of Novgorod rivaled Kiev in power and wealth. Moscow, later to become the center of the great Russian Empire, had not yet achieved a position of prominence and was not mentioned in records until 1147.

The little unity that existed in Russia can be traced to its unusual system of princely rule. The descendants of the early Varangians, together with their bands of armed followers, constituted a ruling military **aristocracy.** The **rota**, a complicated seniority system, determined who would rule where. With the death of a ruler, there would be a shifting of princes. (Only rarely did a woman rule a principality.) A prince in line for a more important principality would take over only after first renouncing his current holding. This would enable princes ranking below him to move up one step, since each shifted to what was for him a more important holding. Because the position of a prince was temporary, the lands he held at a given time were never regarded as his personal possession. All princes, however, regarded the Grand Prince of Kiev as the head of their aristocratic **federation.**

## The Class System

In Kievan Russia, the people of importance were the princes; "prince's men," that is, retainers and warriors; and **boyars**, a class of privileged land owners that arose as farming increased in importance. The boyars, who came from the ranks of the prince's men, played a role in the government. They met together in town councils, which were often consulted by the prince before making a major decision. Indeed, on occasion such a council became so powerful that it could dismiss an unpopular prince and call a new one to take his place.

Ordinary people, though constituting the great majority of the population, had few rights. Some owned livestock and tools, and farmed lands held by the estate. Others worked the lands of boyars or those of the prince, using the landowners' animals and tools. The former were better off than the latter, for should they move, their animals and implements would be a help in making a new start. Peasants who worked on the land of a boyar or prince owned little or nothing. Their position was little higher than that of slaves.

Whether peasants worked state land or private land, they led a difficult life. They lived in crude wooden houses that often were destroyed by fire. Frequently, peasant families were attacked by marauders who took anything of use. Whenever a prince needed men for his army, the peasants were forced to abandon their fields for military service. Because Kievan Russia was a region of comparatively poor soil and a short growing season, crops were meager. Perhaps worst of all, the burden of taxation rested on the peasants. Whether times were good or bad, agents of the prince or boyar came as regularly as the snows of winter to collect taxes and tribute.

## The Wealth of Kievan Russia

Throughout the Kievan period the flow of trade along the River Road greatly increased because of developments to the south. In the mid-seventh century the nomadic peoples of the Arabian Peninsula, inspired by a new faith known as Islam, swept out of the desert to found a mighty empire. Within a century Asia Minor—a peninsula in western Asia between the Black and Mediterranean seas—North Africa, and Spain were in Muslim hands. Not only was Byzantine trade with these areas cut off, but Muslim warships and pirates greatly reduced east-west trade on the Mediterranean. Although a roundabout route, the River Road became the main avenue of trade between western Europe and the Byzantine Empire. The regular Russian exports were supplemented by goods that earlier would have reached Byzantium by sea. As a result, the cities of Kievan Russia prospered.

The long, difficult journey from the Baltic to Constantinople could be made only in the spring and summer, when the Russian rivers were not frozen. Kiev, located on the Dnieper where the forest gave way to the steppe, served during the winter as a gathering point for export goods. As soon as the spring thaws come, the goods were loaded on boats for the southward trip.

The water route to the Byzantine capital had its perils for merchants, however, since it passed through a hostile countryside. Just before the beginning of the Kievan period, the Khazars had controlled the steppes. (See Sidelight, page 43.) The Slavic peoples around Kiev had been forced to pay tribute to the Khazars, but in return had gained the right to transport their goods

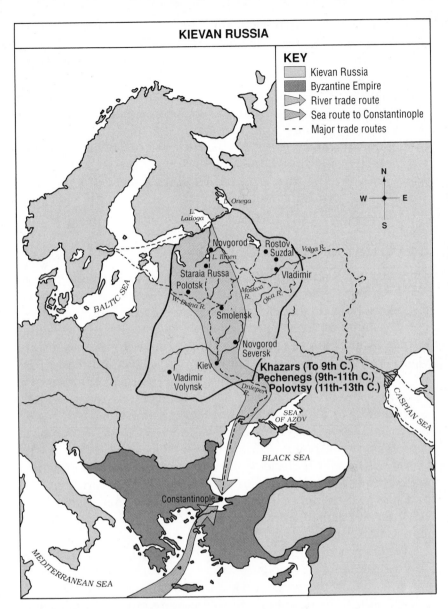

## KIEVAN RUSSIA

**KEY**
- Kievan Russia
- Byzantine Empire
- River trade route
- Sea route to Constantinople
- Major trade routes

*L. Ladoga*

*Onega*

Novgorod
*L. Ilmen*
Rostov
Suzdal
*Volga R.*

Staraia Russa
Polotsk
Vladimir

*W. Duina R.*
*Moskva R.*
*Oka R.*
Smolensk

Novgorod
Seversk

Kiev
**Khazars (To 9th C.)**
**Pechenegs (9th-11th C.)**
**Polovtsy (11th-13th C.)**
Vladimir
Volynsk
*Dnieper R.*

*BALTIC SEA*

*SEA OF AZOV*

*CASPIAN SEA*

*BLACK SEA*

Constantinople

*MEDITERRANEAN SEA*

**INTERACTION: KIEVAN RUSSIA.** The power of Kiev was based largely on its lucrative River Road trade route between the Baltic Sea and the Black Sea. Kievan traders were well rewarded for safely transporting goods from the Varangians to the Greeks. Although boundaries were never stabilized, this map indicates the general area of Kievan power during the 1100's and 1200's. Notice that Moscow is not even a major town during this period.

**41**

across Khazar lands. Indeed, this right was a key factor in the growth of early Russia's important trading towns.

But when the fierce Pechenegs became dominant in the steppe in the 900's, the rights of Russian convoys were not always respected. The Pechenegs, and their successors, the Polovtsy, and still other warlike Asiatic peoples would periodically demand heavy tribute from merchants. At times they would attack unlucky traders and take their wares. The early Varangians and the later Kievan princes made it their business to protect merchants on the river. In return, they received a generous share of the profits.

### Conversion to Christianity

The early Russians, whether Slavs or Varangians, practiced nature worship. Before the coming of the Norsemen, only a very few Slavs had adopted Christianity. But in 987 or 988, Kiev's Prince Vladimir I became a Christian. During his reign Vladimir forced his subjects to convert to Christianity. He tore down their places of worship and built Christian churches, and made Eastern Orthodoxy the official religion of the realm. Centuries after Vladimir's death, the Russian Orthodox Church recognized his contribution to Christianity by declaring him a saint.

The traditional account of how Prince Vladimir came to accept Eastern Orthodox Christianity is preserved for us in *The Russian Primary Chronicle*. It tells how representatives of various faiths came to the prince in an attempt to convert him. The Khazars wanted him to accept Judaism. Muslims tried to convert him to Islam. Vladimir also considered a conversion to Roman Catholicism.

Vladimir had many reasons for choosing Eastern Orthodoxy besides the stately ceremonies and beautiful singing his observers reported witnessing at Hagia Sophia, the great Orthodox cathedral in Constantinople. Russians were already familiar with Eastern Orthodox beliefs and rites since most of Kievan Russia's trade was with the Byzantine Empire. The Russian upper class had a deep admiration for the dazzling civilization of the Byzantine state.

Political considerations were also important. The adoption of the official religion of the Byzantine Empire by the Russian ruler promised benefits for both states but especially for the weaker Russian state. The two states were more likely to stand together against other powers—east and west—because of a common religion as well as close commercial ties.

# IDELIGHT TO HISTORY

## The Khazars

At about the time the Varangians were pressing southward into Russia from their Baltic homes, another people,
the Khazars, were assembling a powerful kingdom in the
region of the lower Volga. The Khazars were most likely a
Turkic people. Excellent warriors and able administrators,
they managed to build a huge domain that endured for
three centuries.

Shrewdly exploiting their **strategic location**, the Khazars were able to build cities and towns that served as
key centers in an elaborate network of trade that linked
Asia and northern Russia with Byzantium to the south.
The Khazar state became very wealthy in time and excited
the envy of many surrounding peoples. The Khazars were
strong enough to prevent westward invasions from warrior
peoples of Central Asia and to check the expansion of
Islamic armies from the south. However, during the 800's
and 900's, the Khazars were weakened by successful attacks from the forces of the emerging state of Kiev, whose
army finally defeated it in 969.

In the process of developing their state, the rulers of
the Khazars made a momentous choice in the mid-700's.
Anxious to rid themselves of nature worship, they looked
about for an alternative. After considering the merits of
Christianity, Islam, and Judaism, they decided to adopt
Judaism. The Khazars were known, however, for the tolerance they extended to other faiths. While it lasted, the
domain of the Khazars was one of the principal political
centers of Judaism. Some people believe the Khazars to
be the ancestors of many Russian Jews.

Vladimir's choice was fateful for Russia. After his decision,
Russian culture steadily took on a distinctive Byzantine glitter.
In the course of time many Russian institutions and practices
were modified, and some completely changed.

Central to the future course of Russian history was the willingness of Church officials to accept a subordinate role in their
relationship with the State. The Church focused on the role of
ritual and life after death. With regard to political matters,
church officials usually took little interest. They did not believe

it was their duty to interfere in nonreligious matters. Of course, some individual clergy aspired to political power, either directly or through their influence on government officials. But the general direction of Church-State relations in Russia was toward the ever-increasing dominance of the State. By the early 1700's the Church had become an arm of the government and high-ranking Church officials were selected by the czar.

### The Russian Alphabet

At the end of the 800's, two missionaries, Cyril and Methodius, later to be canonized saints, were sent by the Eastern Orthodox Church to work among the eastern Slavs. In order to perform their missionary work effectively, the two men had to translate the Bible into the language of the people. Since at that time the Slavs had no written language, the first task was to devise an alphabet. Using the Greek alphabet as a base, Cyril developed the Cyrillic alphabet, which was then used by Methodius in translating the Bible into "Church Slavonic."

The new alphabet included many letters from the Greek alphabet plus a few original symbols to represent sounds unique to the Slavic languages. The Cyrillic alphabet is still used in Russia. Church Slavonic, the language of prayer, became the first written language of the Russians. Indeed all Russian literature was written in Church Slavonic until the 1700's when a less formal style of Russian began to be used.

### Byzantine Art and Architecture

Russia's mass conversion to the Eastern Orthodox faith was accompanied by a great surge of church construction. Princes tried to outdo one another in building places of worship in the Byzantine style, which was adapted rather than adopted. Customs and needs, as well as the availability of materials, made certain changes necessary. Churches in Byzantium were built of stone, but the Russians used wood, which was plentiful. A modification of the Byzantine style was required for the roof, for a steep slope was needed to shed the winter snows. Because many Russian churches served as fortresses, problems of defense also had to be considered in planning.

In time influences from western and central Europe, as well as the Middle East and Asia, came to be reflected in Russian church architecture. Byzantium, nevertheless, gave the churches their most distinctive characteristics—the onion-shaped domes covered with gilt, and the tapering spires. These are the most notable features of Russian church architecture.

**CHURCH ARCHITECTURE.**
The twelfth-century Church of the Intercession (below) is an exquisite adaptation
of the Byzantine style. The Church of the
Transfiguration (left), built six centuries
later, is a true Russian masterpiece in
wood.

Like church architecture, painting came to Kievan Russia
from the Byzantine Empire. Byzantine art had its greatest influence in the production of religious pictures known as **icons**.
Painted on small wooden panels, these images had played an
important part in Eastern Orthodox worship, and came to have
new significance in the Russian church. Icons portraying Jesus,
the Virgin Mary, and the saints were often the central points
of religious services. The Russians believed that by praying to
the icons they could communicate with the figures they represented, who in turn would intercede with God on their behalf.
Icons were especially popular among Russian peasants. Every
Russian household had its icons, which often were credited with
miraculous powers.

At first, Russian icons were done in monochromes or single
colors. Later, painters developed great skill in working with
many colors and shades. Artists of different cities concentrated
on different colors. In Novgorod, for instance, red was widely

Although the twelfth-century *Virgin of Vladimir* was painted in Byzantium, it is more Russian than Byzantine. Mother and child are portrayed with human qualities, rather than as symbols. This style was used because the icon was commissioned for a Russian church. In the fourteenth century the famous *Virgin* was moved from Vladimir to Moscow, as a symbol of that city's spiritual ascendancy.

used. Until the 1917 Revolution, the painting of icons was a leading art form in Russia.

## Kievan Literature

Because most Russians were illiterate, little native literature was produced in Kievan Russia. The most notable written works of the period were *The Russian Primary Chronicle* and a compilation of secular and religious laws known as *Russkaya Pravda*. The latter, Russia's first legal code, probably arose out of the need of early church leaders to reconcile local legal customs with church requirements.

Folktales had been popular among the Russian people even before Kievan times. These tales were passed on by word of mouth from one generation to the next. Every region of the country had its favorite stories, but only the epic called "The Tale of Igor" can be regarded as a Russian classic. It recounts the exploits and final defeat of Prince Igor, who fought the nomadic peoples of the steppes. Like many other Russian folktales, "The Tale of Igor" was recorded in the *Chronicle*.

## Byzantine Influences on Modern Russia

Although the Communists have discouraged the practice of religion, they have nevertheless preserved many aspects of their country's Byzantine heritage. Russians are proud of the magnificent buildings that once were Orthodox churches. Moscow's famous Kremlin, for example, built long after the Kievan period, has elements of Byzantine architectural style. Old Orthodox churches still stand among the huge "look-alike" apartment complexes and office buildings built by the Communists. These churches add life and color to an otherwise drab skyline.

Although most Russian homes no longer have icons, these works of art are prominently displayed in the country's museums. The nation continues to use the Cyrillic alphabet developed by Orthodox missionaries. Notable too, the Communists, like earlier rulers of Russia, have kept the Russian Orthodox Church and other religious bodies subservient to the State.

## Check Your Understanding

1. List the four levels of social classes in Kievan Russia.
2. Why did trade become so important in Kievan Russia?
3. In what ways did Byzantium affect: **a.** Russia's written language? **b.** its architecture? **c.** its art?
4. What evidences of Byzantine influences can still be seen in modern Russia?
5. **Thinking Critically:** Why was Russia's conversion to Eastern Orthodox Christianity so significant?

## 3. The Mongol Hordes

Soldiers were on the march throughout the Kievan period. Princes attacked nearby principalities to acquire slaves. Many of the captured people were put to work on the lands of the prince and his retainers. Others were sold in the slave markets of Russian towns or in Constantinople. Princes living on lands near the steppes often led raids into that region. Some even led expeditions against Constantinople itself, hoping to force tribute from the Byzantines. In light of the rivalry and jealousy within the princely ranks, it is small wonder that the princes were unable to enter into lasting alliances. This inability to unite prevented them from warding off the Mongol invaders in the 1200's.

## Genghis Khan's Army

The people who were to destroy the remnants of the Kievan state had their origins in northeastern Asia. Known in history as the Mongols, they were nomadic hunters and herders who rode over the cold dry plateau north of China searching for pasture and game. They were also fighters, whose frequent expeditions into China led the Chinese to build the Great Wall. In 1206 a clan leader named Temuchin brought the warring clans together under his leadership, and assumed the name Genghis Khan, meaning "ruler of the universe."

Genghis' army was swift and deadly. With his men in units of 10, he organized his attacks by means of signals and messengers. His men relied on heavy bows more than hand-to-hand combat. Their favorite trick was to attack, pretend retreat, and sweep around the enemy to attack from the rear. Their siege tactics were also very successful. The population of a besieged city was given a choice of surrendering or being slaughtered. Those who surrendered soon found themselves serving in the front ranks of the army. Those who fought back were killed or enslaved.

The Mongols' first major conquest was northern China. Following the submission of the Qin emperor, Genghis' army swept westward across Central Asia, carrying with it many nomadic people. Within a few years Genghis ruled Central Asia and Iran and was ready to invade Russia.

The first Mongol horsemen appeared on the southern steppes of eastern Europe in 1223. Despite the spirited resistance of Georgians and other peoples of the Caucasus region, the Mongols advanced rapidly toward Kievan Russia. Recognizing their peril, a few Russian princes banded together in a loose **alliance** with rulers of the steppes. Having won victories in the opening skirmishes, the confident Russians met the Mongols at the Kalka River north of the Sea of Azov. The outcome was a crushing defeat for the allied forces.

Much to the surprise of the Russians, the Mongols did not follow up their victory. Actually the invaders were only a fast-moving reconnaissance force sent ahead of the main armies. Having fulfilled their mission of "spying out the land," this force rejoined the main Mongol army.

## Batu Khan's Victory

Batu Khan, a grandson of Genghis who died in 1227, led a much larger Mongol force into Russia in 1237. Meeting no effective resistance from the Russian princes, the Mongols had advanced by the following spring to within 60 miles of Novgorod. They were stopped there because the spring thaws had made the terrain impassable. Batu withdrew to Sarai, near present-day Volgograd, where he established his capital. During the next two winters the Mongol leader completed his conquest of Russia, taking every major city except Novgorod.

Russia had been attacked many times by nomadic invaders, but previous onslaughts were nothing in comparison with the fury of the Mongols. The fierce Asian horsemen cut a path of terrible destruction across Russia, burning, pillaging, and killing. The suffering of the Russians may be illustrated by what happened to prosperous Kiev. It was occupied and plundered, then put to the torch, and reduced to ashes. A few years later, in the winter of 1245–1246, Friar John of Plano Carpini, a Catholic monk, passed through Kiev. He wrote the following account:

> We found an innumerable multitude of dead men's skulls and bones lying upon the earth. It was once a very large and populous city, but it is now in a manner brought to nothing; for there do scarce remain two hundred houses, and the inhabitants of these are kept in extreme bondage. [Manuel Komroff, editor, *Contemporaries of Marco Polo*.]

Batu's domain, known as the Khanate of the Golden Horde, endured for more than 200 years (1237–1450). In theory a part of the great Mongol Empire that stretched across Asia, the Kingdom of the Golden Horde was actually an empire in its own right. The name came from the fact that yellow was the imperial color of the khan. The Mongolian word *ordu* meant "camp" or tent, and was the origin of the word *horde*. The word has come to mean "great swarms of men."

### Indirect Rule

After the Mongols, called Tatars by the Russians, had terrorized the population of the forested region and imposed their rule, they withdrew southward to the steppes. They had no love for the harsh winters and the vast forests of Kievan Russia. Accustomed to a nomadic life, they felt at home in the grasslands, where they could graze their horses and live as they were accustomed. Batu, as we have seen, established his capital at Sarai, a city in the steppes. Often the only Mongols in a conquered principality were a few representatives of the khan and, perhaps, a small troop of Mongol cavalry.

Frequently Slavic princes served as representatives of the Mongol government in their own principalities. Most princes were required to visit Sarai to pledge their loyalty to the khan. A few, acting in the name of the Khanate of the Golden Horde, had to journey to distant Mongolia to pay homage to the Great Khan, the Emperor of the Mongol Empire. Each prince or Mongol governor had a twofold responsibility to the Golden Horde: to collect and pay an annual tribute, and to raise the assigned quota of soldiers for the armed forces of the Khanate.

Mongol rule became harsh only when people failed to meet their obligations. For the slightest infraction of a rule, the Mongols might destroy a town and massacre or scatter its inhabitants. These occasions, however, were rare. Most princes paid tribute, met their quota of troops, and put down local revolts against Mongol rule.

### Novgorod's Special Position

Novgorod, the one great Russian city not captured by the Mongols, had become the center of an independent state before the coming of the Mongols. About that time Prince Alexander, a young man of 20, came to the throne. When his state was invaded by the Swedes in 1240, Alexander dealt them a stunning defeat at the Neva river. Two years later, he also repulsed German invaders.

Though victorious over Swedes and Germans, Alexander knew better than to challenge Mongol might. Instead he acknowledged Mongol rule and persuaded the powerful nobles of Novgorod to accept the situation. He even adopted a policy of thwarting possible revolts against the Mongols. Novgorod, in return, was given virtually a free hand in running its own affairs.

Some Russian princes, less wise than Alexander, sought help from western Europe in resisting the Mongols. When they eventually had to submit to Mongol rule, they failed to receive the favored treatment that Alexander's policy ensured for Novgorod. The principality of Novgorod maintained its independence until Ivan the Great made it a part of his new Muscovite state in 1478. (See page 57.)

### The Decline of the Khanate

Mongol dominance in Russia came to an end because of internal weaknesses. The Khanate of the Golden Horde had virtually broken away from the great Mongol Empire of Asia, as had many other Mongol groups. Similarly, over a period of years, various Tatar chieftains established their own khanates within the Khanate of the Golden Horde. Still others allied themselves with the emerging Muscovite and Lithuanian states. The death blow to the Golden Horde, however, was delivered by Tamerlane, a Turko-Mongol leader from Central Asia who eventually built a vast empire. For eight years Tamerlane's armies fought the Golden Horde. By his final victory in 1395, every major city of the Horde, including Sarai, had been destroyed.

Although Tamerlane claimed descent from Genghis Khan, he did not attempt to re-establish the old Mongol Empire. However, his grandson Babur established the Mogul dynasty in India. By this time some western Mongols were Muslims, while the eastern peoples were adopting the principles of Buddhism.

By 1500 Mongols were little threat to the Russians, Turks, or Chinese. The Mongolian state had been reduced to its origins on the plateau north of China, and became part of the Chinese empire in the 1700's. Not until 1912 did it achieve freedom, only to come under Soviet domination in 1924 as the Mongolian People's Republic. Although this is now the only Mongol state, all over Asia are people whose ancestors fought with Genghis Khan when he was shaping one of the largest empires the world has ever known.

## The Impact of the Mongols

Historians differ in their interpretations of how the Mongols affected Russia. Some scholars believe that many characteristics of later Russian life can be traced to Mongol influence. In particular, they point to the autocratic tradition of the Russian czars. Since the authority of Kievan princes had been limited by the rights of large landholders and merchants, Russia must have acquired this tradition from the khans. Other historians state that Mongol rule prevented Russia from sharing in the Renaissance, the "rebirth of learning" that was so important to western Europe. They say that Russia might have moved into the orbit of western European culture had it not been for Tatar rule.

The scholars who discount the influence of Mongol rule explain such things as Russian autocracy and the Asian aspects of Russian life on grounds other than Tatar dominance. They point out that the Mongols, although themselves followers of Islam, were tolerant in matters of religion and culture. The Tatars made no attempt to stamp out the Orthodox Church in Russia or to impose Mongol customs on the Russian people. So long as Mongol demands for tribute and soldiers were met, the

Russians could do as they pleased. In time the Mongols paid for their neglect of Russian affairs.

## Check Your Understanding

1. What was the Khanate of the Golden Horde?
2. How did the Mongols rule Russia?
3. Why did Novgorod escape destruction by the Mongols?
4. Why did Mongol rule decline?
5. *Thinking Critically:* Compare and contrast historians' views on the influence of the Mongols on Russian development.

## 4. A Unified State Under Muscovy

In the late 1200's Moscow was a tiny village at the center of the minor principality of Muscovy. The princes of this insignificant state came to be the driving force behind the unification of Russia. The early Muscovite princes, in their wildest imagination, never dreamed of accomplishing such a feat. Yet by the end of the 1300's, the Muscovite princes were already challenging the Mongols as the leading power in Russia. Over the next two centuries Muscovy would lay the foundations for a mighty empire. How and why did this happen?

### Appanage Russia

Muscovite princes were able to take advantage of the breakdown and dispersal of power in Russia. Even before the collapse of the Kievan federation, a new system of rule was taking shape north of the Kievan provinces. There the rota system first fell into decay. Eventually each prince came to regard himself as owner of the territory he ruled, called an **appanage** (AHP-uh-nij.) There were hundreds of great and small appanages in the northeast, since a prince, before he died, generally made provisions for dividing his holdings among his sons or other relatives. Each of these holdings then became a new appanage, which in turn might be divided on the death of its prince.

Northeastern Russia had a handful of grand princes, leaders whose vast holdings entitled them to higher rank than other princes. Under Mongol rule, these grand princes were made responsible for collecting tribute and raising the quota of soldiers in the lesser appanages. None of these grand princes, however, exercised political authority over the lesser princes. Appanage Russia consisted of hundreds of states and, at the outset at least, Moscow was far from the most important of them.

### The Rise of Moscow

During the 1300's, the rulers of Moscow extended their influence in all directions. Many methods were used—purchase, conquest, alliances, treaties, and colonization of unsettled regions. The Mongols did nothing to stop this growth, since they cared little about the affairs of Russian princes as long as their demands for tribute and soldiers were met.

At first, Moscow cooperated with its Mongol overlords. The prince of Moscow became a grand prince with authority to collect and send to the khan the required tribute. Gradually the attitude of the Muscovite rulers changed. Over the years, as the Khanate was weakening, most of the appanages of northeastern Russia became subordinate to Moscow. The time came when Grand Prince Dmitry (1359–1389) collected tribute from lesser princes without forwarding it to the Mongol capital.

In 1380 the reigning khan sent an army to bring the rebellious Dmitry into line. But Dmitry defeated the khan's army in a battle in the region of the Upper Don, thereby winning for himself the title "Dmitry Donskoy," meaning "Hero of the Don." His victory did not free Moscow from Mongol domination. Indeed, just two years after the famous battle, the khan returned with a larger army, sacked Moscow, and forced Dmitry to re-

Dmitry Donskoy's battle with the Mongols at Kulikovo in 1380 became a favorite theme in Russian history, for it was the first victory over the powerful overlords. In this sixteenth century miniature the battle takes on religious meaning, as a struggle between believers and unbelievers. The angels are undoubtedly fighting on Dmitry's side.

sume paying tribute. But the Muscovite ruler had proved that the Mongols were no longer invincible.

## The End of Mongol Rule

Mongol raids into Russia did not stop until near the close of the 1400's. During these years Moscow continued to pay tribute. But the payments became more and more irregular as the Muscovite princes gained strength and the various khans took to fighting among themselves. The year 1450, when the Khan of the Golden Horde was assassinated, is sometimes regarded by historians as the end of the Mongol period in Russia. In 1480 Ivan IV finally declared Moscow's independence from Mongol rule. Actually, by that time his realm had been free from Mongol rule for much more than 30 years.

## Moscow as the Third Rome

An important factor in the rise of Moscow was its position as headquarters of the Russian Orthodox Church. During the Kievan period, the Metropolitan, the head of the Orthodox Church in Russia, lived in Kiev. When that city was nearly destroyed by the Tatars, the Metropolitan moved to Vladimir, a town to the west of Moscow. But he soon began to show a preference for Moscow. It was because of his encouragement that the great Usspenski Cathedral was built in that city. In 1328 the Metropolitan again moved his headquarters, this time to Moscow. Thereafter the Russian Orthodox Church, one of the most influential forces in Russian life, supported the Muscovite regime against competing states.

In 1453 the Byzantine Empire, which for years had been declining in power, fell to the invading Turks. Since the conquerors were Muslims, Constantinople no longer could remain the spiritual center of the Eastern Orthodox Church. Soon after the fall of Constantinople, Ivan III (1462–1505), known in history as "the Great," became Prince of Moscow. He asserted that Moscow was the successor to Constantinople as the religious capital of the world, and that the Metropolitan was now the head of the Eastern Orthodox Church.

But Ivan was not satisfied to claim merely the religious leadership of the world for his capital. He married the niece and heir of the last Byzantine emperor so that he could proclaim himself the successor to the throne of the Byzantines. He also assumed the title of **czar**, probably derived from the Roman title *Caesar*, although his grandson, Ivan IV, was the first ruler to be formally crowned as such. From the days of Ivan III until

**RELIGIOUS ART.** In the *Trinity*, Andrey Rublev's mystical symbolism shows God and the Holy Spirit on either side of Christ (right), as he offers himself as a sacrifice. Its circular rhythm creates the feeling of harmony and love among the three figures.

The late fifteenth century icon on the left was the work of Dionysius. Unlike most icon painters, he was a professional artist rather than a monk. Surrounding the central figure of the Metropolitan Alexius are scenes from the life of this defender of Russian nationalism against the Mongol rulers.

Like the *Trinity* and the *Metropolitan Alexius*, this icon of St. George and the dragon is from fifteenth-century Novgorod (right). This saint is a protector of Russian peasants.

the overthrow of the monarchy in World War I, all rulers of Russia were called czars.

Thus Ivan III sought to claim for Moscow the religious and the secular leadership that was once Byzantium's and, before it, Rome's. By the end of his reign, Russians accepted his claim. Not long after his death, a church official proudly proclaimed:

> Moscow is the successor of the great world capitals; ancient Rome and the second Rome—Constantinople; Moscow is the third Rome, and there will be no fourth. [Quoted in Sidney Harcave, *Russia: A History.*]

### Ivan the Terrible

Ivan IV (1533–1584), called "the Terrible," was probably mad. In any case he could often be cruel, even sadistic. As a child he enjoyed torturing animals. As an adult he had many people put to death. In a fit of rage he even had his eldest son executed. According to legend, Ivan had the builders of Moscow's Church of the Intercession, later known as the Cathedral of St. Basil's, blinded. In this way they would never be able to build another church that would surpass the splendor of this one.

Although some of Ivan's behavior was abnormal, often there were also sound political reasons for the measures he took. Ivan was convinced that the nobles were plotting against him, and sometimes he was correct. Ivan understood that the nobles stood in his way of total control of the Muscovite realm. These hereditary aristocrats possessed power, privilege, and wealth. Ivan resented the boyars' privileged position and was furious because many of them no longer fulfilled their traditional military obligations to the state. The czar's wish to bring the proud boyars into line became an obsession. Many of these aristocrats, including some of his own relatives, paid for Ivan's displeasure with their lives.

In order to have an upper class he could control, Ivan created a new **service nobility**. Admission to this new class was gained through military and political service to the czar. The old boyar class was not eliminated, but the existence of a favored rival group made the old nobles more responsive to the czar's demands. In time, as both the old and the new nobility became dependent on the czar for positions and favors, the two classes became indistinguishable from one another.

### The Growth of Muscovy

By the time Ivan the Great became czar, Muscovy had already expanded from a tiny principality of no more than 500 square miles in area to an empire of 15,000 square miles. Moscow controlled the entire upper basin of the upper Volga and the Oka, with the exception of four or five relatively small principalities. To the northeast, Pskov and Novgorod retained their independence, but they were being threatened by the expansionist-minded princes of Moscow. The rest of the Russian forested region was controlled by Lithuania, with the exception of some German-held land on the Baltic and some under the rule of the Swedes. The Golden Horde still had a precarious hold on the steppe land to the southeast.

**INTERACTION: THE GROWTH OF MUSCOVY.** In the 300 years after 1300, Moscow grew from a small city-state to the foundation of a great empire.

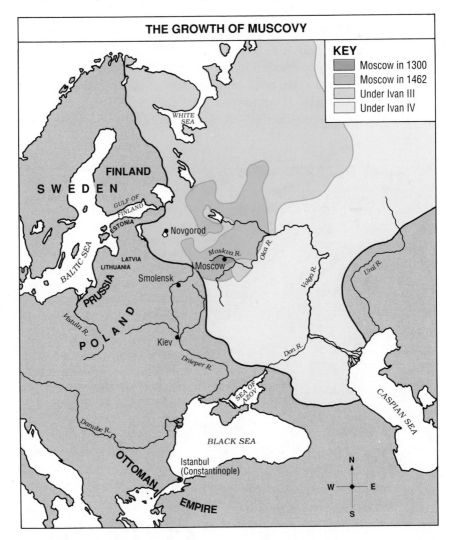

THE GROWTH OF MUSCOVY

KEY
Moscow in 1300
Moscow in 1462
Under Ivan III
Under Ivan IV

WHITE SEA

FINLAND
SWEDEN
GULF OF FINLAND
ESTONIA
Novgorod
Moskva R.
Moscow
Oka R.
Volga R.
Ural R.
LATVIA
LITHUANIA
BALTIC SEA
PRUSSIA
Smolensk
POLAND
Vistula R.
Kiev
Dnieper R.
Don R.
SEA OF AZOV
CASPIAN SEA
Danube R.
BLACK SEA
Istanbul (Constantinople)
OTTOMAN EMPIRE

N
W — E
S

Both Ivan III and Ivan IV were determined to extend the Muscovite Empire even farther. Ivan the Great absorbed the remaining principalities in the Volga-Oka region, made inroads into the Lithuanian possessions, and brought the proud republic of Novgorod into his empire.

Ivan the Terrible spent much of his time fighting a series of wars to expand his realm. Muscovite armies drove far into the steppe region, extending the czar's lands to the Caspian Sea. For many years Ivan IV sought to roll back the Lithuanians, Swedes, and Germans, but met with only partial success. By the time of his death, Moscow's holdings embraced a large part of what is today European Russia. Yet to be conquered were lands along the western frontier and the fertile steppe lands to the south and southwest.

### A Succession of Troubles

On the death of Ivan the Terrible in 1584, Russia entered one of its most trying periods. Because Ivan had killed his eldest son, the heir to the throne, another son, Feodor, became czar. But Feodor was a pale shadow of his father. A weak monarch with little talent or interest in government, he permitted his

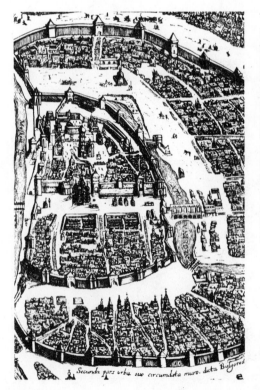

The Kremlin was the heart of Moscow in this seventeenth century engraving. Note the upper half of the central core. The Kremlin's entrance was the Spassky Gate, which is off the marketplace known as Red Square. In the center of this citadel is the Tower of Ivan the Great. The Kremlin and the marketplace, where Ivan IV built St. Basil's Church, were surrounded first by pine and later by stone walls. By 1700 a second and a third wall protected the expanding city of Moscow.

brother-in-law, Boris Godunov, to assume direction of the affairs of state. Since Feodor had no heir, his death in 1598 marked the end of the House of Rurik.

Soon after Feodor died, Boris had himself "elected" czar by the **zemsky sobor**, a council of nobles set up as a consultative body by Ivan IV. Czar Boris remained at the helm of the Russian state for only a few years. An iron-handed ruler, he managed to keep under control the many dissatisfied nobles who did not regard him as a rightful czar. When Boris died in 1605, the nobles quickly deposed his son and successor. The Godunov line of czars had lasted only seven years.

The death of Boris Godunov brought on Russia's "Time of Troubles." With no strong hand to control the government, one person after another advanced his claim to the throne. **Anarchy** prevailed. Boyar families struggled for supremacy, pretenders led armies to Moscow in attempts to gain control of the government, and peasants and Cossacks in the south revolted against landlord-nobles. Once again Russia was invaded by its old enemies from the west. The Time of Troubles continued until 1613, when Michael, the first czar of the Romanov **dynasty**, ascended the throne of "All the Russias."

## Check Your Understanding

1. What were the differences between the appanage and rota systems?
2. How did Moscow manage to break out of Mongol control?
3. Why did Moscow claim to be the third Rome?
4. How did Ivan the Terrible expand the Muscovite state?
5. Explain what is meant by the term *Time of Troubles.*
6. *Thinking Critically:* The Mongols' method of rule led to their downfall in Russia. Do you agree or disagree with this statement? Support your opinion with facts from Section 3.

# CHAPTER REVIEW

## ■ Chapter Summary

***Section 1.*** In early Russia different cultures developed in the forest and steppe regions. Although we know more about the peoples, such as the Scythians, who lived in the steppe region, it was the Slavic peoples who migrated to the forest lands of the north that formed the basis of the later Russian people. By the A.D. 500's, these Slavic peoples, migrating eastward from their original homes in Europe, had settled along the rivers of the forested region. These rivers provided the best means of transportation and, since farming was difficult, the new settlers came to rely on trade. Towns grew up at strategic points along the river routes. In the 800's these towns and their trade came under the domination of the Varangians, Vikings from Scandinavia who long had been active in this river trade. Under the Varangians trade with the Byzantine Empire flourished.

***Section 2.*** Chief among the prosperous river towns was Kiev, strategically located at the southern edge of the forest. During the Kievan period, the culture of the Russian cities was greatly influenced by that of the Byzantine Empire. When the Eastern Orthodox faith was adopted by the Russians in the 900's, that church became the chief transmitter of culture. An alphabet for the Slavic language was developed to make translation of the Bible possible. Russian church art and architecture were heavily influenced by Byzantium.

***Section 3.*** Kievan Russia, never truly unified, gradually declined into bickering principalities. This lack of unity made the towns an easy prey for the Mongol armies of the Golden Horde. Most of Russia was under Mongol rule from the mid-1200's until the breakup of the Khanate of the Golden Horde two centuries later.

***Section 4.*** Eventually most of the Russian states in the Khanate of the Golden Horde fell under the domination of Moscow, a growing state in the Oka-Volga region of Russia. Under Ivan the Great and Ivan the Terrible, Muscovy became the first truly united Russian state. The dynasty of Muscovite rulers ended with the death of Feodor in 1598. Thereafter Russia underwent a period of confusion until the new Romanov dynasty was established in 1613.

## Vocabulary Review

*Define:* national identity, cultural diffusion, tribute, oral tradition, aristocracy, rota, federation, boyar, strategic location, icon, alliance, appanage, czar, service nobility, zemsky sobor, anarchy, dynasty

## Places to Locate

*Identify:* River Road trade routes, Novgorod, Kievan Russia, Moscow, Constantinople

## People to Know

*Identify:* Rurik, Khazars, Vladimir I, St. Cyril, St. Methodius, Genghis Khan, Batu Khan, Tamerlane, Dmitry, the Metropolitan, Ivan III, Ivan IV, Boris Godunov

## Thinking Critically

1. What geographical factors help explain why the history of Russia unfolded in the forest region rather than on the steppe?
2. If Vladimir I had adopted a different faith, how might the history of Russia been different? How might Russian culture have been different? Consider contemporary Soviet life as well as historical developments.
3. Based on your knowledge of world history, what similarities and differences can you see between Mongol rule over its territories and Roman rule?
4. How did Ivan the Terrible's expansion of Muscovy extend his own power?

## Extending and Applying Your Knowledge

1. The story of Boris Godunov has been the source of several well known Russian works of art. Modest Mousorgski (1839–1881) composed the opera *Boris Godunov*, and Alexander Pushkin (1799–1837), Russia's foremost poet, dramatist, and master of prose, wrote an historical drama about him. Obtain a recording of the opera or a copy of the play for a class project. If you use the opera, summarize the story, set the scene, and play the most dramatic scene for the class. To use the play, organize a play reading with several other students. Summarize the story and then read the most dramatic scene for the class.

2. Using art books from the library, choose one work of Russian religious art—either a church or a famous icon—and prepare an oral report on its history and its architectural significance. Show how Russian artisans adapted Byzantine styles to their own uses. Illustrate your talk with either photographs from books or your own drawings.

3. Using a source such as *The Eastern Orthodox Church* by Ernst Benz, prepare a written report on the beliefs and practices of the Russian Orthodox Church.

# 3
# Empire
# of All the Russias

A new ruling family came to the Russian throne in the early 1600's. The Romanov dynasty remained in power for the next 300 years (1613–1917). During its first two centuries of rule, Russia was transformed from a third-rate state into a major power in both Europe and Asia. The Romanov czars put together an empire that stretched from eastern Europe to the shores of the north Pacific. In the early 1700's the official name of Russia was changed from "Grand States of the Russian Czardom" to "Empire of All the Russias."

The Romanovs came to rule the largest country in the world. But more significant than Russia's sheer size was its political and social organization. At a time when the power of monarchs was being limited in many parts of Europe and Asia, the Russian czars were tightening their control over their subjects. Although czarist power was built up at some cost to the nobility and the Church, the peasants, the great majority of the population, suffered even more. Millions of peasants lost their traditional rights and were reduced to serfdom.

As a result of developments in France at the turn of the nineteenth century, Russia came to play a leading role in determining the future of western and central Europe. The French Revolution and the spectacular rise of Napoleon Bonaparte had brought an upheaval in the European political order. Russia's participation in the struggle to halt the French emperor tipped the scales against him. Thereafter Russia became increasingly involved in European power struggles.

# 1. Expansion and Westernization

The Time of Troubles came to a close in 1613 with the coronation of the first Romanov czar. But settling the issue of a new dynasty for Russia did not solve the country's grave internal problems. In many parts of the land the authority of the czarist government was lightly regarded or even ignored. Bandits raided the countryside, and rebels roamed the frontiers. These unsettled conditions seriously hampered agriculture and trade.

The domestic problems of the new czarist regime were compounded by the aggressiveness of neighboring states. Russian border regions in the west, extending from the Baltic to the Ukraine, had been seized by the powerful kingdoms of Sweden and Poland. Both countries were determined to hold on to their new acquisitions and, if possible, further weaken Russia. For much of the 1600's the liberation of the western regions was the dream and despair of the czars. In the south, a formidable foe was ready and willing to block Russian expansion. The Ottoman Empire not only controlled the outlet to the Black Sea, but was expanding northward into the Balkans.

The early Romanov czars attacked the country's problems with zeal and determination. Not every problem was solved, but by the early 1700's Russia's rulers had brought stability to the country and had made important acquisitions of territory, especially along the Baltic.

## The First Romanov Czar

In 1613 the zemsky sobor was called into session for the purpose of selecting a new czar. Its choice was Michael Romanov (1613–1645), aged 16, member of a distinguished boyar family and a third cousin of the deceased Czar Feodor.

One of Michael's first acts as czar was to secure his father's freedom from a Polish prison and establish him as the virtual co-ruler of the nation. Philaret, born Feodor Romanov, had been considered for the throne early in the Time of Troubles. When his bid for power failed, his opponents forced him to enter the religious life, and later arranged for his imprisonment. Since he was both Patriarch of the Russian Orthodox Church and the power behind his son's throne, Philaret was one of the most influential men in Russia.

During the early years of his reign Michael had to govern in consultation with the zemsky sobor, which was determined to keep czarist power under control. But in less than a decade the czar had brushed aside this body, and thereafter Michael,

### Czarist Russia 1613–1815

| | |
|---|---|
| 1613 | Beginning of Romanov dynasty |
| 1639 | Pacific coast reached by Russians |
| 1649 | Peasants' freedom of migration abolished |
| 1667–1671 | Razin's revolt |
| 1685–1725 | Reign of Peter the Great |
| 1689 | Treaty of Nerchinsk |
| 1713 | Capital moved to St. Petersburg |
| 1722 | Table of Ranks |
| 1741 | Alaska reached by Russian explorers |
| 1772–1774 | Pugachev's revolt |
| 1762–1796 | Reign of Catherine the Great |
| 1772, 1793, 1795 | Partitions of Poland |
| 1801–1825 | Reign of Alexander I |
| 1812 | Russia invaded by Napoleon |
| 1815 | Congress of Vienna |

as well as his successors, called it into session only on rare occasions. A major obstacle to autocratic rule had thus been removed.

Russia's many domestic and foreign problems were tackled with equal vigor during Michael's reign. The czarist government took firm action to suppress lawlessness and banditry. In foreign affairs Czar Michael concentrated on recovering the western territories seized by Poland and Sweden. Here, however, he was only partly successful. To promote economic recovery, the czar encouraged foreign trade and tried to persuade artisans and craftworkers from other parts of Europe to settle in Russia. By the time of his death in 1645 Michael was able to pass on to his son Alexis a kingdom that had substantially recovered from its earlier troubles.

### Alexis Romanov

Alexis (1645–1676), a shrewd and capable ruler, was determined to strengthen the power of the czar. His reign was marked by social unrest and religious conflict. (See Sidelight, page 67.)

Even more so than his father, Alexis sought to advance the "Europeanization" of Russia. He encouraged Western technicians and military men to come to Russia. Most of them made their homes in a section of Moscow known as the German Suburb. To the Russians of this period all non-Russian Europeans were "Germans."

Alexis also carried on his father's struggle to expand czarist rule. His primary foe for many years was the kingdom of Poland. Luckily for the czar, the Poles became involved in an intense struggle with their Cossack subjects in the Ukraine at the very time they were faced with internal political and religious dissension. Alexis intervened on the side of the Cossacks. As a result, he was able not only to recover some of the territories Russia had lost in the west, but also to extend his authority into the eastern Ukraine.

### Peter the Great and Westernization

Peter I (1685–1725), called "the Great," was certainly the most inquisitive czar of the Romanov dynasty. Peter's childhood was spent not in the isolated world of royal palaces, but in the German Suburb. There his eyes were opened to western European culture by the German, French, and English technicians

Religious leaders, royalty, and boyars file from the Kremlin into Red Square in this seventeenth-century engraving of a Palm Sunday celebration. Townspeople watch the procession commemorating this religious holiday.

# **S**IDELIGHT TO HISTORY

## The Old Believers

The reign of Alexis was marked by a serious religious conflict. Many Russians of the 1600's—priests and laypeople alike—were pressing for reform in the Russian Orthodox Church. They believed it was necessary for Russian church practices to correspond closely with the Byzantine form, from which Russian Orthodoxy had derived. Over the centuries the Russian Orthodox service, as well as the Russian versions of the Scriptures, prayer books, and hymnals, had departed slightly from the Byzantine patterns. But most Russians, especially the peasants, clung to the familiar rituals and traditions. Illiterate and uninformed about the reasons for change, they considered any difference from the normal service of worship as heresy.

In 1652 Alexis appointed reform-minded Nikon to the office of Patriarch. In an attempt to return the Russian Church to the "right path," Nikon ordered many changes. Opponents claimed these reforms raised questions of basic dogma. For instance, the most heated controversy arose over the question of how to make the sign of the cross. Nikon maintained that it should be made with three fingers as the symbol of the Trinity, which was in accordance with the practice in churches of the Byzantine rite. Conservative Russians known as Old Believers insisted on joining two fingers to represent the dual nature of Christ—God and man. Differences such as these split the Russian church.

The Old Believers soon proved that they would rather die than accept changes in the forms and practices that meant so much to them. During Nikon's tenure they were persecuted for their beliefs, and after he was removed from office in 1666, things became even worse. Thousands of Old Believers died rather than submit to the changes. It became commonplace for a large band of them to gather in an old barn or cottage, set it afire, and perish in the flames. But despite persecution and suicide, the number of Old Believers increased rather than diminished during the 1600's. In fact, the sect has survived into modern times.

**PETER'S WESTERNIZA-TION CAMPAIGN.** Deeming them old-fashioned, Peter outlawed the flowing beards Russians had always tended with pride. Only a special tax would obtain the beard license (above). In the woodcut (left), the unfortunate man appears destined to be beardless despite his protests.

and artists employed by the czarist government. As a young man he traveled in western Europe, observing and learning. His great ambition, from which he never swerved, was to introduce western European ways into his realm. By modernizing the Russian state and society, he hoped to make his country the equal of any European power.

Peter was about seven feet tall and had a powerful build. He possessed an insatiable intellectual curiosity. During his lifetime he mastered more than 20 trades, including shipbuilding, shoemaking, and dentistry. He was also an able military commander, both on land and at sea. But Peter also possessed a darker side. He had a violent temper, drank to excess, and was often quite cruel. Like Ivan the Terrible, for example, Peter had his eldest son executed.

As czar, Peter was determined to serve Russia well. At his insistence many changes were made in Russia. The czar encouraged the building of modern factories. In order to pursue his goals in foreign policy, the czar brought in foreign officers to train the army according to western standards. He gave his full support to the development of shipbuilding facilities, realizing that his country must become a sea power in order to compete for foreign markets. Against great opposition he improved the efficiency of the government. In all his endeavors for reform Peter displayed great impatience and, when his orders were resisted or not obeyed, he did not hesitate to use brutal means.

## Window to the West

Since Peter's dream was to enlarge his country's borders, Russia was at war during most of his 40-year reign. Peter waged war against Sweden, Poland, the Ottoman Empire, and against the Tatars in the Crimea, a peninsula on the Black Sea. Despite early defeats, extensive territories were added to Russia to the northwest and south.

Peter's proudest achievement was the acquisition of land from Sweden along the eastern Baltic. Peter warred for two decades with his northern neighbor to win for Russia a "window to the West" on the Baltic Sea. Alert to the strategic and commercial importance of the area, particularly from the standpoint of his practically landlocked country, Peter decided to build a new port city in the conquered region. In 1703 an army of artisans and laborers began to construct a beautiful city on the disease-ridden marshlands in the delta of the Neva River. Drainage was helped by an elaborate system of canals built within the city, and public buildings were constructed of stone instead of the customary wood. Named St. Petersburg, the new city replaced Moscow as the capital and remained Russia's first city until the honor was returned to Moscow in 1918. It is still the major port for the Soviet Union and the world's northernmost large city. Since 1924 it has been known as Leningrad.

## A Period of Instability

In 1722 Peter the Great issued a ruling that was to confuse the succession to the throne several times during the 1700's. He decreed that a czar could name anyone he chose to succeed him. However, Peter himself failed to name a successor. From 1725 when Peter died to 1762 the czarist succession was determined by political intrigue and chance rather than inheritance. The Palace Guard, composed of noblemen, chose several czars—and unseated some. The only ruler of note during this period was the Czarina Elizabeth (1741–1761).

Elizabeth chose as her successor the son of her sister. When this boy was 17, Empress Elizabeth arranged a marriage with Catherine, a German princess. The young couple lived in the imperial palace for the rest of Elizabeth's reign. When the empress died in 1761, the nephew succeeded to the throne as czar Peter III. But Peter was mentally unbalanced and not competent to rule. A **coup** inspired by Catherine, the young czar's wife, and carried out by the Palace Guard, soon placed Catherine herself on the throne.

## Catherine the Great

Catherine II (1762–1796) called "the Great," was a remarkable woman and an able ruler. Like Peter the Great, she admired the culture of western Europe. She spoke French in addition to Russian and German, and was fond of reading philosophy, history, and literature. She wrote her own memoirs, and carried on an extensive correspondence with prominent persons in other lands. She was particularly interested in the social and political ideas stirring western European intellectuals on the eve of the French Revolution. The empress was a patron of Western art, music, and dance, and made them fashionable at the Russian court. To the leading thinkers, philosophes, as they were called, of western Europe, she seemed a brilliant queen bringing civilization to the eastern barbarians.

Again in the tradition of Peter I, Catherine engaged in ambitious exploits to subdue her neighbors and increase her own territories. During her long reign she struck at Poland, the Ottoman Empire, and the Tatars in the Crimea. Combining force with skillful diplomacy, Catherine managed to achieve most of her goals.

Catherine's most famous international exploits concerned Poland. Taking advantage of that kingdom's internal problems, Catherine joined with Prussia and Austria to take over Polish territory. In each of the "Partitions" of 1772, 1793, and 1795, the participating powers helped themselves to parts of their weak neighbor. (Austria did not share in the Second Partition.) Russia received a large chunk of eastern Poland, most of which was peopled by Byelorussians, Ukrainians, and Lithuanians.

Catherine's other major territorial ambitions were realized along Russia's southern borders. Her war against the Ottoman Empire resulted in Russia's acquisition of useful territory along the northern coast of the Black Sea. In addition, Catherine added the Crimean peninsula to her realm by overcoming the last of the Tatars. These additions to Russian territory greatly increased Catheine's stature at home and abroad. On the other hand, Catherine needed more and more tax revenues to finance her wars.

**THE "GREAT" RULERS.** Peter I and Catherine II were both vitally concerned with strengthening ties to the West and improving Russia's image abroad. Peter planned the city of St. Petersburg according to Western styles to replace the old-fashioned Moscow. European architects built magnificent Baroque (buh-ROHK) palaces such as Peterhof, (below). This palace, with its ornate gold fountains, was intended to rival the Versailles Palace in France.

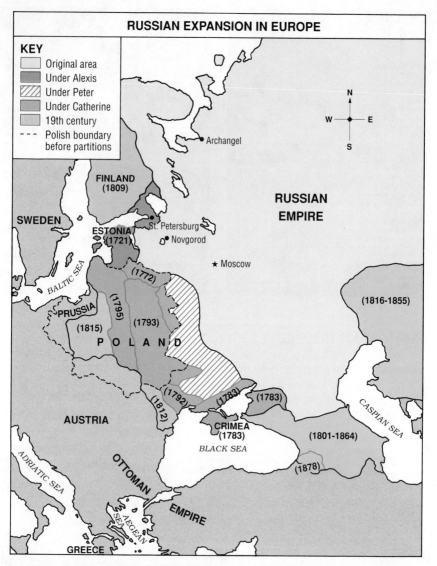

## RUSSIAN EXPANSION IN EUROPE

**KEY**
- Original area
- Under Alexis
- Under Peter
- Under Catherine
- 19th century
- - - Polish boundary before partitions

**INTERACTION: RUSSIAN EXPANSION IN EUROPE.** After the annexation of Poland, expansion in Europe was slowed. Where were the greatest territorial gains made?

## The Legacy of the Early Czars

During the first two centuries of Romanov rule, the czarist monarchy changed from a third-rate state to a major world power. The Russian Empire, including the yet undeveloped region of Siberia, stretched from eastern Europe to the shores of the Pacific. The largest state on the globe, it was also one of the most autocratic. Russia's rulers were unwilling to allow their subjects any power. All any czar would do was make an occasional concession to curb unrest. When they considered Russia's best interest, the Romanovs nearly always took a stand on the side of unlimited autocracy. The Romanovs firmly believed that God had given them the right and obligation to rule. They could not understand why anyone would resent their autocratic ways.

## Check Your Understanding

1. How did each of the following help to develop the principle of autocratic rule: **a.** Michael? **b.** Alexis? **c.** Peter the Great?
2. How did each of the following advance the goal of Westernization: **a.** Alexis? **b.** Peter? **c.** Catherine?
3. *Thinking Critically:* How would you evaluate the changes that Peter brought to Russia? Which were good and which were harmful? Do you think Peter did more good than harm? Support your argument with facts.

## 2. A Base for Autocratic Rule

Not wishing to be puppets manipulated by self-seeking nobles, the czars sought to strengthen the authority of the state and throne. As a result, they aroused widespread opposition among the aristocratic class. They also chipped away at the traditional rights of the peasants and before long reduced them to serfs. Furthermore, the Romanov czars found themselves confronted with an upheaval in the Russian Orthodox Church. Their success in bringing the nobles, peasants, and the Church under imperial control provided a firm base for autocratic rule.

### Less Power for the Nobles

The founder of the Romanov dynasty quickly discovered that he had an unruly nobility on his hands. To bring the nobles into line, both Michael and Alexis stressed the principle of service to the state as a requirement of noble **status**. Like Ivan the Terrible, they also opened the ranks of the nobility to newcomers, giving aristocratic status and the income from landed estates as rewards for service to the state. Naturally, the percentage of boyars in the aristocratic class declined steadily.

Peter the Great continued to expand the ranks of the nobility. He gave major attention to reorganizing the government and the army. Even more than his predecessors, he insisted that nobles fill administrative positions or serve as military or naval officers. In 1722, near the end of his reign, he drew up the Table of Ranks, which classified all servants of the state under 14 civil and military grades. Advancement to the higher levels automatically brought noble rank. Although the system in theory was based on merit rather than birth, abuses were common. Still, the Table of Ranks, with only one major change made in 1834, was in effect until the end of the Romanov dynasty.

The creation and expansion of the service nobility ultimately resulted in a government alarmingly overstaffed with bureaucrats and civil servants. Russian **bureaucracy** was amazingly inefficient:

> Into its [the bureaucracy's] hopper in St. Petersburg poured reports, summaries, complaints, and petitions; and from it poured streams of directives and orders to ministers, school inspectors, police officers, tax collectors, senators, governors, judges, heads of bureaus, government clerks, and— with the introduction of the railway and the telegraph— telegraph operators and station masters. From St. Petersburg to Kamchatka, from Archangel to Odessa, the country was minutely plotted for the channeling of the interminable inflow and outflow of official papers, which at times appeared to be both the raw material and the end product of the machine. [Sidney Harcave, *Russia: A History.*]

Time and again the inability of the bureaucratic machine to operate efficiently created problems for the Russian state.

## A Lessening of Church Influence

Peter was determined to modernize the Russian state and society, and to bring both firmly under his control. But religion had such a firm hold on the people that high Church officials with political ambitions could obstruct czarist plans. Peter's opportunity to break the power of the Church came when the Patriarch died. Refusing to designate a successor, the czar ultimately placed the Orthodox Church under the direction of the Holy Synod, a committee of churchmen answerable only to him.

Peter and succeeding czars tried in other ways to undermine the power of the Church. One of Peter's chief reasons for moving the capital from Moscow to St. Petersburg was to escape from the influence of the "Third Rome." Eventually, the Holy Synod came to be headed by a Procurator, an official appointed by the

**74**

czar. The Russian Orthodox Church was thus under the control of the czar. It became another instrument to support autocratic rule. This situation continued until the end of the Romanov dynasty.

## The New Nobility and Serfdom

In time both social and political climbers and the old boyar families combined to lessen the requirements for achieving noble rank. Members of the aristocracy discovered ways of escaping the obligation to serve the state and of acquiring ownership of an estate and the right to hand it on to their heirs. From the time of Peter the Great such an estate could not legally be divided among heirs, but ways were found around this law, too.

Some of the czars also helped to undermine the service nobility. During the 1700's succession to the throne was hazardous. Some members of the imperial family might conspire to eliminate the heir, and both czars and would-be czars at times fell victim to foul play. To secure the backing of powerful nobles and army officers, contenders for the throne might agree to ignore or modify the requirements for achieving noble status. It is not surprising that during such intrigue the nobles strengthened their hold on their estates and the peasants who lived on them.

The change from peasant to **serf** for the majority of Russia's population was one of the tragic outcomes of the introduction and abuse of a service nobility. Prior to the Romanov period, Russian peasants had not been severely oppressed. They enjoyed many rights and were able to move from place to place. Peasants who were dissatisfied found it possible to migrate to open lands in the south and east. Because the new nobles complained that estates were worthless without an assured labor supply, laws were passed limiting the rights of peasants to move from an estate. Finally, in 1649, peasants' freedom of migration was abolished. Later, laws were passed that extended the time during which runaway peasants could be legally recovered.

By the time of Peter the Great many peasants already were bound to the land. Thereafter their legal status grew progressively worse as landlords were given greater control over their lives. During the 1700's peasants became the property of the nobles. They could be bought and sold like other possessions of the landowner. The process of reducing millions of Russian peasants to serfdom was completed during the reign of Catherine the Great.

*(continued on page 78)*

## Religion in Czarist Russia

The religious makeup of czarist Russia underwent constant change during the Romanov period. Repeated **annexations** of territories inhabited by peoples of diverse faiths were largely responsible.

*Russian Orthodox Church:* The official state church under the Romanovs, its faithful embraced the large majority of the peoples of European Russia. It rejected the supreme religious authority claimed by Rome and the popes of the Roman Catholic Church.

*Old Believers:* Numbering in the millions, they steadily refused to accept the authority of the state church, were from time to time subject to persecution, and often found it necessary to worship in secret. (See Sidelight, page 67.)

*Uniats:* In the late 1500's an effort was made to integrate followers of the Eastern Orthodox Church in the kingdom of Poland-Lithuania into the Roman Catholic Church. The following compromise was reached. The Orthodox agreed to accept the primacy of the Pope and the Roman Catholic position on matters of dogma. In return, the Orthodox were to retain rites of the Eastern Church and were to be permitted to use Church Slavonic instead of Latin in their services. This agreement, acceptable to the hierarchy of the Eastern Orthodox Church in the western Ukraine, was approved in 1596 but was denounced by many members of the lower clergy and laity. Those who accepted the agreement became known as Uniats, or Catholics of the Byzantine rite.

When territories of Poland-Lithuania were later annexed by czarist Russia, the Uniats came in conflict with the Russian Orthodox Church. Many members emigrated in the 1800's, and some of their descendants live today in North America.

*Roman Catholics:* Members of this church were not numerous in Russia until the Russian annexations of Polish territory in 1772, 1793, and 1795. Many Roman Catholics also lived in the regions of Lithuania and Latvia annexed by Russia.

*Armenian (Gregorian) Church:* When Armenia in the Caucasus was annexed in the 1800's, the Armenian Christians were brought under the rule of the czars.

*Gregorian Orthodox:* When Georgia was absorbed by czarist Russia in the 1800's, the Georgians continued to practice their faith.

*Protestant denominations:* Various Protestant denominations were represented in the czarist empire. In Estonia and in much of Latvia, Lutherans had long been the religious majority. In addition, such denominations as the Evangelical Christian Baptists, Seventh Day Adventists, Reformed Calvinists, and Methodists won followings.

*Islam:* With the annexation of large areas in Central Asia by the czars in the 1800's, millions of Muslims came under the rule of the Russian czars.

*Judaism:* Small groups of Jews had lived in Russia since early times. (See Sidelight, page 43.) In the 1500's large numbers of Jews settled in Poland and the Ukraine. In the following century they were subjected to horrible massacres by the Cossack rebel chieftain, Bogdan Chmielnicki. By 1800 the area was part of Russia. Subjected to continuing persecution, millions of Jews fled the country from the late 1800's on, and during the Bolshevik Revolution beginning in 1917. Several million Jews remained in Soviet Russia, however, and many of them were massacred during the Nazi invasion of World War II. It is estimated that more than three million Jews still live in the Soviet Union.

*Others:* In the eastern regions of the Soviet Union a number of Buddhists lived in territories annexed by the Romanov czars. Mention might also be made of the sects that split away from the Old Believers. The Khlysty claimed Rasputin (see page 129) as one of their most famous members. The Dukhobors, a reform and pacifist group of Old Believers, were so relentlessly persecuted that many of them migrated to Canada at the turn of the twentieth century.

Periodic famines caused by weather hit Russia during the days of the czars. This woodblock print shows peasants taking thatch from the roofs of their buildings to feed their cattle. As late as the 1980's the USSR had to import large quantities of wheat to make up for a drought.

### Peasant Revolts

The erosion of traditional peasant rights stirred rebellions, especially in the borderlands of the southwestern Ukraine, the region inhabited by the freedom-loving Cossacks. The most famous of these revolts occurred during the reign of Alexis, the second Romanov czar. In 1669 Stephen Razin, a bold and ambitious Cossack chieftain, headed an army composed of fellow Cossacks and runaway serfs and proceeded to capture town after town along the lower Volga. All along the way he collected booty and **indemnity** from merchants and landowners. More than a year passed before the government could suppress this uprising. Razin himself was handed over to the government by **conservative** Cossack leaders, and executed. But the legend of this revolt lived for generations.

A second major revolt in the Volga region took place during the reign of Catherine. In the early 1770's Emelian Pugachev, an uneducated Cossack, persuaded many serfs and fellow Cossacks that he was Emperor Peter III, the ruler who in fact had been murdered by agents of Catherine. But since the imperial army remained loyal, the revolt was doomed to failure. Pugachev, like Razin, was captured by Cossack leaders, turned over to imperial authorities, and executed.

## Growing Criticism of Serfdom

After the French Revolution the institution of serfdom came under increasing attack. Enlightened Russian nobles sought to ease the peasant's burden, and such writers as Radischev (1749–1802) described the wretched condition of the peasantry and denounced the selfishness of the landholding nobles. Although many critics were exiled to Siberia, their writings influenced many readers. Even more embarrassing to the Russian government were the criticisms of foreign travelers who saw in serfdom proof of the backwardness of Russian society. However, reform was not easy in a country whose economic and social system demanded peasant labor to support a privileged aristocracy. For decades the czars saw no acceptable alternative to serfdom.

### Check Your Understanding

1. Compare and contrast how the service nobility functioned in theory and in practice.
2. How did Peter the Great attempt to undermine the authority of the Church?
3. Why did the life of Russian peasants grow worse during the first two centuries of Romanov rule?
4. *Thinking Critically:* Why was nothing done to improve conditions for Russian peasants?

## 3. The Conquest of Siberia

While the early Romanovs were establishing their rule in European Russia, a slow stream of Russians was flowing into the regions east of the Ural Mountains. Many were runaway serfs seeking an escape from the restrictions imposed by both the state and their landlords. Others were Old Believers fleeing Russia in order to continue rites and practices forbidden by the increasingly autocratic Romanov regime. Most of these refugees settled down on the lands immediately to the east of the mountains and attempted to eke out a livelihood by farming. But the most fearless pioneers were fur traders and trappers. Pushing eastward across Siberia, they reached the shores of the north-west Pacific about a century after the first Russian crossed the Urals.

The conquest of Siberia is a fascinating tale. Within less than 100 years, a territory considerably larger than the United States was added to the Russian domain. This was accomplished large-ly through the efforts of small groups of adventurers. The czarist government did not initiate the exploration of Siberia and gave little help to those who did. Only when Siberia was ready for the taking, did the czarist government move into action.

## Early Exploiters of Siberia

The story of the conquest of Siberia begins with Anika Stroganov (STROH–guh–nuf), the founder of one of Moscow's most influential boyar families. During the early 1500's his agents crossed the Urals in search of furs, giving cheap trinkets and household utensils to the local inhabitants in exchange for the valuable furs. Nor did it take long for the traders to discover the value of liquor in making a trade. Stroganov's traders were the first Russians to reach the Lena River. By 1594 the Stroganovs not only had penetrated deeply into Siberia, but had also established a near-monopoly of the region's fur trade.

At the very time that the Stroganovs were exploiting Siberia in the name of private enterprise, the Russian state was begin-ning to awaken to the region's potential worth. Yermak, a Cos-sack chieftain who had angered Ivan the Terrible, fled eastward to establish the settlement of Orel on the edge of the Muscovite domain. In 1581, Yermak led an expedition from Orel into Siber-ia to find a land of gold rumored to lie beyond the Urals. After an 18-month journey, in which half of his men perished, Yermak reached the river Tura. A Tatar khan ruled the region, but Yer-mak defeated his forces and pressed on to Sibir, the capital of the khanate. Capturing the town, he assumed for himself the title "Prince of Siberia."

Not wishing to irritate his fiery overlord Ivan any further, and not having discovered gold anyway, Yermak offered the new empire to the czar. Soon after Ivan accepted the "gift," the de-feated khan rose up against his conqueror. Ivan sent reinforce-ments to help, but Yermak was unable to defeat the fierce Ta-tars. After Yermak was killed, the Cossacks abandoned their garrisons and returned to Russia. But Ivan, unwilling to give

Yermak's representatives present their Siberian loot to Ivan, while nobles look on.

up his latest acquisition, sent an army to re-establish czarist rule in western Siberia.

Czarist military expeditions fanned out over all of Siberia west of the Ob, subduing the population and bringing the land under Russian control. Fortresses were built that served as bases for the drive east. In 1632 the town of Yakutsk was founded on the Lena River. This became the principal point of departure for further advances.

### The Drive East

Siberia was sparsely populated and, although the local inhabitants often resisted the newcomers from the west, their opposition was easily broken by the gun-bearing intruders. The Russians quickly learned to make use of the tributaries of the great northerly flowing rivers. These waterways provided far more rapid east-west transportation than was possible by land. Forts and trading posts, which later became towns, were set up at strategic points along this vast network of streams.

A small band of Cossacks first reached the Pacific coast in 1639. Based at the mouth of the Ulya River, they explored the coastline. In 1649 other Cossack adventurers established the base that became the town of Okhotsk. For a long time afterwards, this fort was Russia's principal harbor on the Pacific coast. With the opening of bases on the Pacific, Russian explorers were able to attack the unknown reaches of Siberia from the east as well as from the west.

## Discovery of Alaska

During the mid-1600's a number of Russian adventurers left Yakutsk to explore northeast Siberia. In time they reached the Arctic Ocean, where they explored the mouths of some of Siberia's great northward flowing rivers. In the late 1600's Russian explorers penetrated the Kamchatka peninsula in the extreme northeast of the Asia continent. Using this peninsula as a base, other adventurers explored the Kurile Islands from 1711 to 1718.

The inhabitants of northeastern Siberia had often crossed over frozen winter seas to a region they called "the big land." Their accounts were verified in 1741 when Vitus Bering, a Danish sea captain employed by the czarist government, landed on the coast of Alaska. When the survivors of Bering's expedition reported that sea otters and seals were plentiful in the Bering Sea, Russian trappers quickly flocked into the area. For some years chaos reigned in the Alaska regions as Russian adventurers sought by every devious means to obtain the coveted skins. A semblance of law and order was finally established in the late 1700's when the Russian American Company founded permanent settlements in Alaska. Though granted a monopoly over the fur trade by the czar, the company did not enjoy it for long. The company's rich profits invited competition. Soon Spanish, English, French, and American traders were challenging the Russians' position in the north Pacific areas. Still, the prospect for great profits continued to lure Russians to North America.

Russia's foothold in North America was extended far down the Pacific coast. By 1812 the Russians had a settlement and trading post, Fort Ross, just a few miles from San Francisco. To maintain its North American interests, Russia would have had to bring in more settlers or even to become a naval power in the Pacific. For lack of funds, the czar in 1867 sold Alaska and the Aleutian Islands to the United States for the then enormous price of $7,200,000.

## The Amur Valley

Yakutsk also became the jumping-off point for Russian expeditions into the Amur River region. During the early 1600's some

MOVEMENT: RUSSIAN EASTWARD EXPANSION. After Yermak, other explorers in the 1600's pushed the Russian border all the way to the Pacific. With the annexation of Kamchatka and the Amur River region, eastward expansion was complete. In the southwest the czars expanded toward Persia, what is modern-day Iran, at last achieving control over the Khanates south of the Aral Sea.

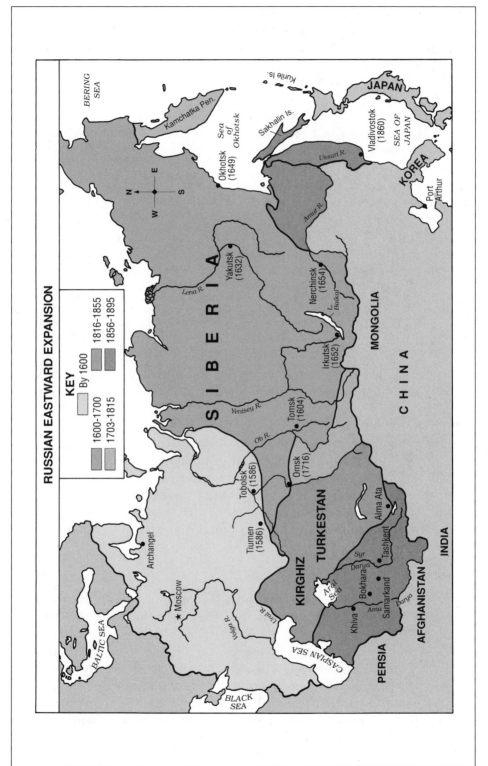

RUSSIAN EASTWARD EXPANSION

KEY

By 1600
1600-1700
1703-1815
1816-1855
1856-1895

BERING SEA

JAPAN

Kamchatka Pen.

Kurile Is.

Sakhalin Is.

Sea of Okhotsk

Vladivostok (1860)

SEA OF JAPAN

KOREA

Port Arthur

Okhotsk (1649)

Ussuri R.

Amur R.

SIBERIA

Yakutsk (1632)

Nerchinsk (1654)

L. Baikal

Lena R.

Irkutsk (1652)

MONGOLIA

CHINA

Yenisey R.

Tomsk (1604)

Ob R.

Omsk (1716)

Tobolsk (1586)

TURKESTAN

Alma Ata

Tiumen (1586)

KIRGHIZ

Syr Darya

Tashkent

Archangel

Aral Sea

Bokhara

Samarkand

Moscow

Khiva

Amu Darya

Volga R.

Ural R.

CASPIAN SEA

PERSIA

AFGHANISTAN

INDIA

BALTIC SEA

BLACK SEA

Russian peasants had migrated to this area, although it paid tribute to the Chinese emperor. The stories about this land that came back from the settlers excited Cossack leaders living on the frontiers of Siberia. Several of them led expeditions into the Amur River Valley, and found it was every bit as fertile as rumored. By 1681 Russians had begun to settle the entire valley as well as the adjoining Ussuri River valley.

The Russians in the Amur region terrorized their neighbors and sowed the seeds of long-lasting Chinese resentment. Fighting broke out. At first Chinese appeals for help brought little response, since a coalition of Manchus and Mongols were busy conquering China. Once the Manchus gained the upper hand in the struggles for the Empire, however, they sent troops into the Amur Valley, destroying Russian settlements and killing many of the inhabitants. But the stubborn Russians, and especially the Cossacks, were not discouraged. If an attack could not be repelled, the Russians would rebuild their homes as soon as the Chinese soldiers left.

The fighting was finally ended in 1689 by the Treaty of Nerchinsk, the first treaty negotiated between the Chinese Empire and a European state. The treaty defined the Chinese-Russian boundary, leaving the western border rather vague. All Russians were excluded from the Amur Valley, and their settlements were destroyed.

The Treaty of Nerchinsk did not end the problem of the Amur. Soon after the treaty was signed Russian traders once again moved into the valley and established settlements. Nor was it long before the Russian government became interested in the Amur River as a possible outlet to the Pacific Ocean for Russian trade. Many Russian explorers charted the Amur region for their government in the years after the Treaty of Nerchinsk was signed.

### Settling Siberia

The motives that caused American hunters, trappers, and traders to explore the frontier also led the early Russians to penetrate Siberia. But in time most Americans who went west began to farm the land and build towns—to create a new and better way of life for themselves. This was much less true of Russians going to Siberia. Some peasants fled to Siberia to escape intolerable conditions in European Russia. They planned to farm and establish permanent homes. But most Russians who went east were adventurers, traders, and trappers—men who hoped to find sudden wealth and then move on.

**84**

A tragic segment of Siberia's population were people exiled for life or for a period of years. The czarist government found the vast region was a good place to "lose" men and women considered undesirable for one reason or another. Many Russian citizens convicted of crimes that called for long-term imprisonment spent their lives working on Siberian prison farms or on government projects in Siberia. Thousands who plotted against, or even spoke against, the czarist regime became exiles in the vast east. The phrase "sent to Siberia" came to be used in other countries when an important person fell out of favor with superiors. Small wonder that few Russians went willingly to Siberia.

## Check Your Understanding

1. **a.** Who were the first Russians to enter Siberia?
   **b.** Why did they come?
2. How did the czars gain their first lands east of the Urals?
3. How were the Russians able to expand so quickly across Siberia?
4. Describe how Russians gained and then gave up Alaska.
5. Why were the czars interested in the Amur and Ussuri valleys?
6. *Thinking Critically:* How did the settling of the American West differ from the settling of Siberia? If the environment of the American West had been similar to that of Siberia, would the pattern of settlement have been the same? Why or why not? Consider the settling of Alaska.

## 4. Russia's Rise to World Power

The outbreak of the French Revolution in 1789 came as a great shock to Catherine the Great. Fond as she was of French social thought and culture, she viewed this upheaval with deep distaste. As an *idea*, "Liberty, Equality, and Fraternity," the slogan of the revolution, was exciting, but as a *program* it aroused Catherine's autocratic disapproval. Yet she did not bring Russia into the conflict to overthrow the revolutionary government that had brought the French monarchy to an end.

Neither Catherine's son Paul nor her grandson Alexander I were able to ignore the wars that followed. Paul was moved to action against England while Alexander, after a brief understanding with Napoleon, turned against the Emperor and helped to bring about his downfall. Alexander's actions established Russia's right to an honored place in the conferences that sought to set up a new order in Europe.

## Involvement in European Affairs

When Paul I (1796–1801) became czar, France no longer was a monarchy. Its revolutionary armies were about to begin a series of military campaigns that would threaten all the old established governments. Paul, a true autocrat, deplored the executions of Louis XVI and Marie Antoinette, and was vehemently opposed to the new republican government in France. To overthrow French **republicanism**, the czar joined a military **coalition** that included Turkey, his country's traditional enemy, as well as Austria, England, and Portugal. Paul agreed to send Russian troops to help drive the French out of the Netherlands and Italy. Never before had Russian armies fought so far from home.

Unfortunately for both Czar Paul and Russia, consistency was not his nature. Paul was probably mentally unbalanced. At any rate, he soon became dissatisfied with English and Austrian contributions toward winning the war. Reversing his foreign policy, the czar opened negotiations with France, and even ordered a Cossack force to strike at British military bases in India. Paul did not live to see the outcome of his ill-conceived plan. In 1801 conspirators assassinated the "mad czar."

## A Policy of Russia First

A contemporary of Alexander I (1801–1825) described him as being "as sharp as a pin, as fine as a razor, and as false as seafoam." But Alexander lived during difficult times, and on the whole served Russia well. When Alexander came to the throne he reversed the anti-English stand of his father. Between 1805 and 1807, Russia sided with England, Austria, and later Prussia, in wars against Napoleon. The Russians fought bravely, but Napoleon won some of his greatest victories in defeating the armies of the czar. Czar Alexander was ready to make peace when the French emperor proposed a conference.

In 1807 Napoleon and Alexander met on a raft in the Niemen River, between Prussia and Russia, near the Prussian town of

Tilsit. Russia agreed to accept the many political changes Napoleon was making in western and central Europe. Napoleon made it clear to Alexander that he did not oppose Russian aspirations to grab Finland and to expand at the expense of the Ottoman Empire. Alexander, in turn, agreed to a secret alliance between the two countries and to a plan for excluding English goods from the continent. This was the so-called "Continental System."

## The Invasion of Russia

Neither Alexander nor Napoleon kept promises made at their Tilsit conference. Undoubtedly differences over the Continental System and the future of Poland were basic causes of the split between the two emperors. In 1812 Napoleon began assembling an army from all over Europe for an invasion of the Russian Empire. In June of that year this huge army crossed the western frontier of Russia. Napoleon expected to dictate his terms of peace in Moscow.

These plans never materialized, even though Napoleon reached Moscow in September. Knowing they were no match for Napoleon's soldiers, the czarist armies had retreated eastward, avoiding battle until near Moscow. Meanwhile the Russians had employed a **"scorched-earth" policy**—burning food and supplies and driving off or killing livestock. The distances were too great for the French to cart in supplies from Prussia, had they been available. The French policy was to live off the land, but in Russia this policy was disastrous.

On September 7 the Russian forces stood firm at Borodino, a town about 75 miles from Moscow. Both sides suffered enormous losses in the showdown, and the Russians resumed their retreat through Moscow and to the east. When Napoleon entered Moscow the city was nearly deserted. To make matters worse, fires broke out that destroyed much of the city.

Napoleon had expected to dictate a peace, but in the end even the truce he proposed was rejected. After remaining five weeks in Moscow, the invasion army began its retreat. The prospect of surviving the terrible Russian winter, which was about to begin, was bleak—especially since the French soldiers would have neither shelter nor winter clothing. Cold, hunger, and constant harassment by Cossacks took a heavy toll of life. The retreat soon became a flight. This terrible campaign cost the French and their allies at least 300,000 dead, while another 100,000 were taken prisoner.

REGION: EUROPE IN 1812.    By 1812 both Napoleon and Alexander had forgotten their alliance formed in 1807, on the raft at Tilsit, (above). Now that Napoleon's empire included nearly all of Europe, the French emperor turned to Russia. His disastrous route is outlined on the map.

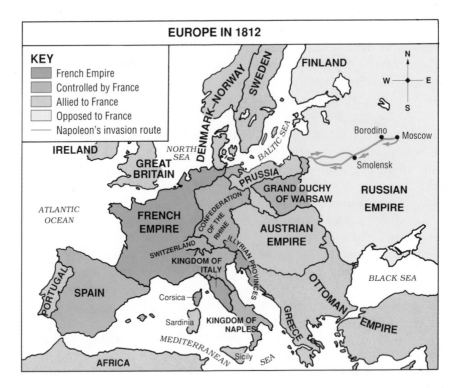

EUROPE IN 1812

KEY
- French Empire
- Controlled by France
- Allied to France
- Opposed to France
- — Napoleon's invasion route

FINLAND

DENMARK-NORWAY

SWEDEN

BALTIC SEA

Borodino

Moscow

IRELAND

NORTH SEA

GREAT BRITAIN

PRUSSIA

Smolensk

RUSSIAN EMPIRE

ATLANTIC OCEAN

FRENCH EMPIRE

CONFEDERATION OF THE RHINE

GRAND DUCHY OF WARSAW

AUSTRIAN EMPIRE

SWITZERLAND

ILLYRIAN PROVINCES

KINGDOM OF ITALY

BLACK SEA

OTTOMAN EMPIRE

PORTUGAL

SPAIN

Corsica

Sardinia

KINGDOM OF NAPLES

GREECE

MEDITERRANEAN

Sicily

SEA

AFRICA

## The War of Liberation

Undaunted by devastating losses in Russia, Napoleon hurried to Paris to raise another army. The long years of almost constant war had taken their toll, however, and the army he assembled included boys as well as men earlier rejected for service. It was a poor fighting force.

Napoleon's enemies had no intention of giving the emperor time to recoup his losses. Alexander brought Prussia into an anti-French alliance with Russia, and these two countries soon were joined by others. The new coalition was determined to continue fighting the "War of Liberation" until all territory outside France was freed from Napoleon's control. For Napoleon it was a great blow when Austria dropped its role of mediator to join the coalition.

The turning point in the War of Liberation came on October 16–19, 1813. In the Battle of Leipzig, also called the Battle of the Nations, the coalition forces defeated Napoleon's exhausted and outnumbered army. During the weeks that followed, Napoleon lost more battles, but refused to consider the terms offered him by the allies. Early in 1814, after coalition forces had crossed the Rhine and were invading France, Napoleon refused a peace offer under which he would have ruled a France with its boundaries of 1792. When the allies entered Paris, the French Senate declared that Napoleon had forfeited the throne. Napoleon then abdicated and was exiled to Elba, a tiny island given him by the allies as a principality.

But Europe had not heard the last of Napoleon. A year later he landed in the south of France. His return to Paris was a triumph as the French troops sent to capture him sided instead with their old commander. For a hundred days the outcome was uncertain even though the nations who had deposed Napoleon were determined to put an end to his regime. The allies agreed to mobilize one million men should that be necessary. But on June 18, 1815, British and Prussian armies under Wellington and Blucher won the Battle of Waterloo. This time Napoleon was sent to the island of St. Helena, where he lived under close guard until his death in 1821.

## The Congress of Vienna

Napoleon's return from Elba took place at the time European rulers and statesmen were meeting in the Congresss of Vienna to work out a new order on the continent. Russia's major role

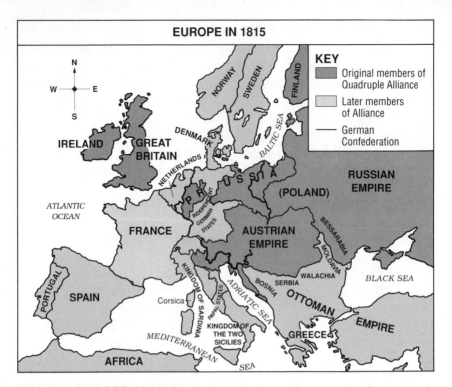

**EUROPE IN 1815**

KEY
- ■ Original members of Quadruple Alliance
- ▨ Later members of Alliance
- — German Confederation

**REGION: EUROPE IN 1815.** In the reshaping of Europe at the Congress of Vienna, Russia received Poland and gained a powerful position in the Quadruple Alliance.

in the defeat of Napoleon made Czar Alexander an important person at the conference. Russia received most of the land included by Napoleon in the Grand Duchy of Warsaw. Since Alexander in 1812 had promised the Poles a kingdom under Russian protection, he now became King of Poland. However, Austria refused to surrender the parts of Poland it had annexed in the late 1700's. It was, therefore, Russian Poland and part of Prussian Poland that made up the new state. Russia had also acquired Finland from Sweden in 1809 and Bessarabia from Turkey in 1812.

In an effort to win the loyalty of the Poles, Alexander granted the new country a constitution. It was to last only 15 years, however. When a revolution broke out in Poland in 1830, Alexander's successor crushed it and abolished both kingdom and constitution. (See page 97.) In 1832 Poland became a province in the Russian empire.

Alexander and the heads of other European states were determined to prevent new political upheavals. The Russian, at times a dreamer compared to such hard-headed realists as Metternich, Austria's prime minister, advocated an agreement among the crowned heads of Europe to conduct their mutual relations on the basis of Christian principles. To please the czar the representatives of most countries agreed to the proposed Holy Alliance, although they saw little merit in the idea.

The Holy Alliance played no important role in international politics, but critics often used that name in denouncing policies of the Quadruple Alliance. This was a compact to maintain the Vienna peace settlement by holding frequent conferences to discuss problems and agree on what to do. In effect it was a continuation during times of peace of the close cooperation that had enabled Britain, Russia, Austria and Prussia to defeat Napoleon. France was invited to join the group in 1818.

## Check Your Understanding

1. What was the result of the agreement at Tilsit?
2. Why did Napoleon invade Russia?
3. How did the Russians defeat the French invaders?
4. How did the invasion contribute to the final defeat of Napoleon?
5. What part did Russia play in the Congress of Vienna?
6. What was Alexander's idea in forming the Holy Alliance?
7. **Thinking Critically:** Why did Russia become involved in the great wars that followed the French Revolution?

## CHAPTER REVIEW

### ■ Chapter Summary

**Section 1.** During the first two centuries of Romanov rule, Russia expanded to become a gigantic state straddling both Europe and Asia. From Michael to Catherine the Great, Russian rulers devoted their energies to strengthening their autocratic rule at home and to furthering their interests abroad. There were few neighbors that Russia did not compete with for land during these centuries.

With the capture of land along the Baltic from Sweden, Peter the Great was able to build his "window to the West." St. Petersburg, now Leningrad, became the major Russian port. By the early 1800's the czarist empire had gained the borders in Europe that it would keep until the early twentieth century.

**Section 2.** The buildup of czarist power was made at the expense of the country's traditional social classes. The Romanovs not only tamed the old nobility but also created a new aristocratic class. This new service nobility accumulated wealth and privileges but remained subservient to the czar. The reduction of the peasantry to serfdom was a fateful consequence of czarist policies. By the early 1700's, the Romanov rulers also had succeeded in bringing the Russian Orthodox Church under the control of the state

**Section 3.** In the 1600's and 1700's Russian penetration and exploitation of Siberia begun by fur traders and Cossacks moved steadily ahead. By taking advantage of the river network for transportation, the Russians were able to cross vast distances comparatively easily. Their expansion into northeastern Asia brought the Russians into direct contact with the Chinese Empire. After some conflict a settlement of the frontier question was reached. The quest for further sources of wealth finally resulted in Russian advances onto the North American continent and into the Pacific Ocean. In the end Russia was forced to sell Alaska to the United States.

**Section 4.** The Russians did not escape the effects of the French Revolution and the rise of Napoleon to power. The upheaval led to the increasing involvement of the czarist empire in the affairs of central and western Europe. The climax of the clash between the czar and Napoleon was the latter's invasion of Russia in 1812. Overwhelmingly defeated in Russia, the French emperor was soon dethroned and exiled. At the Congress of Vienna a new political order was established in Europe. The Russian emperor played a major role in the decisions reached by the great powers, and cooperated in the plans made for maintaining the peace.

■ **Vocabulary Review**

**Define:** coup, status, bureaucracy, serf, annexation, indemnity, conservative, republicanism, coalition, scorched-earth policy

■ **Places to Locate**

**Locate:** Partitions of Poland, St. Petersburg, the Crimea, Yakutsk, Okhotsk, Lena River, Amur River, Borodino, Grand Duchy of Warsaw, Waterloo

*Identify:* Michael, Old Believers, Alexis, Peter the Great, Catherine the Great, Emelian Pugachev, Anika Stroganov, Yermak, Vitus Bering, Paul I, Alexander I, Napoleon

■ **Thinking Critically**

1. Why did the first czars expand to the northwest, the southwest, and the west, but not to the east? Why did it seem a less desirable direction for expansion?
2. Why did Russia enjoy great prestige in western Europe under Alexander?
3. Based on what you have read about the Congress of Vienna and its aftermath, what do you think the term *balance of power* means? How did Russia help maintain the balance of power in Europe? How could it have upset this balance?
4. The czars tried to keep all ideas about freedom, justice, and equality away from the people. Based on what you know about European history, why was this impossible to do in other parts of Europe? How might the course of Russian history have been different if the czars had supported better conditions for the peasants?

■ **Extending and Applying Your Knowledge**

1. Draw a map showing the stages of Russian expansion under the Romanovs.
2. Consult art books and histories of Russian architecture and prepare an oral report on the architecture of St. Petersburg. Use photographs in books or draw your own diagrams to illustrate your art history lecture.
3. The caption on page 71 uses the term *Baroque*. Research and write a brief report on the Baroque style in art and architecture using examples from different countries in Europe.
4. Peter the Great is among the most interesting and unusual individuals in Russian history. His vivid, sometimes contradictory, character has led many historians and biographers to write accounts of his role in Russian history. Read one of these such as Robert K. Massie's *Peter the Great: His Life and His World* and prepare a book report.

# 4

# From Autocracy to Revolution

During the century between the Congress of Vienna and the outbreak of World War I, almost all European states adopted constitutions limiting the powers of the monarchs. But in the "Empire of All the Russias" a system of autocratic government prevailed. While extending Russia's boundaries and enlarging its influence in international affairs, the last four czars reacted strongly against attempts to limit their autocracy at home. Sometimes a czar would recognize the danger signals arising out of his policies, but each attempt at reform was either too little, or too late.

Small groups of professional revolutionaries sought to overthrow czarist rule. Many of these men and women had been influenced by the radical philosophy of the German philosopher Karl Marx. They saw in the country's small but growing industrial population a nucleus for revolutionary change. In the end professional revolutionaries did not bring down the czarist system. The government simply collapsed.

Perhaps no one could have saved Russia from revolution. Each of the czars tried, but centuries of autocratic tradition stood in the way. It is ironic that when the revolution finally came, Russia was beginning to move toward a more just society. Peasants were getting land of their own, poor working conditions in factories were receiving attention, and the **Duma** (DOO-mah), Russia's first representative assembly, was meeting on a fairly regular schedule. But the accumulated problems of the centuries, together with Russia's defeats and heavy losses in World War I, were more than the autocracy could stand. Over 300 years of czarist rule ended in the March Revolution of 1917.

# 1. The Last Czars

In the early 1800's, both Paul and Alexander I were concerned about the problems of serfdom, and the latter even had a passing interest in constitutional government. Lasting reforms were instituted in the nation's administrative and financial systems. But the French Revolution and the threat posed by Napoleon caused all of Europe's monarchs, including the czar to reconsider granting the people powers traditionally exercised by the ruler. Indeed in Russia this growing conservatism found expression in repressive legislation, reactionary domestic policies, and increased police surveillance of "enemies of the state." Neither the czars nor other rulers seemed to realize that the forces of change set loose by the French Revolution could not be suppressed by autocratic methods.

## *The Accession of Nicholas*

With the return of peace following the Congress of Vienna, Russian **liberals** began to form secret revolutionary societies. These are discussed in section three. Because Alexander I had become increasingly conservative, liberals were looking forward to the succession of Constantine, the czar's brother. What very few people knew was that several years earlier Constantine had secretly surrendered his rights to the throne to a third brother, Nicholas. Consequently, for several weeks after Alexander's death in 1825 confusion reigned in St. Petersburg. Neither Nicholas nor Constantine knew quite how to explain to the people this departure from tradition.

Since the liberals had come to believe that Constantine sympathized with their hopes for constitutional government, they were dismayed to learn that Nicholas would be the next czar. On December 26, the date set for officers and soldiers to take an oath of allegiance to Czar Nicholas I, a small number of liberal officers marched on the capital at the head of two regiments of soldiers. These officers and their unsuspecting troops refused to take an oath of allegiance to Czar Nicholas I. Instead they demanded "Constantine and Constitution." Legend has it that the soldiers assumed that Constitution was the name of Constantine's wife. The officers had expected other dissatisfied citizens to join in the protest and were shocked when no one rallied to their cause. Nevertheless, December 26 became for Russian liberals a day to remember—the anniversary of the first attempt to force autocratic Russia to adopt a constitutional government.

## TIMETABLE

### The Road to Revolution

| | |
|---|---|
| 1825–1855 | Reign of Nicholas I |
| 1825 | Decembrist Revolt |
| 1827 | Battle of Navarino Bay |
| 1828–1829 | War with Turkey |
| mid–1800's | Birth of Russian novel |
| 1854–1856 | Crimean War |
| 1855–1881 | Reign of Alexander II |
| 1860 | Founding of Vladivostok |
| 1861 | Emancipation of serfs |
| 1865–1867 | Establishment of zemstvos |
| 1865–1885 | Establishment of control over Central Asia |
| 1869 | *War and Peace* published |
| 1870 | Repudiation of Black Sea agreement |
| 1875 | Possession of Sakhalin confirmed |
| 1877–1878 | Russo–Turkish War |
| 1878 | Congress of Berlin |
| 1881–1894 | Reign of Alexander III |
| 1883 | "Emancipation of Labor" formed |
| 1891 | Trans–Siberian Railroad begun |
| 1894–1917 | Reign of Nicholas II |
| 1898 | Lease on Port Arthur |
| 1901 | Formation of Socialist Revolutionary Party |
| 1903 | Formation of the Social Democratic Party |
| 1904–1905 | Russo–Japanese War |
| 1905 | "Bloody Sunday" |
| 1906 | Meeting of First Duma |
| 1907 | Formation of Triple Entente |
| 1914 | Outbreak of World War I |
| 1917 | Beginning of the Russian Revolution |

The Decembrist Revolt strengthened Nicholas' determination to maintain autocratic rule. Throughout his reign of 30 years, he repressed liberalism and made every effort to stamp out all opposition to czarist rule. The universities, considered hotbeds of radical thought, were carefully controlled. **Intellectuals** were discouraged from traveling abroad where they might observe democratic institutions or study liberal ideas. Strict **censorship** became the rule. Thousands of government officials read all publications and banned any that reflected views they considered anti–czarist or revolutionary.

Nicholas was equally ready to support autocracy throughout Europe. When a revolution broke out in France in 1830, he immediately began to plan intervention on behalf of the king, Charles X. But a revolt in Poland against Russian rule spoiled his plan. Nicholas ruthlessly suppressed the Polish rebellion and took away the constitution and other privileges granted the Poles by Alexander I.

When another wave of revolutions shook Europe in 1848, Nicholas again proved his readiness to support autocracy. The Austrian emperor asked Nicholas for help in crushing the revolt of his Hungarian subjects, and the czar quickly sent a Russian army. Actions such as this caused Nicholas, the "Autocrat of the Russian people," to be called by Western Europeans the "Policeman of Europe."

## War and Reform

As the reign of Nicholas I drew to an end, Russia became enmeshed in the Crimean War. (See page 118.) The czar died while the conflict was still in progress, and was succeeded by his son, Alexander II (1855–1881).

Russian failures in the war surprised people who, after Napoleon's defeat in Russia, regarded that country's army as invincible. The Russians themselves were shocked by the evidence of inferior equipment, inadequate transportation, and corruption among officials and suppliers of war material.

The defeat in the Crimean War was probably the major reason behind Alexander's decision to introduce reforms. But Czar Alexander, like his father Nicholas, was also greatly disturbed by the ever–increasing number of peasant disturbances. Clearly something had to be done about the institution of serfdom. Because many of Alexander's reforms were liberal in nature, the czar acquired a reputation as a liberal that he scarcely deserved. Alexander was an autocrat, and his chief concern was to strengthen and preserve the czarist regime. His every move was made to further his goal. He endeavored to reform the czarist system without changing its inherent flaws.

The emancipation of the serfs in 1861 and the years that immediately followed saw the most far–reaching of the changes

# S IDELIGHT TO HISTORY

## Orthodoxy, Autocracy, and Nationality

In the early 1800's when Western influences were introducing liberal ideas into Russia, Czar Nicholas I attempted to "turn the clock back" to the days when no one dared challenge the authority of the czars. In 1832, when Count Sergei Uvarov proposed a new educational system stressing "the truly Russian and Conservative principles of orthodoxy, autocracy, and nationality," the czar had found his slogan for combating liberalism. *Orthodoxy* signified a common spiritual base, the Russian Orthodox Church. Although it was dedicated to the Christian tradition, the Orthodox Church was also firmly controlled by the state. *Autocracy* was the will of the czar that held the country together. *Nationality* stood for the ethnic and cultural superiority of the Great Russians.

In imposing his program of "Orthodoxy, Autocracy, and Nationality," Czar Nicholas strengthened his control over the Orthodox Church. He demanded enforcement of an earlier rule that compelled all Great Russians, Byelorussians, and Ukrainians to be members of the Russian Orthodox Church. Those who had left the Church had the choice of returning or being punished for their rejection of Orthodoxy. Nicholas also persuaded, and sometimes forced, Protestants, Roman Catholics, Muslims, and Jews within Russia to accept membership in the Orthodox Church.

The interpretation of Nationality did not remain constant. Nicholas at first took it to mean loyalty to the czarist regime, but later used the term to justify the imposition of Russian culture on non–Russian minorities in the Russian Empire.

"Orthodoxy, Autocracy, and Nationality" was the slogan of the czars until the Romanov regime fell in 1917. Although the czars' autocratic rule prevailed, they found it impossible to impose Russian culture on minority groups because these people were determined to follow their own customs and traditions.

introduced by Alexander. Almost 50 million peasants were released from the control of the state and private landlords. Another reform, the establishment of the **zemstvos,** local self–governing bodies, gave the inhabitants of villages, towns, and cities limited rights to manage their own affairs. Improvements were also made in the court system. The czar planned a system of public education to make schooling available to children of all classes. Censorship of news media and travel restrictions were relaxed and, as might be expected, the armed forces were drastically reorganized.

The czar's reforms were sharply criticized by conservatives who argued that the Polish revolt of 1863 was caused by too great an emphasis on freedom. A determined effort was made to stamp out Polish **nationalism**. Thereafter the czar pursued a much more conservative policy at home.

## Assassination and Reaction

Reactionaries applauded the new direction of government, while liberals still urged reforms. In the last years of his life Alexander II seemed ready to consider some of their requests. This never came about because of the conspiracies of underground organizations. The czar survived several attempted assassinations, but in 1881 a terrorist society known as the "People's Will" was successful. Badly wounded by a bomb, Alexander II died shortly after the attack.

Jolted by the assassination of his father, Alexander III (1881–1894) was determined to avoid a similar fate. He would never tolerate dissent, even from trusted and loyal officials. Never were secret police and censors more active. Liberals found little to their liking in Russia's political climate, and some left the country. Those who remained and expressed their views too freely were likely to be arrested, tried, and often sentenced to exile in Siberia. **Radicals** who agitated against czarist autocracy were dealt with even more harshly. But Alexander III made little effort to distinguish between moderates, liberals, and radicals. He condemned anyone who did not support his regime completely and took stern action against all foes.

## The End of the Romanov Dynasty

Whereas Nicholas II (1894–1917) shared his father's views on the role of the czar, in temperament he was a different person. Where Alexander III was unbending and even cruel in his relations with others, Nicholas II was gentle. Alexander III, strong–willed but not too imaginative, did not shy away from

## ART OF CZARIST RUSSIA.

A delicately carved window and fine lace curtains decorate a simple log house (right). Traditional patterns for wood-carving and needlework have been used by Russians for centuries. Common symbols for carving and embroidery are roosters, lions, and mythical animals like those carved on the window frame (above).

Within the Kremlin palace, now maintained as a museum, one sees the Russian love of ornate design. In this room privileged visitors waited to be received by the czar. The bare wooden floors are a stark contrast to the dazzling ceiling. Note the icon.

the challenges Russia faced. Not so Nicholas II. Convinced that the great mass of people loved him as their "Little Father" and gave him unquestioning loyalty, Nicholas was blind to the pressures against czarism that were building in Russia. Moreover, in making important decisions he was often influenced by the impractical czarina Alexandra, who in turn was influenced by the greedy and unprincipled "holy devil," Rasputin. (See page 129.) The advice of competent ministers often went unheeded.

Russia under Nicholas II was seething with discontent and had serious domestic problems that taxed the country's resources. Nevertheless, the state persisted in pursuing a vigorous foreign policy in both Europe and Asia. As a result, Russia antagonized some of the great powers and also became involved in two major conflicts, the Russo–Japanese War and World War I. The added burdens of these wars proved too great for the czarist regime.

## Check Your Understanding

1. What actions did Nicholas I take as a result of the Decembrist Revolt?
2. How did Nicholas I act to suppress liberalism in the rest of Europe?
3. What reforms did Alexander II institute?
4. What events caused Alexander II to become more conservative?
5. What was Alexander III's attitude toward reform?
6. *Thinking Critically:* How did Nicholas I's policy of Orthodoxy, Autocracy, and Nationality offend the nobles, ethnic groups, and non–Orthodox Christians, Muslims, and Jews in Russia? Do you think he knew that this policy would antagonize these groups? Why do you think he would have tried to enforce this policy in the face of opposition?

## 2. Literature and Music in Czarist Russia

During the last century of czarist rule, Russia became a major contributor to Western culture. Russia's writers and composers were among the most talented in the world. How could a country as politically and as economically oppressive as Russia produce such great literature and music? Perhaps it was Russia's oppressiveness that made possible such cultural achievements. Many, although certainly not all, of Russia's great writers and composers came from privileged backgrounds. Leisure gave them the opportunity to be creative. Many of Russia's writers were also deeply disturbed by the injustices they saw all around them. Writing was a way to express their own complex reactions to reality. It was also a way to make their views known.

Russian artists could count on an appreciative though small audience. The majority of Russians were illiterate; however, the upper classes read widely in literature, philosophy, and history. Many of them had extensive personal libraries. They attended the ballet, opera, and concerts.

The Russians had long been impressed with the culture of western Europe. The Romanov czars invited artists to St. Petersburg and encouraged Russian nobles to attend the ballet and opera. As Russians became acquainted with the cultural traditions of other nations, their own talents matured. By the 1800's the writers and composers of czarist Russia were gaining recognition in their own country and in western Europe.

## Literature as Social Criticism

Since Russians were not allowed to express political opinions, especially those critical of the government, they learned to use imaginative literature to debate major issues of the day. Alexander Radischev (1749–1802) was the first of a long line of Russian writers to use fiction as a medium for criticizing the czarist regime.

Radischev's most important work, *A Journey from St. Petersburg to Moscow*, was seemingly a volume of "letters" describing an imaginary trip. It was in reality an attack on the government and the ruling class. Among the radical views expressed was the subtle suggestion that serfdom and autocracy should be abolished. Such writing did not please Catherine the Great, whose "liberalism" had been quenched by Pugachev's rebellion and the great revolution in France. Catherine remarked:

> The purpose of this book is clear on every page: its author . . . is trying in every possible way to break down respect for authority and for authorities, to stir up in the people indignation against their superiors and against the government. [Alexander N. Radischev (Leo Wiener, translator), *A Journey from St. Petersburg to Moscow.*]

Radischev was imprisoned and then exiled to Siberia. When Czar Paul came to the throne, Radischev was allowed to return to his estate, but he committed suicide in 1802. His views influenced the revolutionaries involved in the Decembrist Revolt of 1825.

### The Birth of the Russian Novel

It has been said, with little exaggeration, that in the nineteenth century Russia had no real fiction. Conservatives and liberals, as well as radicals and reactionaries, were all seeking ways to evade the czar's censors. As they became more familiar with Western literary styles, they found in the novel the literary form that let them express their views about Russian life.

As first Russian authors wrote exclusively about the upper classes. During the mid–1800's, however, many of them turned their attention to the condition of the masses. The heroes of this new school of writers were peasants and workers, drunkards and gamblers, thieves and vagrants. The settings for their tales were not palaces or estates but factories, taverns, cheap rooming houses, the marketplace, and the homes of the downtrodden. This style of literary writing, called sordid realism, dominated Russian literature until the end of the czarist period.

Russia's novelists were, above all, superb storytellers. Even though they were writing specifically about their own country, many of their works have a universal and a timeless appeal. The Russian writers frequently dealt with issues that are as relevant today in the United States as they were in nineteenth-century Russia.

### Pushkin as Innovator

Many critics believe that Alexander Pushkin (1799–1837) was the greatest Russian writer of all time. His first works were published while he was still a teenager. By the time he was 21, the government had recognized his importance by banishing him to southern Russia! Like so many writers of the period, Pushkin used the pen to attack autocracy and social injustice.

In his brief lifetime (he was killed in a duel at the age of 38), Pushkin effected great changes in his country's literature, using artistic forms that the Russian language had never known. His classic *Eugene Onegin* (1823–1830) was the first Russian novel in verse form. The first Russian writer to deal extensively with the lives of ordinary people, Pushkin began the trend toward realism, which became increasingly important by the end of the century.

Pushkin refined the Russian language and made it an effective instrument for literary purposes. Under his inspired pen everyday speech became the language of poetry. Two of his major works, *Eugene Onegin* and *Boris Godunov* (1824), later inspired great operas with the same names.

## Romanticism and Realism

Michael Lermontov (1814–1841), czarist Russia's most sensitive writer, was deeply concerned about the problems of good and evil, the ideal and reality, and the complexity of the human mind. This style of writing is known as **romanticism**, but Lermontov's works also included elements of realism. Although his writings were strongly influenced by England's great romantic poet, Lord Byron, Lermontov often took his themes from Russian history or folklore.

Like Pushkin, Lermontov was periodically banished from the capital and met his death in a duel. His most important work was *A Hero of Our Times*, a psychological novel written in 1840. The name of that book's "hero," Pechorin, has become synonymous in Russia with the talented but cynical young person who can find no worthy goal in life.

## Gogol as Master of Satire

Nikolay Gogol (1809–1852), unlike most of his literary colleagues, was a political conservative. His criticisms were directed at incompetence and corruption, not at the government or even autocracy. Gogol's masterpiece, *Dead Souls*, was published in 1842. This satirical novel brings out the shortcomings, injustices, and abuses of the bureaucracy. The "dead souls" are the serfs, although some critics suggest that the phrase is applicable to Russia itself.

When Gogol ridiculed the bureaucracy in *The Inspector General* (1836), unamused censors banned the play. Czar Nicholas I, however, lifted the ban after attending a performance. Perhaps he wanted his subordinates to know that he, too, was aware of their inefficiency and corruption.

Gogol was born in the Ukraine, and some of his writings provided a glimpse of this largely unknown (to Russians) region. His historical novel *Taras Bulba (1835)* is a classic tale of the Cossacks.

## Three Giants of Literature

Towering above all writers of the nineteenth century are three giants not merely of Russian but of world literature: Ivan Turgenev (1818–1883), Fyodor Dostoyevsky (1821–1881) and Leo Tolstoy (1828–1910). Turgenev, having spent much of his life abroad, was more Western in his outlook than his two contemporaries. He was the first Russian novelist to be read widely in Europe.

Although a skilled writer, Turgenev lacked the powerful mind and true genius of Dostoyevsky and Tolstoy. He was recognized as an artist on publication of *A Sportsman's Sketches* (1852), a work that provided a realistic and sympathetic portrait of the serfs. Turgenev's finest work, *Fathers and Sons* (1861), is a novel in which the radical younger generation confronts its more conservative elders.

Although Fyodor Dostoyevsky's first novel, *Poor People* (1846), was widely praised, his great masterpieces appeared following a period of exile in Siberia. For taking part in the activities of a group of liberals, Dostoyevsky was sentenced to 10 years at hard labor and military service in Russia's eastern wasteland. The experience affected him profoundly. Dostoyevsky became a staunch conservative, deeply religious, and intensely interested in probing the human personality. Dostoyevsky's first publication after his return from exile, *The House of the Dead* (1861–1862), detailed his experiences in prison. Other novels, in which he explored the human mind, include *Crime and Punishment* (1866), *The Idiot* (1868), *The Possessed* (1871), and *The Brothers Karamazov* (1880).

Many critics believe that Leo Tolstoy was Russia's greatest writer and acclaim his *War and Peace* (1869) as the world's greatest novel. They rank his *Anna Karenina* (1877) a distant second. War and Peace has as its background Napoleon's invasion of Russia. With nearly 500 characters participating in the complicated plot, the world's social problems come into focus and people's sense of values undergoes careful scrutiny.

Tolstoy was a member of an old and distinguished family and thus lived in comfort and security. But in later years, like Dostoyevsky, he became absorbed in philosophical and religious problems. Whereas Dostoyevsky's work improved because of this change, Tolstoy's suffered. Having experienced a religious crisis in the 1870's, Tolstoy began to preach nonviolence and his own version of Christianity. In 1901 he was excommunicated for attacks on the Russian Orthodox Church.

### Realist Authors: Chekhov and Gorky

Foremost among the realist authors who followed Tolstoy were Anton Chekhov (1860–1904) and Maxim Gorky (1868–1936). Chekhov, educated to become a doctor, gained fame as a writer of short stories and plays. As was common among Russian

**RUSSIA'S LITERARY GIANTS.**
Many Russians believe Alexander
Pushkin (above) had the greatest
mastery of their language. More familiar in the West is Fyodor Dostoyevsky (above, right) whose novels had mystical and psychological
themes. Anton Chekhov and Maxim
Gorky (below, right) are best known
as playwrights. Gorky (on the right)
became a Bolshevik writer. Leo
Tolstoy (below) presented a panorama of life in *War and Peace*.

writers of the period, Chekhov concentrated on mood rather than on action. Often humorous or satirical, his short stories nevertheless are pervaded by a sense of pessimism and melancholy. Chekhov's most famous plays, all written between 1896 and 1904, are *The Seagull*, *Uncle Vanya*, *The Three Sisters*, and *The Cherry Orchard*.

Maxim Gorky's surname was a pen name meaning "the bitter one." It aptly reflects the tone of his writing. In his many plays, novels, and stories, and in his autobiography, Gorky portrayed the unpleasant side of Russian life. He is perhaps best known for *The Lower Depths* (1902), a play that is still popular in the Soviet Union and that has been produced in English in the United States. Gorky, a supporter of the Bolsheviks and a friend of Lenin, became a literary hero following the Russian Revolution of 1917. (See page 143.)

### Russian Composers

Russia got a late start in the field of musical composition because the Orthodox Church forbade the use of musical instruments in church services. It was not until the mid–1800's that Russian music began to catch up with that of the West. Russian composers quickly matched the achievements of those in the West. Today the works of these artists are well-known in concert halls throughout the world.

Nineteenth–century Russia produced a select group of composers who became known as the "Big Three" of Russian music. Nikolay Rimsky–Korsakov (1844–1908) was a naval officer who devoted much of his time to musical composition. Drawing on Russian legends and folktales, he composed many operas. But outside his native land he is best known for *Scheherezade* (1887), an orchestral suite based on the legends of the Arabian Nights. Alexander Borodin (1833–1887), a professor of chemistry, established a place for himself in the scientific community before he became a composer. Although his music is intensely Russian, it reflects even more of the Asian influence than Rimsky–Korsakov's. Modest Mousorgski (1839–1881) also used traditional Russian themes in his works. His *Boris Godunov* (1874), based on Pushkin's play, is often regarded as Russia's finest opera.

Peter Ilych Tchaikovsky (1840–1893) must be placed in a class by himself. His name is known wherever music is played, even in places where other Russian composers may be unknown. Tchaikovsky's symphonies, operas, and ballets are deeply emotional and romantic, and usually are pervaded by a sense of the melancholy. His *Symphony Number 5*; the opera *Eugene Onegin*, based on Pushkin's novel; and the ballets *Swan Lake*, *Sleeping Beauty*, and *The Nutcracker* are loved by audiences throughout the world.

## Check Your Understanding

1. Using examples, show how Russian writers were able to get past censors with their criticism of the government and their discussion of social problems.
2. What characteristics did each of the following contribute to the Russian novel: **a.** Pushkin? **b.** Lermontov? **c.** Gogol?
3. Describe the importance of each of the following: **a.** Turgenev. **b.** Dostoyevsky. **c.** Tolstoy. **d.** Chekhov. **e.** Gorky.
4. Why were the Russians so late in beginning to compose orchestral music?
5. **a.** Name the "Big Three" of Russian music. **b.** Who is the greatest Russian composer?
6. **Thinking Critically:** Do you agree or disagree with the following sentence: It is surprising that nineteenth-century Russians created any great works of literature or music. Support your opinion with facts.

## 3. The Drift Toward Revolution

At the beginning of Alexander II's reign (1855), Russia was economically, politically, and socially backward. This fact was recognized by a small number of intellectuals. They talked about Russia's problems among themselves although they were not allowed to express their criticisms of the czarist regime openly. Alexander, too, was aware of his country's shortcomings—at least those in the fields of economics and social organization. He made efforts to correct them, but he would do nothing to weaken czarist power. Alexander II and his successors, Alexander III and Nicholas II, all sought to introduce western Europe's ideas on industrialization while suppressing the liberal social and political ideas drifting in from the West. But some of the very changes made by the czars in modernizing the country created problems that became threats to Romanov rule. As the intellectuals became bolder and formed secret revolutionary

**108**

groups, the czars found it increasingly difficult to suppress opposition to their rule.

### Slavophiles and Westerners

Two contending groups of intellectuals, the Slavophiles, lovers of things Slavic, and the Westerners, became very active during the reign of Nicholas I. Aware of their country's many shortcomings, both groups were determined to make Russia culturally equal to, if not ahead of, the nations of western Europe. Yet they could not agree on how this should be done.

The Slavophiles wanted to eliminate Western cultural influences, believing them to have a corrupting effect on the Russian way of life. They extolled their country's customs and traditions, and advocated their preservation. Progress, the Slavophiles said, would have to be made within a Russian, not a western European, framework.

The Westerners, on the other hand, argued that Russia had much to learn from such countries as England, France, and Germany. They believed that Russia should follow the same general path as Western civilization and not seek to preserve an independent course. Admiring Peter the Great as a "Westernizer," but opposed to czarist autocracy, they advocated ideas ranging from the mildly liberal to **socialism**.

Neither the Slavophiles nor the Westerners engaged in political action. They were largely talkers and writers. But the issues they posed were debated for years and became seeds for the social and political unrest that appeared after mid-century.

### Emancipation of the Serfs

Alexander II's **emancipation** of the serfs in 1861 served to stimulate the debate over Russia's future, for his Emancipation Edict was filled with grave shortcomings. Almost 50 million peasants received legal freedom, but for most of them the new laws fell far short of their expectations. The state extended credit to enable former serfs to purchase the lands they had worked, but legal ownership of the farming plots was assigned not to individual peasants but to **communes**. Exceptions were made in the Ukraine and other regions where serfs had already begun to acquire land of their own. Peasants were disappointed not to receive outright ownership of a plot of land.

Also, most landlords had kept their best lands for themselves, handing over to the government their poorer lands. Peasants quickly learned that many of the fields sold to the communes had been overpriced. Many peasants also resented the

**PEASANT LIFE.** Life in nineteenth-century Russia was hard, despite occasional amusements like the carnival (above) painted by an English traveler in 1804. Later in the century, the family gathered around the well (right) probably had little time or money for such entertainment. A more common treat would be the sleigh ride (below). This village consists of a swampy street lined with wooden cottages.

fact that they were forbidden to move elsewhere without the permission of the commune assembly. Moreover, nothing at all was done for the millions of serfs who had worked as household servants. Many of these became low-paid employees of their former owners. Others drifted to the cities to find work. Still others became vagabonds. For most peasants, life after the Emancipation was only a little better than before.

The peasants soon discovered they had champions of their cause in the persons of university students. Eager to help the emancipated serfs, this new generation of intellectuals hoped to bridge the huge gulf between themselves and the peasants. From 1872 to 1874 young men and women known as *narodniks*, traveled about the countryside, trying to make themselves useful "to the People." *Narod* means "the people" in Russian.

Unfortunately, they did not understand the peasants and their simple ways. Villagers looked upon the narodniks with suspicion. Nor did the government think very highly of the narodniks. This was Alexander II's period of reaction against liberalism. Considering the narodniks troublemakers, the czarist regime watched their every move. In a short time, the police were cracking down on the youthful idealists. The narodnik movement, never very promising, soon faded away.

### Industrialization and Social Unrest

Alexander III also took on the problem of economic development. Most of Russia's manufacturing was the "cottage" type, that is, work done in homes or in small factories, often by peasants during their off-season. Alexander III decided to change this situation. Because of the country's lack of development, the Russian government could exercise great control over industrial planning. A small, simple economy is much easier to supervise and regulate than a large, complex one.

By offering subsidies and tariff exemptions, Alexander III attracted to Russia foreign **capital** and managers who had contributed to industrial development in other lands. By the end of his reign rapid progress was being made in the exploitation of such resources as iron, coal, oil, and timber; in the creation of steel and textile industries; and in railroad construction. It was Alexander III who started the Trans–Siberian Railroad. (See Sidelight, page 17.) Much of this growth was made possible by foreign capital—mainly French. But all businesses operated under rigid czarist regulations.

Russia's industrial growth created new problems for the czars. For example, the rise of new industries in the western part of the empire led to a great concentration of people in Moscow, St. Petersburg, Warsaw, and Lodz. This meant a concentration of industrial workers, likely to be a source of unrest in any developing country. When revolution broke out in 1905 and again in 1917, it was industrial workers who formed the core of the opposition.

Also, by encouraging foreign investment, Russia's czars created resentment among members of the upper class, who believed that profits from the country's industrial development should go to them and not to foreigners. Moreover, industrialization did little to improve the well-being of the great mass of Russian people. The country remained essentially a land of downtrodden peasants, to which a growing class of discontented urban workers was added.

Opposition to czarist **absolutism** increased throughout the reign of Alexander III and into that of Nicholas II. No class or group was unaffected. Many nobles, unable to adjust to changing economic conditions, became impoverished. They blamed their condition on government actions, especially the freeing of the serfs and the encouragement of foreign investment. Members of the small but growing middle class—merchants, industrialists, and professional people—were annoyed because the czarist regime interfered in their affairs without apparent reason and burdened them with unnecessary restrictions. Although living conditions slowly improved for most peasants after emancipation, many pockets of extreme poverty and great unrest existed.

Religious minorities were oppressed. The czarist regime considered the Orthodox Church an arm of the state and used the Church's power over the people to strengthen its own position. Non-Orthodox minorities, at best, were treated as "second-class" citizens. Often they were persecuted and suppressed. Jews, Finns, and Poles were persecuted both because they were "non-Russians" and because they professed different religious faiths.

Alexander III and Nicholas II were slow to realize that a great threat to czarist rule was building up among the emerging **proletariat**, industrial workers who work for wages. After emancipation, many former serfs drifted to the towns and cities to find work in the new factories. Although industrial workers were in some ways better off than serfs, their work and way of life gave them much to complain about. They complained about long working hours, unsafe working conditions, overbearing foremen, child labor, low wages, and harsh punishment for mistakes. Labor organizers met with some success in persuading factory workers to join unions, and strikes flared up as laborers united in protest against working conditions.

## Rise of Political Parties

Social unrest during the reigns of Alexander III and Nicholas II led to the rise of "political parties." Such groups were illegal and had to conduct their activities in deepest secrecy. The most **moderate** critics, who came to be called the Liberals, placed their faith in the reforms of Alexander II. They wished these reforms to be implemented and extended, and opposed the revolutionary ideas seeping into Russia. Some reform groups operated within the czarist regime itself, hoping to bring about constructive change quietly and without violence. Various revolutionary organizations also emerged, most of them directed from outside Russia by emigrés who had fled the czarist regime. Most fanatical anti-czarists were living abroad, having either left the country to avoid arrest or escaped from prison or exile in Siberia. The most important of these groups were to become the Social Democrats and the Socialist Revolutionary parties.

None of the new political groups was large in terms of membership. The great majority of Russians feared and respected the czars, even though they were unhappy with conditions in the country. Moreover, the secret police was ruthless in dealing with anyone suspected of anti-czarist activity. Since the advocates of change were sharply divided among themselves on most issues, they at times attacked each other more fiercely than their common foe, the czar. Nevertheless, collectively these groups constituted a serious threat to autocratic rule.

## Socialist Revolutionaries

One point the radicals disagreed about was the social group that should constitute the core of the revolutionary movement. Many agitators thought it should be the peasantry, which was by far the largest group. Those who favored this view wanted to replace the czarist state with a democracy, then do away with private ownership of land and establish Socialist **collective farms** owned by groups of peasants. Their ideal society would consist of new communities based on such traditional institutions of rural life as the extended family and the council of elders. They were little concerned with the problems growing out of industrialization. Tracing their origins to the narodniks of the 1870's, the men and women who held such views called themselves Socialist Revolutionaries.

Because the late 1800's was a period when industrial strikes were drawing attention to the plight of the factory workers, the Socialist Revolutionaries attracted little notice at first. Nonetheless, their program, based on the assumed needs of the peasantry, had considerable appeal. In 1901, 49 Socialist Revolutionary groups united to form the Socialist Revolutionary Party. Until the Revolution of 1917, the Socialist Revolutionaries constituted the largest anti–czarist political party.

## Social Democrats

Unlike the Socialist Revolutionaries, the Social Democrats expected little from the peasants. Taking both their name and their ideas from Social Democratic parties in western Europe, they looked to the proletariat for political support. Social Democracy was based on the teachings of Karl Marx (1818–1883), the German economist and philosopher. He preached that the proletariat would overthrow the capitalist system and, under a dictatorship of the proletariat, create a Socialist state that safeguarded the interests of workers. In time, according to Marx, there would be no upper class and no lower class, for all people would be workers. Once this classless society became a reality, the dictatorship would end.

Marx himself questioned whether his ideas were applicable to Russia, which had an agricultural economy. He had a great deal of sympathy for the view of the Socialist Revolutionaries—that in Russia's peasantry lay the greatest hope for establishment of a Socialist state. Russia's industrial class hardly seemed large enough to start a revolution. But Russian Social Democrats firmly believed in the Marxist system and refused to believe that it could not be established in their country.

In 1883, the very year that Marx died, Russian emigrés took steps toward building a Socialist state in their country. At the urging of George Plekhanov, an early leader in the Russian Marxist movement, Social Democrats from the Russian underground and from emigré colonies in other countries met in Geneva, Switzerland. Out of this gathering came the Union for the Emancipation of Labor, the forerunner of a united Social Democratic Party. For the first time, Social Democrats were working together to achieve their common goal.

## Lenin's Bid for Power

Whereas Plekhanov was the guiding light of the early Russian Social Democrats, Lenin (LEN-uhn; 1870–1924), whose real name was Vladimir Ilyich Ulyanov, organized these radicals into an

## Karl Marx and Scientific Socialism

Karl Marx (1818–1883), a German political exile who lived in England, is regarded as the father of modern socialism. Marx's economic views, as modified by Lenin, have become the official views of the Soviet Union.

Marx called his socialism "scientific" to distinguish it from the "utopian" socialism of French reformers and philosophers who preceded him. They failed, according to Marx, because they did not have the support of the working masses, the proletariat. In the *Communist Manifesto*, written with Friedrich Engels, Marx defined past history as a record of class struggles. In *Das Kapital*, he declared the overthrow of capitalist society and the establishment of a classless society as inevitable.

The cornerstone of Marx's economic system was his labor theory of value according to which a commodity is worth only as much as the amount of labor needed to produce it. Since only labor creates value, then all profits should belong to the workers.

At that time, however, workers were being paid a bare **subsistence** while the goods were being sold at the highest price obtainable. Marx called the difference between the selling price of the item and the workers' wages, the "surplus value." By reinvesting these **surpluses**, or profits, the employer could acquire more machinery. This would reduce the number of workers needed and an army of unemployed would appear. As the numbers competing for jobs increased, wages would be forced downward, and there would be general dissatisfaction among the masses. The workers would soon organize, and openly oppose the system exploiting them. Ultimately a revolution would occur. The workers would seize power and establish a "dictatorship of the proletariat."

effective anti-czarist force. Possessing a quick and powerful mind and an iron will, Lenin was fanatically devoted to socialism. Before long he had become the most admired, feared, and hated person in the Social Democratic movement.

Lenin made his successful bid for power in 1903 when a conference was instituted for the purpose of uniting all the Social Democratic groups—both inside and outside Russia—into one Social Democratic Party. Although a single party emerged from the conference, it was not united. Lenin's refusal to compromise divided the new organization into two factions.

The split arose largely over requirements for membership. One group, which included Plekhanov was willing to accept as party members all who supported the party's program. But for Lenin and his followers commitment was not enough. They stubbornly insisted that only revolutionaries who worked full time for the party's goals should be accepted. Lenin had confidence only in the "professional" revolutionary. He called his faction **Bolsheviks**, meaning Majority, even though they were far from a majority, and the other faction **Mensheviks**, meaning Minority. The names stuck, and the two divisions fought bitterly for leadership of the party until the issue was decided by revolution.

## Check Your Understanding

1. Describe the views of the two groups of intellectuals that became active during the reign of Nicholas I.
2. What factors led to an increase in political unrest in Russia in the second half of the 1800's?
3. What were the views of the two radical political parties that developed in response to the unrest?
4. How did the views of the Mensheviks and Bolsheviks differ?
5. *Thinking Critically:* What had the serfs hoped to win by emancipation? How were they disappointed? What similarities were there in their situation and that of freed slaves after the American Civil War?

## 4. Ambitious Goals in Foreign Policy

The boundaries of the Russian Empire in northern and central Europe did not change during the century following the Napoleonic wars, except to incorporate the kingdom of Poland. But in southeastern Europe and in central and east Asia, Russia flexed its muscles. In these regions Russian **imperialism** again and again increased international tensions. During the reigns of Nicholas I, Alexander II, and Nicholas II this activity led to major wars. Combined with the problems the czars faced at home, Russia's involvement in war set the stage for the downfall of the Romanovs.

### Russo-Turkish War

The great powers that took part in the Congress of Vienna, including Russia, seemingly were agreed to stand firm against political change by revolution. This policy, however, soon came in conflict with Russian aims in the Balkans. When the Greeks began fighting for independence from the Ottoman Empire in 1821, they quickly won the sympathy of Czar Alexander I. Here were fellow Orthodox Christians struggling to free themselves from their Muslim rulers. It seemed, moreover, a good opportunity to weaken the Ottoman Empire, whose control of the Bosporus and Dardanelles limited Russia's access to the Mediterranean. But in the end Alexander I accepted the advice of Austria's Prime Minister Metternich, which was to let the Greek uprising burn itself out.

By the late 1820's, however, the situation had changed. Nicholas I, the new czar, decided to support the Greek cause. He joined with the rulers of Britain and France in demanding that the sultan grant an armistice to the Greeks so that the opposing sides could discuss the question of Greek independence. When the sultan rejected the demand, the European powers went into action. In 1827, in the Battle of Navarino Bay, the ships of the three allies practically destroyed the Turkish fleet. The Turkish land forces were forced to retreat. Since Greek independence was practically assured, Britain and France were satisfied.

Not so Russia. In 1828 Czar Nicholas I declared war on the Ottoman Empire. Driving almost to the outskirts of Constantinople, the Russians compelled the sultan to sue for peace. By the Treaty of Adrianople in 1829 Russia acquired territory along its southwestern frontier and won rights of self government for Rumanians and Serbians. The czar was also granted the right to protect the interests of Orthodox Christians in the Ottoman Empire. Most important, the Bosporus and Dardanelles were declared open to the shipping of all "friendly powers."

Favorable as were the terms Nicholas imposed on the Ottoman empire at Adrianople, he could have won greater rewards if he had chosen. The czar restrained himself because he did not wish to anger Britain and France. These powers, both of whom had mounting interests in the Turkish empire, could not be expected to stand by while the czar cut up the sultan's domain. For years England's commerce with the Ottoman Turks had been growing. But of even greater concern was Britain's fear

**117**

that Russian expansion at the expense of the Ottoman Empire would threaten Britain's growing domain in India. France too had political, commercial, and religious interests in Turkey, and had no intention of being squeezed out by the czar.

Like czars before him, Nicholas I repeatedly justified his maneuvers in the Ottoman Empire by claiming Russian responsibility for the protection of Orthodox Christians in the sultan's realm. Devoted to the Orthodox Church, Nicholas felt an obligation to fellow Orthodox Christians in the Balkans and elsewhere in the Ottoman domain. The other European powers, however, were understandably suspicious of Russia. They suspected that religion was a cloak used by the czar to conceal his imperialistic designs on the shaky Turkish empire. They were partly right. Moreover, they themselves had plans for the "Sick Man of Europe," as Nicholas later called the Ottoman Empire.

### The Crimean War

The long-expected showdown over conflicting interests in the Ottoman Empire began with a dispute over religious rights in Palestine, then a part of the sultan's domain. Roman Catholic and Greek Orthodox monks had long competed for control of the holy places in that country. With support from Russia, the Greek Orthodox Church won. But Emperor Napoleon III, to please French Catholics, demanded that control be restored to Roman Catholic monks. No sooner was this crisis supposedly resolved than Nicholas demanded that the sultan grant Russia

TURKEY IN DANGER.

This 1853 cartoon from *Punch* presents the British view of Russia's supposed "protection" of Turkey. The huge Russian bear is in a position to crush the helpless Turkey. Actually, Turkey was not so helpless, since France and Britain became its allies when it declared war on Russia.

a **protectorate** over all Orthodox Christians living in the Ottoman Empire. When this demand was rejected, Russian troops crossed the Danube into Rumania, then a part of Turkey. Britain and France sent warships through the Bosporus and Dardanelles to Constantinople. Thus assured of Anglo-French support, the sultan declared war on Russia. In the spring of 1854 Britain and France entered the war.

Nicholas I was proud of the huge Russian army, and counted on a victory in the Crimean War (1854–1856). But Russia's transportation system was poor, military supplies were of inferior quality, and leadership was second rate. Most of the fighting was in Russia's Crimea, a peninsula jutting out into the Black Sea. The allied forces—British, French, Sardinian, and Turkish—laid siege to the strongly defended Russian base of Sevastopol. When it finally fell after a long siege, Russia was ready to sue for peace.

Czar Nicholas I died while the war was still in progress. It was left to his successor, Alexander II, to tally the cost. Russian military losses amounted to a quarter of a million. Russia's goals in the Balkans had been thwarted. The peace settlement incorporated in the Treaty of Paris (1856) provided that Russia was to give up its claim as protector over Orthodox Christians in the Ottoman Empire; the Danubian principalities, which would become Rumanian, were to be self-governing provinces in the Ottoman Empire; and no great power was to build fortifications along the Black Sea or station a fleet on it.

### Russian Expansion into Asia

Perhaps because their expansionist hopes had met with stiff resistance in the Balkans, the Russians during the reign of Alexander II turned their attention to the regions along their Asian frontier. These efforts to enlarge the czar's domain met with overwhelming success.

As early as the 1700's czarist forces had clashed with Turkish inhabitants of Central Asia. Soon after Alexander II came to the throne, he stepped up Russian penetration of the region. In a series of campaigns the Russians captured such strategic centers as Tashkent, Samarkand, and Khiva. These conquests in Central Asia brought the frontiers of the czarist empire much closer to India, a matter of some concern to the British.

In East Asia Russia made gains at the expense of the Chinese Empire. In 1858 that empire was being attacked by the combined forces of Britain and France. Soon after, Russia, posing as China's friend in time of need, persuaded the Chinese emperor to cede to the czar vast stretches of territory in the Amur River Valley. (See page 84.) In 1860 Russia also acquired from China possession of the present-day Maritime Province. There a port named Vladivostok, meaning "Glory of the East," was built. Though its harbor was blocked by ice for many months of the year, Vladivostok became Russia's principal port and naval base in the Pacific.

## Russian Interference in the Balkans

Despite Russia's rich gains in Central and East Asia, Alexander was not reconciled to his country's diminished role in the Balkans. An opportunity for renewed activity came during the Franco-Prussian War (1870–1871). With Europe's attention focused on that struggle, the czar declared that the Black Sea agreement of 1856 no longer applied to Russia. He then proceeded to restore Russian military and naval power in the Black Sea area.

A few years later an opportunity arose for Russia to flex its muscles in the Balkans. In 1875–1876 Slavs in Bulgaria and in Serbia and Montenegro, both part of present-day Yugoslavia, rose in revolt against ill treatment by the sultan. When the Turks massacred thousands of Bulgarian Christians, Russia in 1877 declared war on Turkey. Although Alexander claimed that he wanted no conquests, the czar sent his armies on a drive toward Constantinople.

## The Congress of Berlin

When the Russian armies met with little resistance, tensions mounted in Britain and Austria. A British fleet was sent to the Bosporus and Dardanelles, and Austria mobilized its army to curb Russian expansion in the Balkans. To avoid a large war, the czar made peace with the sultan. The Treaty of San Stefano (1878) provided independence for Serbia, Rumania, and Montenegro. Bulgaria was to be ruled by a Christian prince as a tributary to the Ottoman Empire and 50,000 Russian troops were to remain as a defense force. These terms were unacceptable to the European powers, especially to Austria and Britain. Both demanded an international conference to revise the Treaty of San Stefano.

With the threat of war hanging heavy over Europe, Bismarck, the Chancellor of the German Empire, acted quickly. He extended an invitation to the great powers to meet in Berlin to work out an acceptable settlement. The resulting Treaty of Berlin (1878) stripped the Ottoman Empire of nearly all its territory and influence in the Balkans, but failed to meet the nationalist hopes of the Balkan peoples. Bulgaria was divided into three parts and denied independence. Rumania, Montenegro, and Serbia became independent, but Bosnia and Herzegovina, kingdoms formerly held by the Turks, were handed over to Austria. Although Russia annexed territory in the Caucasus and from Rumania, it felt humiliated and cheated. The Russians had made great sacrifices in money and in lives to win the war against Turkey. But Russia's gains at the Congress of Berlin were much smaller than those it had obtained at San Stefano.

In the end the Congress of Berlin created as many problems as it solved and greatly increased international tensions. For one thing the problem of Balkan nationalism remained unresolved. More important, the suspicions and hostilities generated at the Congress stimulated the formation of rival alliances.

The results of the Congress of Berlin left Alexander II in a sour mood. European monarchies that formerly had been his country's allies had checked Russian expansionist hopes. Alexander was especially concerned about Austria-Hungary, which increasingly was extending its influence in the Balkans. In 1879 Germany and Austria concluded a defensive alliance to protect either country from attack by Russia. Three years later they joined with Italy in the Triple Alliance, which promised support to that country if attacked by France. Germany received for a similar assurance from Italy.

Under the circumstances it was understandable that France and Russia would draw closer together. Both countries were diplomatically isolated. It did not matter that their political systems were entirely different. Protecting their national security was far more important. During the first half of the 1890's, the two countries reached an understanding. Russia could count on France if attacked by Germany, or Austria supported by Germany. France could count on Russia if attacked by Germany, or Italy supported by Germany. At the time neither side felt sure of Britain. But in 1904 Britain and France reached an understanding. In 1907 Britain and Russia agreed to support each other, completing the Triple Entente. Entente means agreement or understanding. Thus the Triple Entente aligned Russia, England, and France against the Triple Alliance of Germany, Austria, and Italy.

### The Spoils in East Asia

In the closing years of the nineteenth century, the ancient Chinese Empire seemed to be coming apart. The European powers were amazed by Japan's decisive victory over China in 1894 and

1895 and dismayed by the resulting peace terms. China acknowledged the independence of Korea; ceded Formosa, the Pescadores, and the Liaodong peninsula (south Manchuria) to Japan; and paid a large indemnity. In the interest of preserving the "integrity of Chinese territory," Russia, France, and Germany lodged protests that caused Japan to return the peninsula in exchange for additional indemnity.

Within a year, Russia managed to get concessions in the Yalu River valley from Korea and the right to extend the Trans-Siberian Railway across Manchuria from China. Then in 1898 China "leased" Port Arthur on the Liaodong peninsula to Russia and received the right to build a railroad connecting Port Arthur with the Trans-Siberian railway. What the Japanese had been unable to win by war the Russians had gained through diplomatic pressure.

### Russo–Japanese War

Fearing that Manchuria as well as Korea were earmarked for annexation by the czar, the Japanese began to prepare for a showdown. On the diplomatic front they concluded the Anglo-Japanese Alliance in 1902. If Japan went to war with Russia, Britain agreed to be **neutral**. If a third power, meaning France, came to Russia's aid, Britain would join the war on the side of Japan.

Since Russia failed to withdraw from Manchuria as promised and continued to meddle in the affairs of Korea, Japan began an all-out war in 1904. The Russian squadron at Port Arthur was attacked and blockaded. Fighting far from their bases in Europe, the czar's naval and land forces met with crushing defeats. In January 1905, the Russian fortress at Port Arthur fell after a long siege. In May a Russian fleet, which had sailed halfway around the world, was annihilated in the straits between Japan and Korea. These crushing setbacks contributed to the dangerous unrest in Russian cities. (See page 125.) Since Japan's resources were hardly equal to a long war, it, like Russia, was soon willing to negotiate peace.

The peace treaty concluding the Russo-Japanese War was negotiated at Portsmouth, New Hampshire, in 1905. Russia recognized Japan's paramount interest in Korea, and transferred to Japan its lease of the Liaodong peninsula and part of the railroad leading north from it. Russia also ceded to Japan the southern half of Sakhalin, the large island just north of Japan. What Japan had wanted and needed badly, but did not get, was an indemnity.

United States President Theodore Roosevelt mediated the end to the Russo-Japanese War in 1905. The Treaty of Portsmouth, signed in Portsmouth, New Hampshire, won Roosevelt the Nobel Peace Prize, but seriously damaged Russia's plans for territorial expansion in the Far East. What was one cause of Russia's defeat?

The defeat came as a great blow to Russian pride. Russian leaders had expected victory, and so had their counterparts in other European countries. But in retrospect it is easy to see that fighting a war on a front thousands of miles away when supplies have to be bought in over a single-track railroad presents problems. Perhaps the chief mistake made by the Russians and other Europeans was to underestimate the Japanese.

After this war all the powers realized that Japan's international interests in East Asia could no longer be treated lightly. Russian diplomats after 1905 soon ironed out differences with Japan through negotiation. Russia abandoned its designs upon Korea, but its special interests in north Manchuria and Inner, or southeastern, Mongolia were recognized by the Japanese.

### Russia in World War I

In June, 1914, Archduke Franz Ferdinand, heir to the Austro-Hungarian throne, was assassinated by a Bosnian. When the Austrian government made harsh demands on Serbia, which it blamed for the continued unrest in Bosnia and Herzegovina, Russia became alarmed. It suspected that Austria would try to exploit the crisis to bring about changes in the Balkans that were disadvantageous to Russia. Despite setbacks suffered in earlier efforts, the czarist government still dreamed of dominating the Balkans and controlling the Bosporus and Dardanelles. Russia, therefore, gave assurances of support to Serbia. These, in turn, were matched by German promises to Austria-Hungary. The result was tragic. Within a matter of weeks Russia, France, and Britain were all at war with Austria-Hungary and Germany. World War I had begun. Before fighting ceased, the czar would no longer rule "All the Russias."

## Check For Understanding

1. How did Alexander I's policy toward the Greeks differ from that of Nicholas I?
2. **a.** List the causes of the Crimean War. **b.** Explain the reasons for the actions of each of the powers involved.
3. What new territories did Russia add to its empire after the Crimean War?
4. **a.** What events gave Alexander II the opportunity to extend Russian influence in the Balkans? **b.** Describe the reaction of other powers.
5. How did Russia come into conflict with Japan?
6. *Thinking Critically:* How were the expansionist policies of Peter the Great and Catherine the Great the same as and different from the policies of the czars of the nineteenth century?

## 5. Revolution of 1905 and Czarist Concessions

During the first years of the 20th century, there was growing opposition to czarist institutions and autocracy. The setback suffered in the Russo-Japanese War called attention to inefficiency in the government and corruption. Peasants, disillusioned because emancipation had not brought them economic freedom, took out their frustration on the great landlords. Crops were illegally harvested or burned, owners murdered, and manor houses destroyed. Czarist troops brutally subdued the lawless peasants. City workers, going on strike with disturbing frequency, held huge rallies that were broken up by police. The fact that striking workers were wounded or killed only increased the people's determination to take whatever action was needed to improve working and living conditions. The growing middle class openly resented government restrictions and interference. Several radical political parties were waiting for the right moment to start a revolution. All that was needed for a nationwide revolt was an incident that would unite the dissatisfied and rally mass support. The spark that fired such an uprising occurred in the first month of 1905.

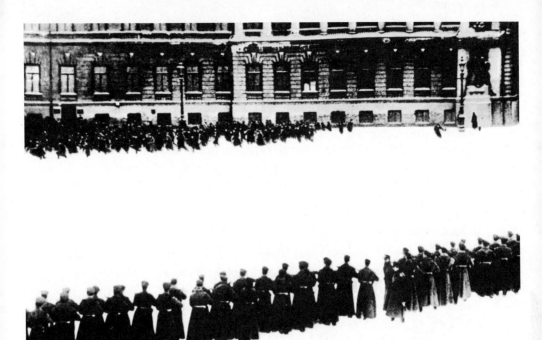

A prelude to the 1917 revolution was the "Bloody Sunday" massacre of peaceful petitioners to the czar in January 1905.

## Bloody Sunday

On Sunday, January 22, 1905, thousands of workers in St. Petersburg marched to the imperial palace. Led by an Orthodox priest, Father Gapon, they hoped to present a petition to the czar. Their requests included **constitutional government**, the right to organize into unions then forbidden by law, and improved working conditions. Actually the czar was not in the city. Although the marchers were unarmed, the troops guarding the palace opened fire. Several hundred marchers were killed or wounded in the tragic affair.

Word of the massacre quickly spread throughout Russia. All over the country factory workers went on strike, peasants rose in revolt, and even soldiers and sailors mutinied. The largely spontaneous nature of these widespread incidents testifies to the depth of resentment felt by millions of Russians against the autocratic government.

The climax of this movement came in October, nine months after Bloody Sunday. A strike by typesetters in Moscow triggered a nationwide strike that brought the country to a standstill for

**125**

ten days (October 20–30). The bakers followed the lead of the printers, and in turn were followed by railroad workers. When the railroads stopped running, mills and factories closed down, and then industrial workers joined the strike. Before long clerks in offices and stores, postal and telegraph workers, actors and cab drivers, house servants and janitors, as well as professional people and civil servants stopped work. Surprisingly, even middle-class industrialists and businessmen who profited from government contracts joined in the work stoppage. Some even paid their workers for the days they were on strike. Never in Russian history had there been anything like the strike of 1905.

### The October Manifesto

The widespread unrest and the general strike compelled the czarist government to recognize the need for reform. On October 30, 1905, Czar Nicholas II issued the October Manifesto in which he made three promises: (1) the people were to enjoy freedom of conscience, speech, assembly, and the press; (2) a Duma was to be established, to which the people would have the right to elect representatives; and (3) all laws must be approved by the Duma.

This imperial proclamation seemed to promise personal liberties and the introduction of constitutional government. But not all Russians were impressed by the vague language of the October Manifesto. Among the least satisfied were the members of the St. Petersburg Soviet, an organization established by revolutionary leaders during the general strike to give direction to the activities of the strikers. Its president, Leon Trotsky, expressed the doubts of many Russians:

> So a constitution is granted. Freedom of assembly is granted but the assemblies are surrounded by the military. Freedom of speech is granted, but the censorship exists as before. Freedom of knowledge is granted, but the universities are occupied by troops. Inviolability of the person [freedom from arbitrary arrest and imprisonment] is granted, but the prisons are overflowing with the incarcerated . . . . A constitution is given, but the autocracy remains. Everything is given—and nothing is given. [Bertram D. Wolfe, *Three Who Made A Revolution.*]

The czarist regime responded to such criticisms as Trotsky's by suppressing the writing of radicals, curtailing the activities of the Social Democrats and Socialist Revolutionaries, and arresting and exiling to Siberia the most aggressive leaders of the revolutionary movement. Trotsky, one of those exiled, soon escaped to western Europe. But opposition was not limited to professional revolutionaries. Late in December workers in Moscow revolted, and peasants in many parts of the country also took part in uprisings. These challenges were crushed by the czarist army, which had received concessions to keep it loyal to the czar. Most Russians, however, accepted the October Manifesto as a major step forward in the direction of constitutional government.

### The First Duma

Nicholas II fulfilled one of his promises on May 10, 1906, when he called into session the First Duma. It soon became clear, however, that this legislative body would have no real power. For on May 6 the czar had issued the "Fundamental Laws," a proclamation that reaffirmed his autocracy; gave him control over the executive department, the armed forces, and foreign policy; allowed him to appoint half the members of the Duma; and reserved to him the right to legislate by decree when the Duma was not in session.

The various revolutionary groups, Bolsheviks, Mensheviks, and Socialist Revolutionaries, anticipating some such action by the czar, had boycotted the election of representatives to the First Duma. When it met, therefore, the liberals, divided among several parties, occupied most of the elective seats. However, even the liberals rapidly became disenchanted with the Duma. They then demanded a ministry responsible to the Duma, much as the cabinet is to Parliament in Britain. As a result, the czar abruptly dissolved the Duma.

Between 1907 and 1916 three more Dumas were convened. In the Second Duma the strength of the radicals was greatly increased, since Bolsheviks, Mensheviks, and Socialist Revolutionaries had taken part in the election. Thereafter, by changing the electoral system, the czarist regime made sure that the Dumas would be "more responsible." In the Third and Fourth Dumas, therefore, conservatives and reactionaries, supporters of czarist autocracy, were in the majority.

The Duma was not a Western-style legislative body. Indeed its role was consultative rather than legislative, since nearly all legislation was introduced by the czarist regime. In other words, the czar and his ministers still determined policy. Nevertheless it should be recognized that the Duma provided an opportunity for critics of the czarist regime to voice their grievances publicly. This was a sharp contrast to the conditions before the October Manifesto.

## State-sponsored Reform

The limitations on the power of the Duma might have provoked greater opposition, had not the czarist regime itself instituted some reforms. Determined that the Duma should not undermine autocracy, Nicholas II and his ministers pondered steps to regain the confidence of the people. Some of the czar's advisors still favored secret police, spies, arrests, exile, and executions. Others, however, recognized the need to reduce the causes of widespread discontent. Peter Stolypin (stuh-LIH-pyin), Prime Minister from 1906 to 1911, was the chief spokesman for this policy.

Under Stolypin many reforms were introduced. Industrial growth was stimulated and foreign trade was expanded. But the keystone of his program was land reform. The peasantry had long been a source of support for the czarist regime. Up to the Revolution of 1905, most of their anger had been directed at the aristocracy. Stolypin sought to regain the peasantry's confidence by changing the laws regarding landholding. Since the great dream of millions of villagers was to own their own farms, Stolypin reasoned that peasants who were property owners would never listen to agitators and revolutionaries.

Despite strong opposition from both reactionaries and revolutionaries, Stolypin brought about the enactment of new land laws. This legislation abolished the controls exercised by the communes and permitted the peasants to acquire title to their land. In truth, Stolypin had begun to launch a conservative counter-revolution!

Stolypin did not live to see the fulfillment of his plans. He was assassinated in 1911. During the years the new land laws were in effect, millions of peasants became private land owners. Unfortunately for the czarist regime, the time left for introducing reforms was limited.

## What if...

Czarist Russia had experienced many changes in the quarter-century of Nicholas II's reign. The old absolutism had given way to what, at least in theory, was a limited constitutional government. Industry and foreign trade were booming. Conditions in rural areas, though still bad, were improving.

## Rasputin

The fall of the Russian Empire was hastened by a rough peasant who gained a strange power over the ruling family. This man came to St. Petersburg from a small village in western Siberia, where he had been called Rasputin (ras-PYOO-tin), meaning "dissolute", or unrestrained in his conduct. The man deserved this name even after he became a wandering monk of an Old Believer sect, for he believed that sin must come if salvation is to follow. This flamboyant "holy man" with the powerfully piercing eyes became well known in St. Petersburg society. In 1905 he was presented to Empress Alexandra, the wife of Nicholas II.

To Alexandra, whose religious beliefs bordered on the mystical, Rasputin was God's messenger sent to protect the Russian monarchy. She sought his advice on public as well as personal matters. Alexandra's confidence in Rasputin was strengthened by his ability to help her son Alexis, who was tragically stricken with hemophilia, a hereditary disorder that prevents blood clotting. Seemingly endowed with the power to heal, Rasputin on several occasions stopped the boy's bleeding when doctors could not.

Alexandra and Nicholas often discussed "Our Friend," as they called Rasputin. Nicholas was reluctant to heed his political advice, but Alexandra trusted him in all matters. During World War I when Nicholas went to the war front, leaving the conduct of domestic affairs in his wife's hands, Rasputin was able to exercise considerable influence in the government. If an official criticized the "holy man," the czarina would promptly remove the person from office. She discussed all appointments and important decisions of state with Rasputin.

Desperate nobles who saw the damage Rasputin was doing finally agreed that he must be killed. He survived huge doses of poison, even gun shots fired at point-blank range. Finally Rasputin was tied with ropes and thrown into the river. Since Rasputin's death occurred on December 17, 1916, the hated "holy man" did not see the revolution that his scheming had unknowingly helped to bring about.

**THE LAST DAYS OF THE ROMANOVS.** The self-styled monk Rasputin played an important part in the reign of Nicholas II. The czar blesses the Russian troops with a holy icon, thus continuing the tradition of "Nationality, Orthodoxy, and Autocracy."

It was World War I that changed the course of Russian history. The Romanov dynasty doubtless would have survived a short war. But contrary to the expectations of all, the war developed into a long and incredibly costly conflict. Of all the major participants, Russia was the least prepared and suffered the greatest losses. As the war dragged on, the internal weaknesses of the czarist empire once again were mercilessly exposed. Its armies fought bravely, but guns and ammunition were in short supply. The transportation system was overtaxed, and Russia's main ports were closed by enemy blockades. The economy was strained to the breaking point. Instead of remaining in St. Petersburg to give direction to the government, Nicholas II delegated this responsibility to the czarina. He himself joined the army in the field where Britain and France were calling for Russian offensives to relieve the German pressure on the western front.

The year 1917 was critical for Russia. Troop morale was low. Deserters drifted home faster than they could be replaced. Popular support for the struggle wavered as shortages of food and fuel aroused discontent in the cities. Yet few Russians were prepared for the startling events of March. Without warning and planning, demonstrations by workers and soldiers broke out in St. Petersburg. Thus began the Russian Revolution, one of the most profound and important upheavals in history.

## Check Your Understanding

1. What circumstances led to Bloody Sunday?
2. Why was the October Manifesto issued?
3. Why were some Russians unimpressed by the October Manifesto?
4. What was the chief importance of the Duma?
5. Why did the czarist government introduce reforms in the early 1900's?
6. What reforms did Peter Stolypin introduce?
7. How had Russia changed during the reign of Nicholas II?
8. *Thinking Critically:* Was World War I a disaster for Russia?

## CHAPTER REVIEW

### ■ Chapter Summary

**Section 1.** During the final century of Romanov rule, the czars tried to preserve their autocratic system of government. With varying degrees of firmness and consistency, they attempted to stamp out all opposition. Nicholas I, for example, supported a system of "Orthodoxy, Autocracy, and Nationality" that strengthened his authority over the Church, forced ethnic minorities to learn Russian and adopt Russian culture, and made his will supreme. Although Alexander II might have supported some reforms, he was killed by an assassin and his son Alexander III condemned anyone who did not support his regime.

**Section 2.** One way to show discontent with the regime and to criticize its actions was through literature. The great works of such Russian writers as Pushkin, Dostoyevsky, and Tolstoy often reflected the mood of their times.

**Section 3.** While the czars were attempting to strengthen their hold on the nation, opponents were organizing radical political parties and participating in conspiracies, uprisings, strikes, and demonstrations. The emancipation of serfs, which did not provide the security and equality the serfs had hoped for, along with the rise of industrialization worsened conditions and fueled the unrest in the country. The Socialist Revolutionaries and the Social Democrats vied for power among the nation's discontented. Among the Social Democrats, Lenin rose to power advocating violent overthrow of the czars.

**Section 4.** The last czars devoted considerable energy to policies designed to enlarge their imperial domain. Czarist efforts to extend their territory and influence in the Balkans aroused the opposition of other European powers, but the czars managed to acquire extensive territory in Central Asia and the Far East. Imperialistic schemes in Europe and Asia involved Russia in wars, and finally contributed to its involvement in World War I.

**Section 5.** Discontent with czarist rule reached a climax in the early 1900's. The Revolution of 1905 forced the czar to make concessions to the growing demand for reform. A Duma was established and provided a platform for criticizing the regime. But the Duma lacked the powers exercised by legislative bodies in Western countries. It was unfortunate for the czar that the outbreak of World War I cut short the time for solving the nation's many problems. Under the great strains of that terrible conflict, the government collapsed. The Russian monarchy was overthrown by revolution in 1917.

■ **Vocabulary Review**

**Define:** Duma, liberal, intellectual, censorship, zemstvo, nationalism, radical, romanticism, socialism, emancipation, commune, capital, absolutism, proletariat, moderate, collective farm, subsistence, surplus, Bolshevik, Menshevik, imperialism, protectorate, neutral, constitutional government

■ **Places to Locate**

**Locate:** Bosporus, Dardanelles, Crimea, Tashkent, Samarkand, Khiva, Vladivostok, Port Arthur

## People to Know

*Identify:* Nicholas I, Decembrists, Alexander II, zemstvo, Alexander III, Nicholas II, Radishchev, Pushkin, Lermontov, Gogol, Turgenev, Dostoyevsky, Tolstoy, Chekhov, Gorky, Rimsky-Korsakov, Borodin, Mousorgski, Tchaikovsky, Karl Marx, Lenin, Rasputin

## Thinking Critically

1. Based on what you know from studying world history, why do you think the czars were fearful of the ideas of the French Revolution?
2. What factors led the czars to expand into the Balkans, Central Asia, and East Asia? How did their imperialist ambitions affect their country?
3. What common themes are apparent in the works of the writers of the late czarist period?
4. Based on what you have read about the policies of Nicholas II, do you think he could have eliminated Russia's discontent had World War I not intervened? Support your opinion with facts.

## Extending and Applying Your Knowledge

1. The final days of the Romanovs make interesting reading. Read Robert K. Massie's *Nicholas and Alexandra* and write a book report focusing on how their personal lives affected the course of Russian History.
2. Select a piece of music by a composer discussed in this chapter and prepare an oral presentation for the class. Do research on the life of the composer and on the themes of the piece you chose. Explain what influenced the composer in writing this music and describe the themes before playing a record or tape of it.
3. While the Romanovs were trying to suppress liberal ideas, these same ideas were lighting fires of rebellion across Europe and Latin America. Make a timeline, beginning with 1789, of political events in these two areas of the world. Use it as the basis for a paragraph comparing developments in these areas with developments in Russia.

# 5

# The Communist Dictatorship

In 1917 two revolutions in Russia rocked the world. The first, in March, toppled the czarist regime. The second in November, brought the Bolsheviks to power. It was this November Revolution that changed the course of history. The Bolsheviks, led by Lenin, not only reshaped Russia into a Communist state and society, but did their utmost to export communism to other countries.

It proved far from easy to construct a Communist way of life in war-torn Russia. Lenin had to postpone building a socialist society to concentrate on economic recovery. Stalin, the next Soviet leader, introduced centralized economic planning. He willingly sacrificed the well-being of farmers and peasants to achieve rapid industrialization. Simultaneously, the Communists were attempting to fashion a new government and culture. The "dictatorship of the proletariat," in reality the Communist Party, replaced the czarist political system. The actual results were a far cry from the ideals of communism.

Russia under the leadership of Stalin became a police state, more rigid than the Russia of the czars. The Soviet Union, intent on stirring up other revolutions, helped to organize Communist parties in other lands. These parties worked toward the overthrow of existing governments but at times also cooperated with nationalist and anti-imperialist movements. In the 1930's, the pressures exerted by **totalitarian** regimes in Germany, Italy, and Japan compelled the Soviet Union to cooperate with former foes to preserve their country.

## Creation of the Conmmunist State

| | |
|---|---|
| 1917 | March Revolution |
| | Bolshevik Revolution |
| 1918 | Treaty of Brest-Litovsk |
| | Constitution of 1918 |
| 1918–1921 | Russian Civil War |
| 1919 | Founding of Comintern |
| 1921 | New Economic Policy |
| 1922 | Stalin as General Secretary |
| | Formation of USSR |
| | (Constitution approved in 1924) |
| 1924 | Death of Lenin |
| 1925–1927 | Removal of Trotsky as War Commissar and from Politburo, and expulsion from Communist Party |
| 1928 | Adoption of First Five-Year Plan |
| 1929 | Trotsky deported |
| 1931–1932 | Famine |
| 1935 | "Popular front" idea endorsed |
| 1936 | Stalin Constitution approved |
| 1939 | Nazi-Soviet Non-Aggression Pact |
| | German invasion of Poland |

## 1. The End of Czarist Russia

By 1917 the overthrow of the czarist regime was the goal of various Russian groups and organizations. Some were revolutionary groups such as the Bolsheviks, Mensheviks, and Socialist Revolutionaries. But a group of influential aristocrats called the Union of Nobles was considering a palace revolt, and the Duma itself was at the point of open rebellion. Nicholas II, however, rejected every proposal for change, whether made by a noble, members of the Duma, or one of his own ministers. When the revolution came in March 1917, anti-czarist groups were almost as surprised as the government. After all, the czarist state had been in power for several hundred years. Moreover, the opposition was weak and divided. Few Russians realized how

**135**

During the food shortages of early 1917, St. Petersburg, renamed Petrograd, was filled with lines of people attempting to buy the little remaining food.

completely the czarist regime had lost the confidence and support of the people.

### War and Revolution

Developments during the winter of 1916–1917 had greatly increased popular discontent. The war was going badly for the czarist forces. The poorly armed, ill-fed, and inadequately clothed Russians were suffering heavy casualties. Every third family in Russia had lost or was to lose a son, brother, or father in the war.

Moreover, the winter had been unusually severe, creating problems for the people in the cities as well as for the armed forces. The nation's transportation system was more inefficient than ever because locomotives and railroad cars were wearing out after years of constant use. High snow halted traffic and slowed the delivery of food, which at best was in short supply. Hunger was widespread in the cities. Urban workers, disgruntled because of low pay and difficult working conditions, blamed their hardships on the czar. Their discontent was encouraged by Mensheviks and Bolsheviks, who counted on a working class revolution to bring them to power.

### The Beginning of the Revolution

On the morning of March 8, 1917, women workers from Petrograd's textile district poured into the streets in a mass demon-

Nicholas II and his wife Alexandra pose with their five children. With the coming of the revolution Nicholas abdicated, but in July 1918, the entire family was killed by the Bolsheviks.

stration. It was the beginning of their long-planned "Women's Day," a protest against working conditions in the factories. The women were soon joined by thousands of men who had been "locked out" of their jobs after striking for higher wages. Noting that the band of protesters was growing rapidly, revolutionary leaders formed a strike committee. Since members of this committee had influence with workers in most of Petrograd's industries, they confidently ordered all workers into the streets. The exodus of workers virtually emptied the city's factories.

By the afternoon the workers were in an ugly mood. Hungry and desperate because of winter-long shortages of food, they began crying "Give us bread." When bakeries were looted, troops were ordered out of their barracks to disband the crowds. To the amazement of the government, the soldiers showed little interest in breaking up the demonstration. Many of them had been drafted from the very factories that had been emptied of workers. They were in sympathy with the strikers and joined them. During the next few days the situation rapidly worsened. Most of the soldiers in or near the city mutinied, the jails were emptied by demonstrators, and government offices were forced open and their records scattered or destroyed. Government officials, fearing for their lives, fled the city or went into hiding. Without troops to maintain order, the government was helpless.

### Formation of a Provisional Government

Czar Nicholas II did not realize the seriousness of the situation in Petrograd, and he discounted reports from desperate officials that the situation was getting out of hand. It was not until "The Government of His Imperial Majesty" was replaced with the revo-

**137**

lutionary Provisional Committee of the Duma on March 12 that Nicholas realized what was happening. He boarded his private train to return to Petrograd, only to discover that the railways were under the control of revolutionary leaders. His train was halted, boarded by representatives of the **Provisional Government** and the czarist regime. All aboard advised the czar that only his abdication could save the nation. On the night of March 15, in the drawing room of his private train, Nicholas II abdicated in favor of his brother Michael. More aware of the temper of the people than Nicholas, Michael refused the crown.

The new Provisional Government was dominated by the Constitutional Democrats or Cadets, a party that wished to establish a democratic government in Russia similar to Great Britain's. The head of the Provisional Government was Prince Lvov, an aristocrat of mediocre ability. The Cadet regime, regarding itself as a caretaker government serving until national elections could be held, pursued a do-nothing policy. For eight months this government did little to restore law and order or to halt the rapid disintegration of the nation's economy. Needing strong leadership at this time of crisis, Russia found itself with a weaker government than that of the czar.

### The Soviets as a Rival Force

Complicating the Provisional Government's task was the existence of rival, self-appointed, and Socialist-oriented groups. When the czarist regime disintegrated, revolutionaries quickly formed committees or **soviets** to represent the interests of workers and soldiers and, later, peasants. These soviets became the accepted speakers for the masses. Closely linked throughout the country, the soviets were an effective instrument for exercising political power.

At the core of the soviet structure was the committee representing the workers and soldiers in the capital. The Executive Committee of the Petrograd Soviet, known as **Ex Com**, was formed the same day as the Provisional Government. The latter soon discovered that it could make no move without the consent of the Ex Com, since the soldiers and workers in the capital looked to Ex Com for leadership. Although the Provisional Government gained recognition as Russia's official government, the Ex Com exercised far greater control over the revolution.

### Provisional Government's Policies

One decision that the new government could not escape was what to do about the war. In the capital views were sharply divided over the issue. The various Socialist groups were advocating a policy of peace at any price. To their thinking the senseless war was designed only to advance Western **capitalism** and imperialism. They wanted peace so that they could begin to work toward the fulfillment of Socialist goals.

To leaders in the Provisional Government, on the other hand, the "country's honor" meant much. Also, like their czarist predecessors, they had their eyes on Constantinople. Were Russia on the winning side, it could expect to receive this valuable gateway as a prize of war. The Allies were exerting strong pressure on the Lvov government to stay in the war. If Russia pulled out, German armies on the eastern front would be used against France and Britain.

The government was not long in making its decision. Despite strong pressure from the Socialists, it chose to side with the Allies and to keep the country at war.

During this time, the Provisional Government made an effort to relieve some of the most serious domestic problems. To satisfy some of the minority peoples who resented domination by the Great Russians, the new government recognized Poland and Finland as independent states and granted self-rule to Estonia. To win support among the Russian masses, Prince Lvov's government announced a sweeping program of social reform. Religious and racial discrimination were outlawed, amnesty was granted to all those convicted of political crimes by czarist officials, an eight-hour work day was established in factories, and civil liberties were guaranteed. Unfortunately, most of the new laws were ignored because the new government had no way to enforce its program.

Under the best conditions, the Lvov government could not have quickly solved the economic problems that had plagued Russia for centuries. Among peasants the chief demand was for land reform. For centuries they had dreamed of owning their own land, and the revolution had given them hope that this dream would come true. But the best the Provisional Government could do was to refer the problem to the proposed constitutional convention. By deciding to keep Russia in the war, the new government lost the confidence of war-weary soldiers and civilians. The Russian people had never lived well, and now they were suffering more than ever.

### Lenin's Return

Leaders of the Bolshevik branch of the Social Democratic Party had no part in the overthrow of Czar Nicholas. The heads of this revolutionary group were in exile in either Siberia or abroad. Lenin himself was in Switzerland. He had not been in Russia for ten years. Trotsky, who had played a major role in the 1905 uprising, was living in New York City. He was not yet a Bolshevik. The turmoil following the fall of Nicholas opened the way for radicals to return to their homeland.

The German government, recognizing that prolonged unrest in Russia was to its advantage, offered transportation to exiled Russians wishing to return home. In early April the German high command provided a private train to transport Lenin and other revolutionaries from Switzerland across Germany to Russia. This train reached Petrograd on April 16, 1917.

Lenin's arrival aroused mixed feelings. The Provisional Government, which represented the bourgeois element Lenin hated, was unhappy to see him return. The Mensheviks remembered that Lenin had forced the split in the Social Democratic party. Socialist Revolutionaries considered Lenin too radical. Even many Bolsheviks were uneasy. They thought it wise to cooperate with the Provisional Government until the war was over, a policy Lenin rejected. Still Lenin was a famous exile, and a large crowd was on hand at the Petrograd station to welcome him.

At the time of Lenin's arrival in Petrograd, no group was eager to accept the responsibilities of leadership. The Provisional Government saw itself in a caretaker role until a constitution could be written, hence the name Provisional. The Socialists posed no threat to the Provisional Government because neither Mensheviks nor Socialist Revolutionaries wished to assume the responsibilities of government.

Interpreting the teachings of Karl Marx literally, the Socialist groups were content to await the first step on the road to socialism. According to Marx this step was a capitalist state governed by the middle class. This was doubtless the kind of government that would be created by the constitutional convention. Only then, according to Marx, would the time be right for the proletariat to overthrow the capitalist government and establish the socialist state. Meanwhile the Socialists were content to influence the government through the soviets. There they had a say in government without being held responsible for the government's failures.

Lenin believed there was no better time for action than the present. Whatever strategy promised to put the Bolsheviks in power could be used. Lies, deceit, unfulfilled promises, double-dealing, murder, violence, suppression of individual rights—anything was justified if the end result would be a Bol-

# SIDELIGHT TO HISTORY

## Old Style or New Style

During his reign, Peter the Great abandoned the Russian tradition of dating time from the creation and instituted the Julian calendar. This system, introduced by Julius Caesar more than 17 centuries before, was based on a year of $365\frac{1}{4}$ days. Like our present calendar, this "Old Style" calendar added an extra day every four years to adjust for the fraction.

The slight error of the Julian calendar—11 minutes and 14 seconds per year—particularly bothered medieval religious leaders. The error added an extra day every 128 years, so it became more and more difficult to celebrate holy days at the proper time. By 1582 the calendar had gained ten days, and Pope Gregory XIII persuaded the Catholic nations to omit the extra days and establish a procedure to correct future error.

The solution was to omit three leap days every 400 years since three days were gained in that period. This improved Gregorian calendar was ignored by non-Catholic countries for many years. Britain and its colonies finally adopted it in 1752. Russia, who had not even adopted the "Old Style" calendar until 1699, finally converted to the "New Style" when the Communists came to power.

In the style of Rip Van Winkle, the Russian people went to bed on February 7, 1918, and awoke on February 21. The disappearance of those 13 calendar days resulted in the confused dating of the events of the Revolution. "Old Style" dates were adjusted to conform with the new calendar after 1918. Thus the revolutions that occurred in February and October of 1917 are now referred to as the March and November Revolutions. To avoid confusion, this text has used only "New Style" or post–1918 dates.

shevik takeover of government. Within a few hours after his arrival in Petrograd, he set forth his program: (1) all powers of government were to be transferred from the **bourgeois** Provisional Government to the soviets; (2) Russian participation in the war was to cease immediately; (3) peasants were to seize the lands they worked; and (4) factories were to be taken over by committees of workers. The last three points were likely to have such wide appeal that the first would readily be accepted.

## Check Your Understanding

1. What were the immediate causes of the overthrow of the czarist regime?
2. Why did the Ex Com exercise greater control over the revolution than the Provisional Government?
3. How did Marxist theory limit the actions of the Socialists during the revolution?
4. What actions did the Provisional Government take to deal with the problems it had inherited from the czarist government?
5. List the terms of Lenin's plan.
6. *Thinking Critically:* Why did the Socialists prefer a situation in which they had some say in what the new government did but were not held responsible in any way?

## 2. The Bolsheviks in Power

Under ordinary conditions the Bolsheviks would have posed no great threat to the Russian government. But the months from March to November of 1917 were not ordinary times for Russia. The government seemed incapable of action, economic conditions grew steadily worse, hunger and even starvation were common, and the people were becoming increasingly opposed to the war. At this desperate moment in history, Russia sorely lacked strong leadership. The Bolsheviks supplied it, seized control, and built a police state harsher than that of the czars.

### Continued Unrest

During the weeks following Lenin's return, the plight of the Provisional Government steadily worsened. In May, when the decision to keep the czar's war commitments was announced, Prince Lvov's cabinet came under bitter attack from both the moderate and radical Socialist leaders. This uproar was quelled only by reorganizing the cabinet to include a number of Mensheviks and Socialist Revolutionaries.

When this new government's July offensive turned into a humiliating defeat for the Russian Army, armed demonstrations broke out in Petrograd. The rioters took as their cry "All power to the soviets!" This July uprising did not, however, get out of hand, and another governmental reorganization temporarily restored calm in the capital. This time the Mensheviks gained control and Alexander Kerensky (kuh-REN-skee), the only Socialist in the original Provisional Government, replaced Prince Lvov as Prime Minister.

The next challenge came not from the radical left but from the conservative right. In September General Lavr Kornilov, the Commander-in-Chief of the Russian armies, staged a military coup to seize power. His effort failed, but it further weakened the authority of the Provisional Government.

### The Bolsheviks' Coup

While the Provisional Government was disintegrating, Lenin was making plans for a takeover. For several months he made little headway because other leaders and their programs enjoyed greater popularity. The liberal parties, led by the Constitutional Democrats or Cadets, had control of the Provisional Government until the Mensheviks took over in July. Among the Socialists, the Socialist Revolutionaries had the largest following. The Bolsheviks ran a poor third behind the Mensheviks. Steadily worsening conditions at home and at the front were causing growing unrest and dissatisfaction. Lenin hoped this discontent would make the people ready for drastic change.

Bolshevik leaders regarded the soviets as the key to power and set out to control them. Maneuvering for strategic positions on the various committees, they bombarded the delegates with proposals for reforms to be introduced under Bolshevik leadership. Trotsky, who had returned to Russia in May, doubtless was the Bolsheviks' most effective speaker. At first the Bolsheviks enjoyed little success. Time and again they were shouted down and their ideas rejected. But throughout Russia many soviets, especially those composed of soldiers and industrial workers, came to believe in Lenin's program. By October the Bolsheviks enjoyed a majority in the strategically important and influential Petrograd Soviet, and Trotsky had become its new chairman. At last the stage was set for the Bolshevik Revolution.

The Bolsheviks chose the night of November 6–7, 1917, to make their move. Acting under the orders of Trotsky's Military Revolutionary Committee of the Petrograd Soviet, units of armed workers, soldiers, and sailors moved swiftly to take over the city. By morning they were in control of the rail lines, telegraph offices, and main bridges. It was impossible for the Provisional

On November 7, 1917, workers stormed the Winter Palace in Petrograd, where the Provisional Government was lodged.

Government to move troops into the city. So far the Bolsheviks had met with little opposition from forces loyal to the government.

Although caught off guard by the Bolshevik revolt, Kerensky managed to slip out of the city, disguised as a sailor riding in an automobile owned by the United States Embassy. Hastening to the front, he managed to persuade several army commanders to dispatch troops to Petrograd. By then it was too late. Having skillfully exploited their initial success, the Bolsheviks were firmly in control not only of Petrograd but also of other strategic centers. Troop trains were not permitted to reach the capital.

The Bolsheviks moved fast to secure their victory. In a statement issued by the Military Revolutionary Committee on the morning of November 7, they announced:

> The Provisional Government is overthrown. The state power has passed into the hands of the organ of the Petersburg [Petrograd] Committee, which stands at the head of the Petersburg garrison and proletariat. The cause the people have been fighting for—the immediate proposal of a democratic peace, the elimination of private property in land,

workers' control of production, and the formation of a Soviet Government—is assured. Long live the revolution of the workers, soldiers, and peasants! [N. N. Sukhanov, *The Russian Revolution, 1917; Eyewitness Account,* 2 vols.]

Even as the Revolutionary Committee was issuing this declaration, the Second All-Russian Congress of Soviets was preparing to meet in Petrograd. On the evening of November 7, the ruling council, up to that time controlled by Mensheviks and Socialist Revolutionaries, was replaced by one dominated by the Bolsheviks. The next evening the Congress elected Lenin's hand-picked Council of People's Commissars to rule Russia until a Constituent Assembly could be elected. Thus in a matter of two days the Bolsheviks seemed to have gained control of both the soviets and the central government.

### The Fight for Power

Actually Bolshevik control of the situation was less firm than it appeared during the early, emotion-packed hours of the Congress of Soviets. This became clear when elections for the Constituent Assembly were held later in the month. Most of the elected delegates were Socialists, but less than one fourth were Bolsheviks. The majority of the delegates had no intention of accepting Lenin's proposal—that the Assembly meet just long enough to delegate officially the powers of government to the Council of People's Commissars.

After repeated delays caused by Bolshevik stalling tactics, the Assembly finally convened on January 18, 1918. Despite constant harassment from the Bolsheviks, the Assembly managed to outline plans for a new government. This blueprint was not even considered by the Bolsheviks because it failed to give them supreme power. When the Assembly gathered for its second day of deliberations, armed guards were in control of the convention hall. These Bolshevik military units dissolved the assembly, and non-Bolshevik members wisely scattered. Some went into hiding. Others left the country. Thus ended Russia's all too brief experiment with democracy.

### Ending the War with Germany

The Bolsheviks realized that they could not hope to remain in power unless they could end Russia's participation in the war. They needed peace to free themselves for battle against enemies at home. In early December of 1917, the Bolsheviks met with the Germans at Brest-Litovsk to discuss peace terms. The Bol-

Here Lenin speaks to supporters of the Revolution in Sverdlov Square, Petrograd. On the steps below him to the right is Leon Trotsky, commander of the army and Lenin's right-hand man.

sheviks hoped to reach a settlement under which Russia would neither lose territory nor pay **reparations**. Trotsky, now Russia's Commissar of Foreign Affairs, was given the task of winning German approval for this plan. To his dismay the Germans pointed out that since they were winning the war on the Eastern Front, there was no reason to stop fighting unless substantial concessions were made.

The price for peace demanded by Germany was staggering. Russia was to give up the vast, fertile lands of the Ukraine, as well as its Baltic territories. All told, Russia would lose one third of its people, one fourth of its territory, a third of its crop land, one fourth of its income, and more than half of its industries. Despite strong opposition from many Bolsheviks, including Trotsky, Lenin persuaded the governing councils of the Bolshevik Party and the Congress of Soviets to accept the harsh terms. On March 3, 1918, the Soviet Government signed the Treaty of Brest-Litovsk. Eleven days later it was ratified by the Congress of Soviets.

### Civil War

Having removed Russia from World War I, the Bolsheviks, now called Communists, turned to the task of establishing their supremacy over all of Russia. Wherever they turned, they were confronted by armed foes. Some of the most determined opposition came from the "White" armies. Led by former czarist generals, they were dedicated to the overthrow of the "Reds," as the Communists were called. Not only did the "Whites" hold out for years in such widely separated regions as Crimea, Central Asia, and eastern Siberia, but at times they threatened to roll back the Bolshevik armies. The striking power of the White armies depended heavily on aid furnished by anti-Bolshevik foreign governments. Angered by Russia's betrayal of the Allied cause at Brest-Litovsk, and fearful lest communism undermine their own governments, the Allies were ready to supply money and arms to the "Whites." For some years, too, British, French, American, and Japanese troops occupied various parts of Russia.

Less serious resistance to the Bolsheviks was raised by minority peoples who dwelt in the Caucasus regions and in Central Asia. They often attempted to set themselves up as independent states, but the Bolsheviks used the strength of the Red Army to crush their hopes.

By late 1921 the Russian Civil War was over. The Bolsheviks had either made peace with or taken over the fledgling independent states and crushed the White armies. At last the Communists exercised complete military and political control over what remained of the former empire of the czars.

### How the Bolsheviks Gained Power

The Bolshevik triumph in 1917–1921 astounded the world. Representing such a small part of the Russian population, Lenin and his followers were given little chance of imposing their will on a state the size of Russia. Overlooked was the superb organization, high morale, and utter ruthlessness of the Bolsheviks. Though few in number, they were fanatically dedicated to their goals. In Lenin and Trotsky the Bolsheviks had, respectively, a skillful strategist and an outstanding organizer. The latter created a Red Army that strict discipline and continuous indoctrination shaped into a mighty striking force completely loyal to the Communist Party and its leaders.

The Bolsheviks carefully exploited popular grievances for political advantage. Urban workers, long underpaid and overworked, responded enthusiastically to the Bolsheviks' cry to oust their employers and take over the factories. The peasants, who for centuries had dreamed of owning their own land, were encouraged to overthrow their landlords and take their property. War-weary soldiers were promised an end to the war. It is not surprising that these glowing promises attracted many followers.

The major reason for the military success of the Bolsheviks, however, lay in the shortcomings of their enemies. Had the many "White" armies been united, they might have defeated the Reds. But anti-Communist forces often were as hostile to one another

Each day long lines of Soviet citizens pay homage to Lenin at his tomb, which stands between the two towers of the Kremlin wall. Until Khrushchev's de-Stalinization campaign in 1961, this tomb also honored Stalin.

as the Bolsheviks. Moreover, Lenin's political opponents failed to assess accurately the Bolshevik strength. They reasoned that since the Bolsheviks were supported by only a small minority, the people would reject Lenin's leadership in favor of the more democratic program of the Socialist Revolutionaries and their allies. By underestimating their opponents, and by failing to cooperate with one another, the anti-Bolshevik forces lost their chance to defeat the Bolsheviks.

## Lenin's Death

Badly wounded in 1918 by a would-be assassin, Lenin never regained his full health and strength. In 1922 and 1923 he suffered several strokes, leaving him semiparalyzed and unable to speak or write. Lenin's death on January 21, 1924, left his followers in Russia and all over the world with a feeling of irreplaceable loss. The funeral of the giant who had given direction to the Bolshevik Revolution and had founded the Communist state was memorable. One of his biographers has described it:

> Lenin's body lay in state in the Hall of Columns. For four days, while the northern city [Moscow] was in the deepest freeze it had known in years, hundreds of thousands of women, children and men queued for hours night and day

in the icy streets to get the split-second look allowed them as they passed the open coffin. Moscow mourned. Many millions elsewhere mourned. Meanwhile, a temporary wooden mausoleum was being built behind a fence in the Red Square near the Kremlin wall. Into it Lenin was borne on the 27th. Later, however, he was carried away to a laboratory, his organs and body fluids removed and preservative liquids substituted by a complex never-disclosed chemical process to keep him life-like to this day. [Louis Fischer, *The Life of Lenin*.]

The temporary mausoleum was later replaced by an imposing stone tomb. People from all over the Soviet Union and from many other lands as well still line up patiently to catch a fleeting glimpse of Lenin's body. On all important holidays the leaders of the Communist world stand atop the tomb to review the parades that pass on the broad plaza known as Red Square.

### Stalin's Rise to Power

No Communist ever challenged Lenin for leadership of the Russian state and the Communist Party. But during his illness party leaders gave thought to what their role would be once Lenin was dead. Eventually the field narrowed to two: Trotsky and Stalin. The former, a brilliant planner and a spell-binding orator, had made contributions to the Bolshevik cause second only to those of Lenin himself. Much of the early support given Bolshevism by the soviets was the result of Trotsky's activities. Trotsky had helped plan the successful November Revolution, and it was Trotsky who had organized and led the Red Army to victory in the Russian Civil War.

Stalin, like Trotsky, was a veteran of the revolutionary movement. Active in agitation among railroad workers in southern Russia, Stalin had been jailed for his actions and deported to Siberia. After escaping, he organized groups that raised money for the Party by robbing banks. This activity caught Lenin's eye, but it also landed Stalin in Siberia again. Shortly after the November Revolution, the shrewd and aggressive Stalin became Lenin's administrative assistant.

In 1922 Stalin became Communist Party Secretary, a position carrying great power. Within a year Lenin, then in the early stages of his fatal illness, had recognized Stalin as being "too rough" for the office and urged his fellow Communists to find some way of deposing him. But the warning went unheeded. After Lenin died, Stalin secured complete power by imprisoning or exiling all rivals. Trotsky lost his official positions in 1925

## Leon Trotsky

Before the overthrow of the czar in 1917, Russian revolutionaries, often one step ahead of the police, found it necessary to adopt aliases. Thus Vladimir Ulyanov took the name of N. Lenin. Josif (Joseph) Dzhugashvili became known as Joseph Stalin, meaning "like steel." Lev (Leon) Davidovich Bronstein (1879–1940) became Leon Trotsky during his escape from Siberia to London in 1902. This was the name of the chief jailer of the model prison in Odessa where Trotsky had been imprisoned.

An early convert to revolutionary socialism, Trotsky was a man of many talents, who worked out his own set of revolutionary and ideological beliefs. Not until the Russian Revolution was well underway did he join Lenin and the Bolsheviks. Trotsky was one of the principal engineers of the Bolshevik seizure of power. Lenin held him in the highest esteem and entrusted him with important posts in the infant Communist state.

In the deadly struggles within the Communist Party after the death of Lenin, Trotsky was challenged by Stalin. Trotsky had long been a believer in revolution, insisting that Communists always had to be on the offensive, ready to seize every opportunity that presented itself to advance the cause of Socialist revolution. Stalin, on the other hand, believed that Soviet Russia had to become a fortress of socialism before undertaking risky revolutionary ventures abroad. This was the doctrine of "socialism in one country." In the critical maneuvers within the Communist Party between 1924–1927, Stalin and his views prevailed. Trotsky was gradually squeezed out of his positions of leadership and finally expelled from the Party.

Trotsky was exiled to Alma Ata in Central Asia in 1928 and banished from the USSR in the following year. After living in Turkey, France, and Norway, he finally settled in Mexico in 1937. Because Trotsky produced a flood of books and articles that attacked Stalin's regime, Stalin sent an assassin who worked his way into the Trotsky circle and mortally wounded Trotsky on August 21, 1940.

Russian creative expression was greatly restricted by the Soviet ruling that all works should dwell on socialist themes. In art, this "socialist realism" produced works with a message, but with little artistic merit. This 1949 painting entitled "Creative Fellowship" depicts the cooperation of science and industry for the state's benefit.

and 1926, was expelled from the Communist Party in 1927, and was deported in 1929. Stalin was undisputed master of Russia and the leader of world communism. The Stalinist Era lasted until the **dictator's** death in 1953.

### Stalin's Use of Power

On the flag of the Soviet Union there is emblazoned a hammer and a sickle. The first figure stands for the worker, and the other, the peasant. Opponents, however, used to say that the hammer signified Stalin and his methods. By one means or another the soviet dictator eliminated all opposition. The entire country was honeycombed with agents of the dreaded secret police. Spying on Party members and officials, workers, and peasants, the secret police arrested people on the slightest suspicion.

Stalin's ruthlessness reached a climax in the **purges** that began in 1935–1936. Hundreds of leading Communists in the government, including many members of Lenin's original "inner circle" who had survived earlier harassment, were "liquidated." The greatest of these were subjected to humiliating public trials in which they were compelled to confess their "crimes" against the Communist regime. They were then executed. Even Stalin's associates from revolutionary times who had aided him in his rise to power were killed.

## THE UNION OF SOVIET SOCIALIST REPUBLICS

**PLACE: THE UNION OF THE SOVIET SOCIALIST REPUBLICS.**

The Soviet Union was created in 1922, when the Russian Soviet Federated Socialist Republic formed a union with the Ukrainian, Byelorussian, and Transcaucasian Republics. During the next 15 years the Turkmen, Uzbek, Tadzhik, Kazakh, and Kirghiz Republics of Central Asia joined the Soviet Union. In 1936 Transcaucasia was divided into three republics—the Armenian, Azerbaijan, and Georgian. Finally,

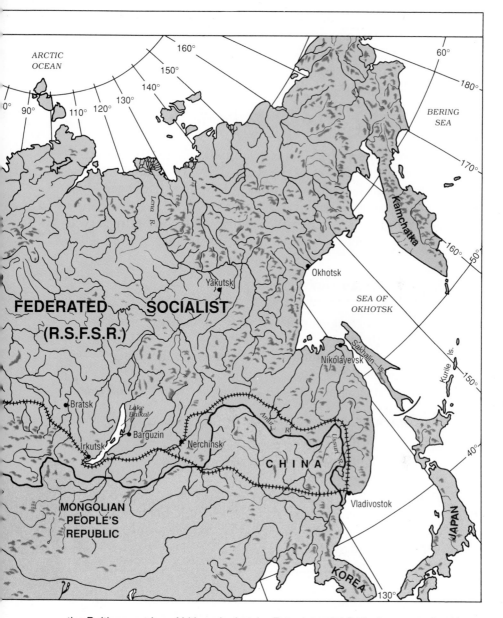

ARCTIC
OCEAN

BERING
SEA

FEDERATED      SOCIALIST

(R.S.F.S.R.)

Yakutsk

Okhotsk

SEA OF
OKHOTSK

Kamchatka

Nikoláyevsk

Sakhalin Is.

Kurile Is.

Bratsk

Lake
Baikal

Barguzin

Irkutsk

Amur R.

Nerchinsk

CHINA

Ussuri R.

MONGOLIAN
PEOPLE'S
REPUBLIC

Vladivostok

JAPAN

KOREA

the Baltic countries of Lithuania, Latvia, Estonia, and Moldavia were gained in
World War II. Although each of the 15 republics has its own constitution, the
Communist Party controls the government. The Russian S.F.S.R. dwarfs all the
others in land area, and contains more than half the Soviet people, most of them
concentrated west of the Ural Mountains.

The purges were soon extended to all levels of Soviet society. The exact number of victims will never be known. At a minimum, one million people were shot. Another 12 to 15 million were sentenced to long-term imprisonment in the forced labor camps of Siberia. Perhaps three million or more of these prisoners died in the camps. Most purge victims had been innocent of any wrong-doing against the government, or even of having opposed it.

The pace of the purges slowed dramatically in 1939. By this time the Party, the officers of the army and navy, the bureaucracy, and the professional and intellectual elites had been decimated. But Stalin's position was now more secure than ever. Historians continue to debate the motivation for the purges. Was Stalin mad? Or was he simply taking no chances?

## Check Your Understanding

1. What was the Bolshevik strategy for seizing power?
2. Why did the Bolsheviks succeed?
3. Why was Lenin willing to pay the price for peace with Germany?
4. What groups opposed the Communist takeover of the government?
5. How did the Communists win the support of peasants and industrial workers?
6. How did Stalin establish himself as the dictator of the Soviet Union?
7. *Thinking Critically:* Based on what you have read in this chapter, do you think that if Stalin had challenged Lenin for power he would have succeeded? Why or why not?

## 3. The Struggle to Develop a Socialist Economy

The Bolsheviks had plunged Russia into bloody revolution to clear the way for a new social order. On the ruins of the czarist system they meant to build a workers' state—a country in which workers' interests came first—and a Communist way of life. To describe communism, Karl Marx had used the phrase "From each according to his abilities, to each according to his needs." But in 1921 Russia was not ready for Marx's ideal society. The desperate state of the economy had to be improved before the

After the Bolshevik takeover wealthy Russians were reduced to poverty. Deprived of their fortunes, widows of former aristocrats peddled their last bits of finery on the Petrograd streets. Their expressions indicate little sympathy for the new Socialist state.

ideal state could be built. Both Lenin and his successor, Joseph Stalin, inaugurated bold new plans to put the country back on its feet.

### A Rethinking of Communist Goals

During the Russian Civil War, Communist leaders had tried to introduce "instant communism" with a system of controls called War Communism. But the plan was a failure, and by the end of the Civil War the economy was in utter chaos. Industrial production was at its lowest level in years. Money, made almost worthless by **inflation**, was accepted by neither merchants nor peasants. The railroads, a vital part of Russia's economy, were operating in haphazard fashion. Two-thirds of the freight cars and locomotives were out of service because of poor management or lack of repairs. Cities had lost a third of their population because hungry workers had returned to the farms, hoping to find food. The peasants, ordered to feed soldiers as well as urban workers without payment, refused to produce food. The coming of government food collectors invariably brought on riots. Between 1917 and 1921 agricultural production fell to half its prewar level.

Some Communist leaders accepted these depressed economic conditions as the necessary price for achieving "pure communism." What was important to them was the fact that some progress was being made toward this goal. A moneyless economy was in sight, and the working class had "triumphed" over "bourgeois" factory owners. "From each according to his abilities, to each according to his needs" was being applied. But more realistic Communist leaders such as Lenin realized that War Communism was rapidly leading the country into economic ruin. Lenin therefore called for a strategic retreat, lest mounting disorder threaten Communist rule. Until current unrest could be brought under control, the Communist state would have to wait.

## The New Economic Policy

Lenin's first move was to enact a law in 1921 inaugurating the New Economic Policy (NEP), and mark the beginning of the end of War Communism. As the NEP took form, it became clear that Communist ideology was being revised to fit the distinctive needs of the moment. Lenin's new economic axiom was: "From each according to his ability, to each according to his work." Thus the NEP combined features of capitalism and socialism.

Communist leaders realized that they needed middle class support to stimulate economic recovery. Such help would not be forthcoming unless the "bourgeoisie" could be induced through profits to take part in the NEP. Peasants, merchants, and owners of small factories, therefore, were allowed to sell their products and services on the open market for whatever they could get. The state, however, retained ownership and management of the large industries and businesses, such as mines, mills, transportation facilities, banks, and foreign trade.

Lenin made a further concession to capitalism by inviting foreign investments in Russian economic projects. In czarist times, foreign investments had been needed to supplement funds supplied by wealthy Russians and the government. After the Communist takeover, Russian capital dried up. Wealthy Russians had been ruined by the confiscation of factories and estates and intimidated by Communist threats to destroy capitalism. Many had fled the country. Few who remained had either the funds or the desire to invest in Russian socialism. Lenin knew that he must have the backing of foreign capital.

Many dedicated Communists were critical of Lenin's plan for economic development. Some thought the Communist goal of **central planning** of the economy based on **heavy industry** was being shelved in favor of a "free market" economy based on agriculture and **light industry**. Some opponents were fearful that if capitalism were encouraged it would stifle Russian socialism, which had not yet taken root. Others argued that the NEP might hurt the group on which socialism depended most, the industrial workers. For not only did the plan favor the peasants, but it allowed merchants and owners of small factories—the very groups that "exploited" industrial workers—to earn profits.

**156**

Lenin did not deny the charges leveled at the NEP. He simply argued that any plan that could save the Socialist revolution must receive consideration. Though an arch foe of capitalism, he had no qualms about using capitalist means to attain Communist goals. Lenin pointed out that the attempt to establish communism immediately had been a great mistake. The transition from capitalism to communism must be made in stages. The "dictatorship of the proletariat," the Communist Party, would guide the people through the various stages. As long as the Party retained control of heavy industry and foreign trade, he saw no possibility of capitalism overthrowing the Socialist revolution. Instead, he reasoned, the resources of the capitalist enemy could be used to bring about conditions leading to its ultimate destruction.

## Stalin's Five-Year Plans

During the NEP period (1921–1928), the Soviet economy had grown steadily. But many Communists feared that a further rapid expansion of the economy was unlikely. Most important, under the NEP, heavy industry had not grown quickly enough. To step up sharply the pace of industrial development, Stalin, in 1928, abandoned the NEP in favor of centralized economic planning. Production goals for agriculture and industry would be established by the Soviet government, which would also determine the means for reaching these goals.

The State Planning Commission, known as *Gosplan*, put together a five-year plan for the Soviet economy. Under centralized planning, heavy industry received major attention. Because the Soviet Union was determined to catch up with the more industrialized West, Gosplan placed chief stress on the production of iron and steel, coal, oil, and hydroelectric power. To meet its quotas, Gosplan tapped many previously undeveloped resources. In the Magnitogorsk region of the Ural Mountains great iron mines were opened, and the coal fields of the Kuznetsk Basin in south-central Siberia were worked for the first time. Later the mineral wealth of the Arctic region, as well as its timber, fish, and furs, was exploited. New railroads and canals were built to connect the various industrial regions in Asia with one another and with European Russia. A great pipeline was laid linking the oil fields in the Caucasus region to the port of Batumi on the Black Sea. Powerful hydroelectric installations harnessed the flow of the Soviet Union's great rivers.

In manufacturing, such items as tractors, trucks, and machines received high priority. These were essential to both in-

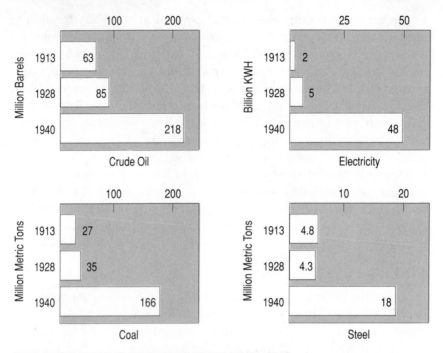

**SUCCESS OF THE EARLY FIVE-YEAR PLANS.** During the Russian Revolution, production fell sharply, but by 1928 it had passed pre-Revolutionary levels. The first two five-year plans had brought significant increases by 1940.

dustry and agriculture. But **consumer goods**, such as washing machines, radios, refrigerators, automobiles, clothing, and cosmetics, were regarded as less essential. The Soviet people were expected to sacrifice comforts in order to bring the level of industrialization of their country up to that of industrial developments in capitalist countries.

When the First Five-Year Plan was instituted, it was recognized that all types of machinery would have to be imported. Since the Soviet economy was based on agriculture, the money to pay for these expensive machines had to come from the export of food products. Stalin's government, therefore, had to produce large farm surpluses to ensure having the grain needed for export.

The Soviet government's solution was to merge the country's farms into gigantic enterprises under centralized management. Each of these huge collective farms was to be cultivated cooperatively by its many members. The Communists placed great faith in the collectives, expecting them to revolutionize Soviet agriculture. With government direction and financial assistance, outmoded farming methods would be eliminated, and with mechanization, agricultural production greatly increase.

## ПО ПЛАНУ СТАЛИНА-ПРЕОБРАЗУЕМ ПРИРОДУ!

Posters urged increased agricultural production during the five-year plans. "We shall transform the face of the earth according to Stalin's plan," vows this poster of a thoughtful Stalin advising dedicated Soviet farmers.

### The Slaughter of the Kulaks

From the onset of the five-year plans the peasants had opposed the state's program. Throughout history they had dreamed of owning their own land. This dream apparently became a reality in the days following the Bolshevik Revolution, when millions of peasants seized the lands they worked, evicting or even killing the landlords. Under the NEP peasants had kept these lands and had been able to sell any surplus food. Now, the same Communist government not only was forbidding them to work their lands as **free enterprise**, but was taking the land itself.

The most determined resistance came from peasants known as **kulaks**, meaning "fists." For centuries this term had been applied scornfully to peasants who had more land or livestock than their neighbors and who exploited their fellow peasants. In the period of the NEP, when government restrictions were rather lax, the kulak class had grown. Hiring other peasants to work their lands for low wages, leasing tools and livestock for high rentals, and loaning money at exorbitant interest rates, the kulaks had made enemies of less fortunate neighbors. They were unpopular with the government for another reason. Since they controlled much of the land, their cooperation was needed to achieve government quotas.

Workers, most of them women, gather for lunch on a collective farm in the 1930's. A horse-drawn wagon brings food to the fields.

The Communists decided to destroy the kulak class. In practice, they identified as a kulak any peasant who opposed collectivization. During the period of the first three five-year plans, at least five million peasants lost their lives. Some were simply murdered. Others were deported to Siberian prison camps, where they later died. Many peasants perished during the famine of 1932–1933. A drought had brought on a devastating crop failure in the normally fertile Volga region. The government made no effort to feed the starving peasants. Indeed, it viewed the famine as a convenient way of breaking peasant resistance to collectivization.

### Continued Agricultural Problems

The results of collectivization fell short of Communist hopes. Though the opposition of the kulaks was brutally smashed, the peasants as a whole showed little enthusiasm for the state's program. Fearful of displaying their resentment openly, they cooperated halfheartedly. By refusing to exert themselves and by resorting to sabotage, they frustrated the hopes of the state for increased farm production. The state responded to this defiance by intimidation and the use of force. Supplies of food were

**160**

taken from the peasants at unreasonably low prices, declared "surplus," and made available to urban workers. The effectiveness of collectivization also suffered because of shortages of mechanical equipment. Since factories were unable to turn out the necessary tractors and other farm machines, inefficient methods of cultivation had to be continued. Today, more than half a century later, Soviet agriculture is still not totally mechanized.

By the end of the Second Five-Year Plan almost all the country's peasants had been forced to give up private farming. But life on the collective farms was less harsh than private farming. Once collectivization was achieved, the government allowed peasants to have small plots on which they could raise produce for their own use and for sale. This policy greatly reduced opposition to government policies.

## Mixed Economic Results

Before World War II interrupted the scheme of five-year national planning, two five-year plans had run their course and a third was underway. Agricultural gains had been negligible. Enough food for subsistence living was grown, and some was exported, but the hoped-for surpluses were not achieved. Production of consumer goods was well below the level of other industrialized countries. Only in the area of heavy industry could Communist leaders take heart. Not only was production in this field increased in existing factories, but many new manufacturing enterprises were founded. Most encouraging to Communist leaders was the steady rise in the production of iron, steel, coal, oil, and electric power.

One important result of the five-year plans was the eastward shift in Soviet manufacturing. In czarist times most of Russia's factories and mines were in Europe. The vast resources east of the Urals were almost entirely undeveloped. During the period of Stalin's five-year plans, millions of workers were relocated to Siberia, and "enemies of the state" were exploited as slave labor in Siberia's forests, mines, and industries and on road and railroad projects. Great cities developed where a few years before no sign of human habitation was found. Ever since the 1930's the new centers of Soviet industry have been built to the east of the Ural Mountains.

By World War II the USSR's overall economy was strong, if not healthy. The emphasis on heavy manufacturing had made the USSR a great industrial power, as shown on the chart on page 158. The cost in terror and human suffering had been enormous, but this did not bother Stalin and his fellow Communists. They were reaching their goals.

## Check Your Understanding

1. Why was War Communism replaced with the New Economic Policy?
2. Why did Stalin abandon the NEP?
3. How did Stalin seek to speed the USSR's: **a.** industrial development? **b.** agricultural production?
4. Why did the peasants resist collectivization?
5. How successful had Stalin been in reaching his goals for: **a.** industrial development? **b.** agricultural production?
6. **Thinking Critically:** Even if the farm machinery had been available, do you think that peasants on collective farms would have turned out surpluses? Why or why not?

## 4. World Communism vs. Soviet Interests

One of the many issues dividing Stalin and Trotsky was the direction that the Communist revolutionary movement should take. The daring Trotsky spoke out for "permanent revolution." Communists should promote revolution throughout the world. The cautious Stalin, seeing the risks of pressing immediately for the overthrow of capitalism in other countries, favored a policy of "socialism in one country." First, Communists should build up Russia, the only existing Socialist state. Stalin's rigidly-controlled five-year plans were instituted with this end in mind. Under his direction Communist activity in other countries was encouraged unless it conflicted with the interests of the Soviet Union. Always, the well-being of the USSR had to come first.

### Formation of the Comintern

In 1919 the Bolsheviks created an organization for the promotion of revolution in other countries. This was the Communist Third International, known as the **Comintern**. It was the successor to the First (1864) and the Second International (1889) that came apart during World War I. Communist parties in other lands could join the Comintern only by accepting the conditions laid down by Lenin. In effect this meant accepting the leadership of the USSR in working for the overthrow of capitalism.

Lenin firmly believed in international communism. In many of his writings he had condemned Communists who put national interests first. But once in control of the Soviet Union, he saw things in a different light. Of primary importance was the success of the Communist movement in the USSR. The establishment of socialism in other lands could wait.

During the period of the NEP, the Soviet-dominated Comintern was under orders not to antagonize Western powers by actively promoting revolution in those lands. Lenin, and later Stalin, did not want to discourage the inflow of much-needed foreign investment. But with the onset of the Great Depression in 1929, the situation changed. Hunger and misery came to Western countries. Factories closed, millions of workers were out of work, and falling agricultural prices made it impossible for farmers to make payments on their mortgages.

Communists decided to take advantage of this misery. The Comintern began to agitate and conspire to bring about the overthrow of established governments. Even though Communist parties in many countries gained strength, nowhere were the Communists able to seize power.

### The Nationalist Revolution in China

Communism's greatest advance during the 1920's was in China. Sun Yat-sen (SOON YAHT-SEN) and his Nationalist Party, the Guomindang (GWOH-min-DAHNG), were attempting to bring a unified government to a land that had known only chaos since 1911, the year the centuries-old Manchu Dynasty fell. In 1923 Sun met with Adolf Joffe, a Soviet who represented the Comintern. Joffe promised Sun that the Comintern would help the Guomindang in its struggle to unite China.

Sun Yat-sen was an old man. Though not a Communist, he was willing to do almost anything to secure victory for the Guomindang before he died. With Soviet assistance, the Nationalist movement became stronger. A veteran Bolshevik, Michael Borodin, became one of Sun's most important advisers. The Soviets helped the Nationalists establish a military academy where men could be trained for a new national revolutionary army. Before his death, in 1925, Sun had seen his movement transformed into a vital force through Soviet aid.

Sun's successor, Chiang Kai-shek (jee-AHNG ky-SHEK), did not trust the Communists. Convinced that they were planning to seize control of the revolutionary movement, he decided to strike first. In 1927 Nationalist forces rounded up hundreds of Communists, together with labor leaders and others suspected of being radicals. Some were immediately executed. Many others were arrested and imprisoned. However, a number of Communists escaped the purge and went into hiding. Among them was Mao Zedong (MAH-oh dzuh-DONG), who found refuge in the mountains of southeast China. Here he organized a revolutionary base that slowly grew in strength.

### The Spread of Nazism and Fascism

The surfacing of strong rightist and anti-Communist movements in the 1930's compelled Stalin and the Comintern to reconsider established policy. **Fascism** under Benito Mussolini had gained control in Italy in 1922, having ousted that country's democratic government. In 1936 Mussolini alarmed the world by conquering Ethiopia. In Germany, the National Socialists, the Nazis, came into power in 1933, with the appointment of Adolf Hitler to the post of Chancellor. The Nazis soon destroyed the democratic Weimar Republic and suppressed all other political parties. Many Communists were killed, and the Party continued to function only as an underground movement. In Japan the military was expanding its control over the civilian government.

A threat to French Communists in 1934 led the Comintern to adopt a new strategy. After fascist riots in Paris, the French Communist Party joined with the Socialist and Radical parties to form a **popular front** against fascism. In Communist usage, fascism included nazism. On July 25, 1935, just days after the agreement was signed, the Comintern assembled in Moscow.

The delegates were then officially informed that the Communist Party in any country threatened by fascism should seek to organize a popular front. It was hoped that this would include all anti-fascist political parties in the country—democratic and Socialist as well as the Communist Party—in a coalition against the extreme right. Communist parties throughout the world would cease their maneuvers to overthrow established regimes. Instead their task was to persuade governments and peoples to join the Soviet Union in a worldwide struggle against the common enemy. The capitalists were to be allies in destroying the fascists.

### The Iron Discipline of Communism

Communists everywhere obediently, if at times unhappily, accepted orders from the Comintern to cease revolutionary activity. But only in France did a popular front government hold office long enough to exert much influence over political affairs. In Spain, a civil war broke out in 1936 when Fascists sought to overthrow a popular front government that included Socialists and Communists. The Comintern and the Soviet Union supplied aid to the government in power. But Germany and Italy supplied more to its allies, and the Fascist leader, General Francisco Franco, gained control of the country. In China the forces of Mao Zedong cooperated with Chiang Kai-shek's Nationalist government in the war against Japan.

The objective of the popular front policy was to safeguard the Soviet Union. Still in the midst of its efforts at industrialization, the USSR had no desire to get involved in a major war. To protect his country, Stalin was ready not only to cooperate with the "bourgeois democracies" but, if necessary, to sacrifice Communist parties and their leaders in other lands.

### The USSR and Its Neighbors

For years following World War I Russia was friendlier with its old enemy Germany than with the victorious Allies. Although the Treaty of Brest-Litovsk (see page 145) was repudiated, Russia had lost extensive territory in the postwar realignment of national boundaries. The fact that Britain, France, and the United States had cooperated with the White armies in the Russian Revolution did not help the situation. Germany, furthermore, had soon recognized the Communist regime, while some of the Western democracies, including the United States, refused for years to do so. An added insult was that until 1934 the League of Nations refused membership to the Soviet Union.

Stalin gradually became convinced that France and Britain were trying to push Germany into war with the Soviet Union to escape having to fight Hitler in the west. When Hitler made clear his designs on Czechoslovakia, a country bordering the USSR, Stalin understandably was concerned. British and French statesmen preferred **appeasement** of Hitler to negotiations with Stalin for joint action. To safeguard his country's interests, Stalin decided on a drastic step.

### Stalin's Pact with Hitler

During the 1930's, the Soviet Union's efforts to contain Fascist aggression won friends for that country in non-Communist lands. It came as a shock, therefore, when the Nazi-Soviet Pact was announced in 1939. In this historic pact Nazi Germany and the Soviet Union pledged not to attack each other. It mattered little to Hitler that the treaty conflicted with the Anti-Comintern

Pact he previously had negotiated with Italy and Japan. Nor did it bother the Soviet dictator that he had come to terms with the sworn enemy of communism. News of the pact had a profound effect on peoples in other lands. Disillusioned Communists in Western countries withdrew from their parties, while Communist sympathizers who had been influenced by the USSR's anti-Nazi stand were horrified.

Both Stalin and Hitler had good reasons for agreeing to the pact. Stalin hoped that the non-aggression agreement would turn Nazi expansion westward. In any event he was buying time to strengthen the Soviet Union against a future German attack, which he was sure would come. Hitler found the understanding useful in terms of his plans for conquest. Already preparing his forces for a lightning attack or *blitzkrieg* on Poland, he did not wish to risk a Soviet attack from the east. Germany had learned the folly of a two-front war between 1914 and 1918. Both dictators would gain at the expense of Poland. That unfortunate country was divided by secret agreement into German and Russian **spheres of influence**.

On September 1, 1939, eight days after Stalin and Hitler reached their "thieves' agreement," Nazi armies crashed across the Polish frontier. Soon Soviet troops moved in to occupy the

In a display of doomed, hopeless courage, aristocrats like these in the Polish cavalry charged German tanks during the *blitzkrieg*, and were slaughtered.

Soviet sphere of influence. The Poles fought bravely but without hope of victory. Although both France and Britain declared war on Germany, neither could provide effective aid in time to save Poland. World War II had begun.

## Check Your Understanding

1. Why did the Comintern not aggressively seek to further its goals in the 1920's?
2. Why did the Comintern change its policy in the 1930's?
3. Why were relations between the Soviet Union and the Western democracies cool between World War I and World War II?
4. How was the Nazi-Soviet Non-Aggression Pact advantageous for **a.** Germany? **b.** the Soviet Union?
5. *Thinking Critically:* Why was the Nationalist Revolution in China considered a success for communism?

## CHAPTER REVIEW

### ■ Chapter Summary

*Section 1.* The March Revolution of 1917 brought to an abrupt end three centuries of Romanov rule. This dynasty was replaced by a Provisional Government that attempted to keep Russia in the war. This policy, together with worsening conditions on the home front, enabled the Bolsheviks to gain influence in the soviets by espousing a policy of peace, land, and socialized industry.

*Section 2.* The Bolsheviks made their successful bid for power in November, 1917 and early the next year made their position secure by disbanding the constitutional convention called to give Russia a new government. In order to concentrate on the problems at home, Lenin accepted Germany's very harsh peace terms. Many Russians opposed the Communist takeover. These "White Russians" received military aid from the Western allies. It was only after four years of bloody civil war that the Communists became masters of the former czarist empire.

**167**

**Section 3.** Having achieved victory in the Russian Civil War, Lenin realized that all resources must be mobilized to rebuild the shattered country. His plan, the New Economic Policy (NEP), sacrificed Marxian dogma for immediate results. The NEP sought to attract investment capital from foreign lands and combined capitalist and socialist methods. Slow economic progress under the NEP led Stalin to introduce a system of central planning. The five-year plans placed major emphasis on heavy industry and went into effect in 1928. While industrial production increased, farm output lagged because of peasant opposition to collectivization.

**Section 4.** Lenin originally believed that the success of the Bolshevik Revolution depended on revolutions in other countries. For a while the Soviet Communists actively supported worldwide revolution through the Comintern but scaled down anti-capitalist activity during the period of the NEP. When Stalin recognized the potential threat to the USSR of fascism in Italy and Germany, he encouraged Communist parties in other lands to take part in popular front governments to block the threat from the right. But in 1939 he did an about-face and joined Hitler in a mutual non-aggression pact shortly before the Nazi leader sent his army into Poland and began World War II.

## ■ Vocabulary Review

*Define:* totalitarian, provisional government, soviet, Ex Com, capitalism, bourgeois, reparations, dictator, purge, inflation, central planning, heavy industry, light industry, consumer goods, free enterprise, kulak, Comintern, fascism, popular front, appeasement, sphere of influence.

## ■ Places to Locate

*Locate:* The 15 republics of the Union of Soviet Socialist Republics

## ■ People to Know

*Identify:* Leon Trotsky, White Army, Red Army, Joseph Stalin, Sun Yat-sen, Chiang Kai-shek, Mao Zedong, Benito Mussolini, Nazis, Adolf Hitler

## ■ Thinking Critically

1. Considering the situation in early 1917, could the czarist regime have survived if it had followed different policies? What changes would Nicholas have had to make?

2. Compare the policies of Lenin and Stalin. Why did each adopt the economic policies he did? How did these policies differ from the teachings of Karl Marx?
3. Was Stalin justified in entering into a non-aggression pact with Hitler? Based on your knowledge of world history, why did he fear and suspect Britain and France in the years before World War II?

## ■ Extending and Applying Your Knowledge

1. Create a timeline listing major domestic and foreign policy events in Soviet history from the Revolution of 1917 to September 1, 1939. Include events in which the Soviet Union aided Communist parties in other countries as well as those in which the USSR was directly involved.
2. *Dr. Zhivago* by Boris Pasternak is an excellent fictionalized account of the Russian Revolution. Read it and prepare a report discussing how the novel portrays the different social classes caught up in the revolution.
3. With several classmates do additional research on the Russian Revolution and prepare newspaper articles describing the opponents, their plans for Russia, the amount of support for each side, and their chances for success.

# 6

# The USSR
# as a World Power

For the Soviet Union June 22, 1941, was a dark day indeed. German military forces had unleashed a furious assault against the nation. Except for Great Britain, no other world power was actively fighting Adolf Hitler at this time. Moreover, the Soviet Union was the sole Communist country in the world. However, the war to defeat Nazism forced the Soviet Union and the Allies into an uneasy alliance.

Despite extensive wartime devastation, the Soviet Union emerged from World War II as a **superpower**, second only to the United States. The conflict had shattered the strength of Germany and Japan. The exhaustion of Great Britain and France was reflected in their diminished postwar roles in Asia and Africa. Under Stalin's direction, the Soviet Union made an amazingly rapid economic recovery. Simultaneously the country tightened its political control over the areas in Eastern Europe that Soviet military forces had occupied during the war. The United States had hoped that the Soviet Union would honor agreements it had made during the war to allow occupied nations to determine their own futures. Soon, however, the United States found itself confronted with the task of checking further Soviet expansion.

Stalin died in March 1953. After a power struggle lasting several years, Nikita Khrushchev emerged as the leader of the Soviet Union. He instituted many important domestic changes and pursued an aggressive foreign policy. His removal from power in October 1964 caught the world by surprise.

### World War II and After

| | |
|---|---|
| 1941 | Russo-Japanese neutrality pact |
| | German invasion of Russia |
| 1944 | Dumbarton Oaks Conference |
| 1945 | Yalta Conference |
| | The end of World War II |
| 1947 | Truman Doctrine announced |
| | Marshall Plan announced |
| 1950 | Beginning of the Korean War |
| 1953 | Death of Stalin |
| | Korean armistice |
| 1953–1958 | Khrushchev as First Secretary |
| 1955 | Warsaw Pact |
| 1956 | Hungarian uprising |
| 1957 | First Soviet satellite launched |
| 1958–1964 | Khrushchev as Premier |
| 1961 | Berlin Wall erected |
| 1962 | Cuban Missile Crisis |

## 1. The Soviet Union's Wartime Role

The Nazi-Soviet Pact gave the USSR nearly two years to prepare for the expected Nazi attack. To strengthen its western frontiers, the USSR annexed not only eastern Poland (see page 168) but also the Baltic states of Estonia, Latvia, Lithuania, and Moldavia. Although Stalin's attempt to overrun Finland failed, he nevertheless acquired strategically important territory in the southern part of that country. The Soviet Union also absorbed lands along the Russo-Rumanian frontier. To the Soviets, the occupation of these lands signified a restoration of Russian rule over territories lost in World War I, not imperialist expansion. In 1941 Stalin concluded a neutrality treaty with Japan as assurance against a Japanese attack on Siberia in the event of war with Germany. Stalin's understanding with Hitler bought him time to increase the Soviet Union's industrial production and to build up the nation's armed forces. Meanwhile, Hitler was making his preparations for the invasion of the USSR.

## The Nazi Invasion

By the summer of 1940 Hitler's forces had overrun France, Belgium, Holland, Norway, Denmark, Yugoslavia, and Greece. They were poised for an invasion of North Africa. Because its navy controlled the English Channel and its air force shot the Nazi bombers from the skies, only Britain had been able to stop Hitler. Recognizing that invasion of Britain was impossible, Hitler decided to strike at the Soviet Union to get the food and natural resources Germany needed. Probably, too, eastward expansion had always been Hitler's goal. He was confident that the German armored columns would roll swiftly across the great plains of Russia, crush the Soviet armies, and bring Nazi Germany its most glorious victory.

The Nazi drive against the Soviet Union, on a front that extended from the Baltic to the Black Sea, began in late June 1941. The huge Soviet armies, numbering almost six million troops, for a time were unable to check the onslaught. The German armies advanced steadily eastward, occupying important cities and industrial centers as well as rich farmlands.

Despite the two-year "breathing spell," the Soviet Union was not fully prepared for the powerful attack launched by the enemy. In the course of "purging" the government and army of all persons who might weaken his hold on Russia, Stalin had "eliminated" many able senior officers. But while the Red Army struggled to slow down the enemy advance, the Soviet government worked frantically to mobilize the country for total war. Factory equipment, supplies, and millions of refugees were evacuated as far east as Siberia. The production of war materials was speeded up and the distribution of food and other consumer goods was strictly rationed. The Soviet people were warned to prepare for great sacrifices.

Hitler had hoped for a quick victory with comparatively little destruction of the occupied country. But in retreating, the Soviets pursued a scorched-earth policy. Buildings, machinery, supplies, and food were destroyed or rendered useless. Bridges were blown up, communication lines torn down, and roads mined. Farmers and townspeople fled to the forests where many of them became guerrillas ceaselessly harassing the Nazis. To cope with this determined and widespread resistance, the Germans were compelled to leave many army units in occupied territory, thereby reducing the number of troops at the front. The German Air Force, having suffered heavy losses fighting Britain, was not able to provide the air support that had been a crucial factor in earlier Nazi campaigns.

**172**

Invading German soldiers found that the Soviets had devastated their own land to deny its usefulness to the enemy. During what other invasion had the Russians used this scorched-earth policy?

Despite the troubles his armies were having on the Soviet front, by fall 1941 Hitler believed that victory was near. Soviet military might apparently had been shattered, the furiously resisting Red Army had suffered terrible casualties, and perhaps a million Soviet soldiers had been captured by the Germans. Actually, the Nazi advance had been halted by do-or-die opposition outside Leningrad, Moscow, and Sevastopol.

Once the forward rush of Hitler's armies had been checked, their problems began to mount. The onset of winter was a major factor. German troops on the northern and central fronts had to endure the most bitterly cold weather that had struck Russia in many years. The Soviets, heartened by the news of the successful defense of Moscow and Leningrad, stiffened their resistance. Hitler's hopes for a quick victory in the USSR and total victory in Europe were dimmed.

### Military Developments Elsewhere

At the time a stalemate began to develop on the USSR's western front, Stalin received encouraging news from other parts of the world. His fear of attack from the east lessened when Japan attacked the United States naval base at Pearl Harbor on

## The Siege of Leningrad

The German attack on the Soviet Union had begun on June 22, 1941. By early September, German forces in the north had encircled Leningrad (formerly St. Petersburg) and were preparing to storm the city. At this point Hitler decided against a frontal attack and instead ordered that the city be razed to the ground by artillery fire and aerial bombardment. Thus began the 880-day siege of Leningrad.

At the war's beginning Leningrad had a population of about three million. During the siege more than one million residents died—mostly from starvation. Food reserves were quickly used up at the beginning of the siege. During the winter, the Soviets were able to bring in some food over frozen Lake Ladoga. But it was not enough, and the government had to impose severe rationing. A worker might receive a half pound of bread per day. The old and children were allotted far less. People were quickly reduced to eating whatever they could find: pets, wallpaper, leather, sawdust. But starvation was not the only horror. There was no fuel for heating purposes. Thousands of people simply froze to death in their homes. By the time the siege of Leningrad was lifted in January 1944, probably every resident of the city had lost at least one family member.

Many experts believe that the siege of Leningrad was a tragedy that did not have to happen. The German army had been able to advance so fast and so far in part because Soviet forces were woefully unprepared for battle. The purges of the 1930's had cost the Red Army many of its ablest officers. For several months prior to the German attack, Stalin had been receiving information that German troops and tanks were massing along the Soviet border. But he refused to believe these reports. He stubbornly insisted that a German offensive would not come until 1942. Even when the invasion actually began, Stalin ordered his forces to hold their fire. Perhaps he thought it was all a mistake.

December 7, 1941. More important, the assault brought the United States into the war against Nazi Germany as well as against Japan. Fortunately for the Soviets, American strategists gave priority to the struggle against Hitler. Before long massive American military and economic aid began to flow into the USSR. By the end of the war, the United States had provided the Soviet Union with more than eleven billion dollars' worth of supplies. Furthermore, Britain and the United States soon went on the offensive against Germany.

## A Second Nazi Campaign

Hitler launched a gigantic offensive against the Soviet Union in the spring and summer of 1942. Not only was military pressure applied along the front, but a special effort was made to take over the rich oil fields near Baku in the Caucasus. German forces struck deep into the mountainous area to the east of the Black Sea, but were stopped short of their goal. As the German lines became overextended, Soviet armies went on the offensive in a winter campaign. A large German army was encircled at Stalingrad on the lower Volga River and destroyed. This Soviet victory proved to the world that the Nazi armies were not invincible. The epochal Battle of Stalingrad (November 1942–February 1943) proved to be the turning point of the war.

## Germany's Defeat

For more than two years Stalin had urged the Allies to open a second front against the Nazis in France. The Allies agreed in principle with the plan but felt that priority should be given to ensuring the safety of the Suez Canal and Allied shipping on the Mediterranean. Britain and the United States did not believe that they had the military strength necessary to invade France. Stalin was furious at the delay, believing that his allies were not doing their fair share.

In November 1942, combined Anglo-American forces began their campaign to sweep the German-Italian armies out of North Africa. Allied landings in Sicily and Italy followed in the summer of 1943, which put increased pressure upon the Nazis and forced Italy to withdraw from the war. Then, as the Soviets began a series of offensives on the eastern front, the United States and Britain stepped up preparations for the invasion of Nazi-occupied western Europe. In June 1944, Allied troops landed in Normandy, France, secured beachheads, and began their advance into the interior. A series of campaigns liberated France,

**THE LEGACY OF WAR.** While Stalingrad heroically resisted numerous German attacks, Soviet soldiers surrounded the German army there and annihilated it. The photograph above shows the center of the city completely destroyed by the fighting. Now rebuilt and renamed Volgograd, it is filled with monuments honoring its brave defenders. Characteristic of the Soviet heroic style of sculpture is the "Stand to Death" monument in the foreground below.

Belgium, and Holland. Before war's end, troops of the Allies had pushed into Germany as far as the Elbe River.

Hitler's armies, unable to cope with mounting pressures on both fronts, began a stubborn retreat toward Berlin. Following relentlessly on the eastern front, the Red Army suffered huge casualties but hurled the Nazi troops out of the Baltic countries, Poland, and the Balkans. Finally the Soviets invaded Germany itself and took Berlin. Hitler committed suicide on April 30, 1945, and Germany surrendered unconditionally on May 7. Thus closed the most destructive war in the long history of Europe.

### The Dumbarton Oaks Conference

During the war against Hitler, President Franklin D. Roosevelt of the United States and Prime Minister Winston Churchill of Britain gave thought to creating a safer and more secure post-war world than the one that had followed World War I. President Roosevelt's great desire was to establish a strong international organization to take the place of the League of Nations. When his proposals for such a body were favorably received by Stalin and other Allied leaders, a planning conference was scheduled for fall 1944. To the meeting at Dumbarton Oaks in Washington, D.C., came representatives of the United States, the Soviet Union, Britain, and China.

Although the participants reached a broad level of agreement at the Dumbarton Oaks Conference, there was a deadlock on some issues. The Soviet Union, for example, wanted each of the republics of the USSR to be granted membership in the new international organization. Stalin hoped thereby to ensure that the Communist bloc would have a strong voice in the body. A more important problem concerned the right of permanent members of the proposed Security Council to exercise veto power over any question before the Council and thus defeat it. The USSR believed that it could not adequately protect its interests without this right.

### Concessions at Yalta

When another conference was held at Yalta in the Soviet Union during February 1945, Hitler's downfall was almost certain. But the war against Japan, in which the Soviet Union was not as yet involved, seemed to offer no prospects for a quick victory. The purpose of the meeting was to reach agreement on major military and political issues.

At Yalta, Churchill, Roosevelt, and Stalin discussed plans for the war's end and the return of peace. Stalin won concessions in eastern Europe and East Asia, and a compromise was reached on Soviet UN membership. Why did Churchill and Roosevelt agree to Stalin's demands?

Stalin adopted a stiffer position than he had shown at earlier meetings. He made it clear that the Soviet Union was opposed to the re-establishment of the prewar political order in eastern Europe. Both Churchill and Roosevelt agreed to political and territorial changes in eastern and central Europe and to the Soviet leader's insistence that his country receive concessions in Manchuria and take over southern Sakhalin and the Kurile Islands. As for Germany, the leaders decided that four zones of military occupation—American, British, French, Soviet—would be established. Berlin in the Soviet zone, would be under the joint control of the four powers. With reference to Poland and Yugoslavia, Stalin agreed to add non-Communist representation to the governments then in power in those countries. This promise was never kept. Stalin also agreed to enter the war against Japan within three months of the end of the war in Europe.

Stalin further agreed that the USSR would cooperate in the forthcoming United Nations—for a price. He withdrew his demand that the USSR have 16 votes, settling for three—one each for the USSR, Byelorussia, and Ukraine. It was understood that the USSR and the other permanent members of the Security Council—the United States, Britain, France, and China—would have the crucial power of veto.

The agreements in Eastern Europe were not all that Stalin wanted, but he knew he was in the "drivers seat" in that area. Soviet troops had advanced into Germany and had occupied parts of Hungary and Czechoslovakia. Tito's Communist guerrillas were driving the Germans out of Yugoslavia. Meanwhile American troops were having little success pushing the Germans out of Italy, and had just recovered from their setback in the Battle of the Bulge. By being agreeable to most of Stalin's demands, Roosevelt and Churchill hoped to obtain the Soviet Union's membership and cooperation in the UN. But as the war

**MOVEMENT: SOVIET TERRITORIAL GAINS, 1939–1945.** During the war the Soviet Union reannexed much territory that had formerly been part of the czarist empire. How was Stalin able to accomplish this?

SOVIET TERRITORIAL GAINS, 1939–1945

KEY
- USSR, 1939
- Annexed 1939-1945

N
W — E
S

NORWAY
SWEDEN
FINLAND
ESTONIA
DENMARK
LATVIA
LITHUANIA
BALTIC SEA
USSR
NETHERLANDS
GERMAN
• Berlin
DEM.
REP.
GERMAN
FEDERAL REP.
NORTHEAST
PRUSSIA
POLAND
BELGIUM
LUX.
CZECHOSLOVAKIA
NORTH
BUKOVINA
BESSARABIA
SWITZERLAND
AUSTRIA
HUNGARY
RUTHENIA
RUMANIA
ITALY
YUGOSLAVIA
BLACK SEA

against the Nazis neared the end, it became clear that Stalin was determined to advance Soviet interests and Communist power.

## Japan's Defeat

May 8, 1945, VE Day (Victory in Europe Day) was a time of rejoicing throughout the world, even though Japanese resistance continued. The United States dropped an atomic bomb on Hiroshima on August 6, 1945. On August 8, in keeping with his agreement at Yalta, Stalin entered the conflict against the already defeated Japan. On August 9 the United States dropped a second atomic bomb, this time on Nagasaki. Meanwhile Soviet troops were moving into Manchuria, Korea, southern Sakhalin, and the northern Kuriles. On August 15 the Emperor of Japan broadcast his message of surrender.

## Check Your Understanding

1. Why did Hitler invade the Soviet Union?
2. What difficulties did the Nazis encounter in their invasion?
3. How did events on other war fronts affect the situation in the Soviet Union?
4. How did the Soviet Union contribute to Germany's final defeat?
5. What concessions did Stalin gain for the Soviet Union at the wartime conferences?
6. *Thinking Critically:* Considering the war against Japan was almost over, why did Stalin declare war against Japan?

## 2. Extending Soviet Power and Influence

Although the Soviet Union and the other Allies cooperated to destroy Hitler's Germany, neither side in the alliance overcame its distrust of the other. Britain, France, and the United States believed that the USSR's goals at the wartime conferences were to further its own interests rather than to achieve a just and lasting peace. The Western democracies hoped that in the postwar world the Soviet Union nevertheless would identify with UN policies.

Stalin, however, thought that the Soviet Union had suffered by far the greatest losses in the war and had made the greatest contribution to victory. Therefore, he believed, his country was entitled to reparations and rewards. He also felt resentment toward the Western powers because, to him, the delay in the Allied invasion of France reflected a willingness on their part to let the USSR suffer appalling losses. When the war ended, there were many issues on which the two sides continued to have serious disagreements.

### Communist Domination of Eastern Europe

The growing friction between Stalin and his wartime allies grew out of the Communist leader's plans to create a Europe, and for that matter a world, that would be "safe for communism." Stalin and his successors were determined to have a buffer of **satellites**, or Soviet-controlled states on the nation's western borders. In the event of invasion from the west, fighting would occur in those satellite nations and not in the Soviet Union itself. Never again would the Soviet Union experience the devastation of World War II. As we have seen, Stalin absorbed a part of Finland, the eastern portion of Poland, the border regions of Rumania, and the Baltic states of Estonia, Latvia, and Lithuania. These three nations had become independent after World War I. When the Allies questioned Stalin's right to these lands, Stalin claimed they were rightfully Russia's because they had been a part of czarist Russia. But more damaging to East-West relations was Stalin's attempts to impose a new political order in eastern and central Europe.

Stalin was determined to eliminate "hostile" regimes along the Soviet Union's western border and to bring them within the Soviet sphere of influence. He was remarkably successful in his efforts. Within five years after the war there were Communist regimes in Poland, Bulgaria, Rumania, Hungary, and Czechoslovakia. That the majority of peoples in these countries had no wish for a Communist way of life did not bother Stalin or those who carried out his orders. By intimidation, military threats, and terror the countries were made satellites, linked to the Soviet Union by economic and political ties.

### Defeats in Central Europe

The USSR had hoped to dominate central Europe as well as eastern Europe. But since Germany and Austria were jointly occupied by American, British, French, and Soviet troops, Stalin failed to achieve this goal. In Germany the Western powers wished to hold free elections and to re-establish a united country. They realized the urgent need for a barrier against Commu-

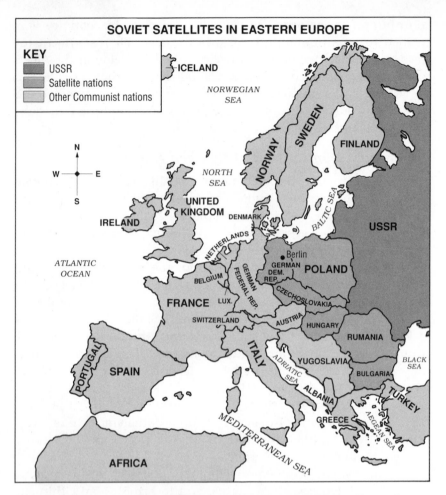

**SOVIET SATELLITES IN EASTERN EUROPE**

KEY
- USSR
- Satellite nations
- Other Communist nations

ICELAND

NORWEGIAN SEA

NORWAY

SWEDEN

FINLAND

NORTH SEA

BALTIC SEA

USSR

UNITED KINGDOM

DENMARK

IRELAND

NETHERLANDS

Berlin

GERMAN DEM. REP.

POLAND

ATLANTIC OCEAN

BELGIUM

GERMAN FEDERAL REP.

CZECHOSLOVAKIA

FRANCE LUX.

SWITZERLAND

AUSTRIA

HUNGARY

RUMANIA

ITALY

YUGOSLAVIA

BLACK SEA

PORTUGAL

SPAIN

ADRIATIC SEA

ALBANIA

BULGARIA

TURKEY

MEDITERRANEAN SEA

GREECE

AEGEAN SEA

AFRICA

**REGION: SOVIET SATELLITES IN EASTERN EUROPE.** Except for Albania and the non-aligned Yugoslavia, the Soviet satellites in Eastern Europe were under strict control from Moscow.

nist aggression westward. Stalin, however, rejected both the earlier agreed-upon plans for elections and the new proposals to unite Germany. Doubtless he feared a revival of German militarism, but he also wished to continue to exploit Germany in rebuilding the Soviet economy. Vast amounts of German machinery had been shipped to the USSR to aid in its recovery. Stalin recognized that if the Soviet zone became part of a united Germany, it too would be outside the Communist bloc.

In June 1948 Soviet troops blocked all surface routes into West Berlin. Two million West Berliners were cut off from the Western zones and from food and other supplies. Within two days the Allies were flying in supplies and flying children and others to safety. This became known as the Berlin Airlift. When

**182**

it became apparent that the Western powers were not going to surrender their right to be in Berlin, Stalin lifted the blockade in May 1949.

In 1949 the American, British, and French zones of occupation were merged to form the Federal Republic of Germany, commonly known as West Germany. The eastern part of the country, occupied by the Soviets, was transformed into a Communist state, the German Democratic Republic or East Germany. Berlin, the old capital, was similarly divided. East Berlin, the former Soviet zone, became the capital of the Communist state. West Berlin became part of the Federal Republic and was given a democratic government.

In Austria an impasse similar to that in Germany continued for some years after the war. Stalin did not like to have Western troops stationed in a country that jutted into the Soviet sphere of influence. (See map, page 182.) It was not until after his death, however, that the problem of Austria was resolved. In 1955 an agreement for the neutralization of Austria was reached. All foreign troops were withdrawn and the country was united under a non-Communist government.

## Trouble in the Balkans

Stalin's plan to include the Balkans among the Soviet Union's Communist satellites was only partly realized. In Bulgaria and Rumania, which had been occupied by the Red Army, as well as Albania, pro-Soviet governments came into power after the war. But in adjoining Yugoslavia Stalin met with an unexpected setback. The Communist partisans led by Marshal Tito (TEE-toh) had received support from the USSR during the war and at its end had organized a Communist state. But unlike other heads of Communist governments, Tito refused to subordinate his country's interests to those of the Soviet Union. The quarrel led to a break with Stalin in 1948, and caused Tito to take a neutral stance in the growing division between West and East. This development alarmed Stalin. Soon trials began in the satellite countries. From 1948 until Stalin's death hundreds of prominent Communist leaders in satellite countries were accused of "Titoism," that is, of trying to be too independent of Moscow. Many were executed. Others were sentenced to long prison terms.

Communist plans for Greece also failed to materialize. Under a wartime agreement, British rather than Soviet troops liberated the country from the Nazis. When the monarchy was restored, Communist guerrillas began a civil war to gain control of the government. The British, who supported the monarchy, felt unable to assume the financial burdens of suppressing the revolt and made clear its troops would withdraw.

President Truman took up the cause of independence and in what came to be called the Truman Doctrine stated ". . . it must be the policy of the United States to support free peoples who are resisting attempted subjugation by armed minorities or by outside pressures." This policy was applied equally to Turkey and Greece. American economic and military aid enabled the Greeks to defeat the Communist guerrillas in a bitter struggle that raged from 1947 to 1949. Tito of Yugoslavia also contributed to the defeat of the Greek Communists. He stopped military supplies from filtering in from Yugoslavia and refused to grant asylum to Greek rebels.

### The Cold War

By 1947 whatever good will had characterized relations between the United States and the Soviet Union had evaporated. Thereafter international relations became polarized as many governments came to side with one or the other of the two superpowers. The **cold war** had begun.

A major conflict did not erupt because leaders in both the United States and the Soviet Union exercised restraint. Uprisings, revolutions, and small wars occurred, but the superpowers made certain these were limited. The restraint was due in part to memories of the horrors of World War II. A major factor, of course, was the threat of nuclear weapons. With the development of atomic and hydrogen bombs by the United States and the USSR, and of increasingly sophisticated systems for their delivery, it became obvious that a nuclear war would be mutually disastrous. The nuclear stalemate helped to preserve an uneasy peace.

As American-Russian relations deteriorated, the cold war took on a new form. In summer 1947 General George Marshall, the American Secretary of State, made a dramatic proposal. If European nations would do what they could to rebuild their own countries, the United States would provide funds to help meet their needs. In effect this policy was an extension of the wartime aid funneled to the Allies. The Marshall Plan was designed to eliminate the conditions of poverty and despair on which communism thrived. Starting in 1948, Congress began to appropriate billions of dollars each year for the European Recovery Program. ERP proved to be a major factor in rebuilding the economies of many European countries and in arresting the expansion of communism.

The Soviet Union and its satellite states had been invited to share in the economic benefits of the Marshall Plan. Although Czechoslovakia at first expressed interest in receiving American aid, the Soviet Union refused to have anything to do with the program. Moscow made it clear that this was also to be the position of its satellites. Much as he needed to strengthen the economies of the Soviet **bloc** countries, Stalin feared the political influence that would be an inevitable by-product of American economic assistance. He therefore denounced the Marshall Plan as merely another way of furthering "American imperialism."

## *Containment*

Stalin's efforts to expand communism were matched by American steps to ensure **containment** through diplomatic, political, economic, and even military measures. The unification of the Anglo-French-American zones in Germany, the Truman Doctrine, and the Marshall Plan have already been discussed. A further step was taken in 1949 with the establishment of the North Atlantic Treaty Organization (NATO), the outgrowth of an earlier regional defense agreement among Britain, France, Belgium, the Netherlands, and Luxembourg. When the United States expressed interest in joining, the broader organization took shape. Eight countries on the European continent joined with Britain, Iceland, Canada, and the United States in a pact providing that an attack on one would be considered an attack on all. The United States undertook to maintain military forces in Europe and to help other NATO members to rearm. During the difficult years when European nations were struggling to rebuild their economies, NATO served as a shield of military security.

The Soviet response to this Western alliance was to organize a military coalition of Communist states. Soon after World War II Russia began efforts to coordinate the military forces of the Communist bloc. In 1955, two years after Stalin's death, this relationship was formalized in the Warsaw Pact, a military alliance uniting the Soviet Union, Poland, East Germany, Czechoslovakia, Hungary, Rumania, Bulgaria, and Albania. Communist Yugoslavia, which under Marshall Tito pursued an independent course in foreign affairs, refused to join the Warsaw Pact. Albania withdrew in the 1960's after philosophical differences with the USSR over the future course of communism.

In this American cartoon, Stalin is seen as the cupid who inspired strong friendship among the frightened members of the NATO alliance. How did Stalin's insistence on governing Eastern Europe work to his disadvantage?

## Soviet Intentions in Japan

Stalin's purpose in sending troops into southern Sakhalin, the Kuriles, Korea, and Manchuria was to strengthen the Soviet Union's position in East Asia. This hope was offset when the United States assumed major responsibility for preparing Japan for the postwar world. Stalin pressed for an active role in the administration of occupied Japan but was denied it. The Japanese were exposed only to democratic institutions and practices during occupation. Japan became a democracy, and the Communist Party of Japan, although allowed to exist, never became strong.

The United States had no desire to prolong its military occupation of Japan, and as early as 1947 began to discuss plans with its allies for a peace treaty. When the USSR and Nationalist China claimed the right of veto on any issue, the United States proceeded on its own without their cooperation. Of the 52 powers that took part in the 1951 peace conference in San Francisco, only the Soviet Union, Poland, and Czechoslovakia refused to sign the treaty. Japan lost Korea, Formosa, southern Sakhalin, the Kuriles, and its mandates over some Pacific islands. Continued Soviet occupation of southern Sakhalin, which had been surrendered to Japan by Russia in 1905, aroused lasting resentment among the Japanese. They were irritated also by the USSR's takeover of the Kurile Islands. It was not until 1956 that Japan and the Soviet Union agreed to "normalize" their relations.

## Communism's Victory in China

At the end of the war the Soviet Union as well as the United States and Great Britain underestimated the strength of the Chinese Communists. With the end of the war against Japan, a grim civil war broke out between the Communists and the Nationalists, also know as the Guomindang. Both sides were eager to occupy Manchuria, from which the Japanese had been ousted by the Soviets. The Communist troops were nearer to the region than the Nationalists and seized it. After acquiring the arms and military supplies left behind by the Japanese, Mao Zedong's Red Army was ready for a showdown with the Nationalists—years of fighting resulted in the disintegration of the Kuomintang regime and its armies. Mao gained control of all mainland China and, later, Tibet. In 1949 Chiang Kai-shek and many of his followers fled to Formosa.

In early 1950 Stalin concluded a treaty of alliance with the new Chinese government. The agreement was aimed particularly at the United States, which refused to recognize Mao's regime. The Chinese Communists followed the Soviet example in mobilizing resources to speed industrialization. At first the Soviet Union provided technical assistance, machinery, and other forms of aid. But after a time, relations between the Soviet Union and Communist China worsened. (See page 203.)

## The Korean War

With the defeat of Japan, Allied troops occupied Korea, which had been a part of the Japanese Empire since 1910. The Soviet Union was made responsible for accepting the surrender of Japanese forces north of the 38th parallel. The United States was given the same task south of the dividing line. Stalin had hoped to establish a Communist Republic of Korea, an idea unacceptable to the United States. Consequently, by 1948, two completely different governments evolved in the divided country, each claiming to be *the* government of Korea. Communist North Korea had a Soviet trained army of over 100,000, and South Korea, a small American trained force.

In summer 1950 the North Korean Communist army, using Soviet tanks and aircraft, invaded South Korea. This bold act of aggression was encouraged and supported by Stalin. But the Soviet dictator was mistaken in assuming that the United States and its allies would not aid South Korea. The UN Security Council called on North Korea to withdraw its troops. When that country failed to respond, the Security Council urged UN members to support the government in the south. United Nations forces, largely American, joined South Korean troops in a counterattack which, in time, pushed the North Korean invaders far north of the 38th parallel.

When the UN forces neared the border with China, Chinese Communist armies intervened. This led to a long and bitter conflict. After three years' fighting, an armistice was concluded. Korea remained divided at roughly the 38th parallel.

## Stalin's Impact on Eurasia

Five years after the World War II ended, the USSR was ringed with Communist countries. Stalin had not waged war simply to defeat Nazi Germany. Wherever Soviet troops were victorious, Stalin had laid the foundations for a Communist regime. Only Austria managed to escape Communist rule. All other countries subjected to Soviet occupation either became Soviet satellites or were drawn into the orbit of the Chinese Communist state. From the small core of dedicated revolutionaries led by Lenin, the Communist cause had grown into a movement that controlled well over half of Eurasia.

## Soviet Economic Recovery

While expanding Soviet power and influence abroad, Stalin was also rebuilding the Soviet economy. The USSR certainly suffered the greatest losses of any country during World War II. The number of war-related deaths will never be known, since the Soviet government refused to publish casualty figures. But estimates run as high as 20 million. Other millions of Soviet citizens were displaced from their homes in the war zone and never returned. Property damage was beyond reckoning. For many years after the war foreigners were not permitted to travel in some parts of the country lest they observe the extent of war damage. Official Soviet figures listed 1,700 towns and 70,000 villages destroyed. Some 31,000 factories had been smashed into heaps of rubble. Food was in short supply. Thousands of acres of farmland had been devastated, while livestock losses were in the millions. Perhaps a fourth of all property in the Soviet Union had been destroyed or rendered unusable.

Stalin launched an energetic program to speed economic recovery. Like Germany and Japan, which also had been devastated during the war, the Soviet Union made remarkable economic progress in an amazingly short time. The goals of the Fourth Five-Year Plan (1946–1950) were not only to repair the war damages but to expand production beyond prewar levels. To attain these goals extensive use was made of industrial equipment brought in from eastern Europe and Manchuria. When Stalin died in 1953, halfway through the Fifth Five-Year Plan, the Soviet economy had fully recovered.

## Check Your Understanding

1. Why did Stalin seek to create a buffer of Soviet-controlled states along the USSR's western border?
2. What were Stalin's goals in: **a.** Central Europe? **b.** the Balkans? **c.** Japan? **d.** China? **e.** Korea?
3. Explain whether Stalin was successful or not in each area listed in question 2.
4. What were the causes of the cold war?
5. What were the results of the policy of containment?
6. *Thinking Critically:* Stalin believed he had a right to reparations and rewards because of the losses the Soviet Union had suffered in World War II. How did his views differ from those of the Western powers?

## 3. Domestic Changes in the Khrushchev Era

Stalin's death marked the end of an era. For a quarter of a century Joseph Stalin had guided the development of communism in both the Soviet Union and abroad. At home, he had created a police state, in the process killing off much of the idealism of an older generation of revolutionaries. In fact, nearly all the important leaders of the Bolshevik Revolution had died or been killed. Millions of other Soviet citizens had been killed or imprisoned as well. But it cannot be denied that under Stalin's leadership the economy had grown rapidly. In world affairs Stalin had made the Soviet Union a superpower. Stalin had achieved many of his objectives, but the cost in human suffering was so great that few mourned his death.

## The Problem of Succession

Over the years Stalin had been careful to remove from positions of leadership all potential rivals. Therefore, when he died in early March, 1953, no one could claim the right to lead the country. The chief contenders were top officials in the government, in the Communist Party of the Soviet Union (CPSU), in the secret police, and in the Red Army. At first, the direction of the USSR was entrusted to a collective leadership that had representation from all four agencies. But the nucleus of power rested in three men: Georgy Malenkov, Chairman of the Council of Ministers, also called Premier; Nikita Khrushchev, General Secretary of the Communist Party; and Lavrenty Beria, head of the secret police. Beria, however, had too many powerful enemies. He was soon arrested and put to death.

By 1958 Khrushchev was in control of the Soviet state. A Russian, Khrushchev joined the Communist Party in 1918 and participated in the revolutionary struggle in southern Russia. Thereafter he advanced both in the Communist Party of the Ukraine and the Communist Party of the Soviet Union. Able, shrewd, and ruthless, Khrushchev was careful to stay in favor with Stalin. He became a trusted follower of the dictator and helped to carry out his policies.

Elected General Secretary of the CPSU in September 1953, Khrushchev, like Stalin before him, used the office to strengthen his position in the Party. Malenkov was induced to resign his premiership in 1955 and was replaced by Nikolay Bulganin. In 1958 Bulganin, too, was ousted from power, and the post went to Khrushchev. Thus once again one man was both head of the Soviet government (Premier) and chief of the CPSU (General Secretary).

## End of the "Cult of Personality"

With the change of leadership in 1953, Stalin's heavy-handed political practices were somewhat relaxed. Not only top-ranking officials who had survived his purges but most other Soviets had disapproved of Stalin's use of force and terror. Thus except for Beria, leaders ousted from power were no longer exiled or executed, but were given lesser positions. Malenkov became Minister of Power Stations; Bulganin was sent to the Caucasus in a minor capacity; and Molotov, one of the eight most powerful leaders in the Soviet Union in 1953, was made ambassador to Mongolia. Not even Khrushchev had the power that Stalin had exercised.

This Turkic woman uses the ancient skill of rugmaking to create a piece of Soviet propaganda. In addition to traditional designs, the rug shows Khrushchev surrounded by four smiling astronauts. Although he decried Stalin's "cult of personality," Khrushchev did not forbid personal tribute to himself.

Throughout his time in power, Stalin had sought to glorify himself and his achievements. He ordered histories of the Communist movement and of the Soviet Union rewritten, even falsified if necessary, to magnify his contributions to the revolution. It was not enough that his policies were supported. They had to be publicly commended. Stalin had statues, paintings, and pictures of himself placed in the public squares, government buildings, and schools of towns and cities throughout the land. Stalin's self-glorification was later called the "cult of personality."

Khrushchev used this term in attacking Stalin's policies on February 25, 1956, at a session of the Twentieth Congress of the CPSU. He denounced the late dictator as a brutal and unscrupulous tyrant who had not hesitated to use violence to advance his own ambitions. Stalin was also accused of making serious mistakes, such as failing to heed warnings of an impending Nazi attack on the Soviet Union. Ironically, many of the crimes attributed to the late dictator in earlier years had been praised in official publications by none other than Nikita Khrushchev himself.

## "De-Stalinization"

The campaign to see Stalin in a true perspective continued for several years. Once again history books in the Soviet Union were rewritten. Statues of Stalin were removed from public places and his portraits were replaced by those of other distinguished Communists. A further step in the program of "de-Stalinization" was taken in 1961 when Stalin's body was removed from Lenin's tomb and buried in a simple grave alongside the Kremlin wall.

## Khrushchev's Industrial Policies

Although the USSR was second among the world's industrial powers when Khrushchev took power, its economy was unable to provide an adequate standard of living. Khrushchev's goal was that the Soviet Union catch up with and overtake the American economy by 1970. That achievement, he suggested, would convince people everywhere that socialism was unquestionably superior to capitalism.

During Khrushchev's years in power, Soviet industrial production did increase steadily. As in Stalin's time, however, priority in the allocation of labor and resources was given to heavy industry. The output of iron, steel, coal, oil, and electric power mounted. Soviet factories turned out large numbers of trucks, tractors, railroad locomotives, and industrial equipment. Yet by 1964, when Khrushchev was forced out of office, the Soviet economy was no closer to world leadership than when his tenure began.

## Consumer Goods

Unlike the United States, the Soviet Union chose to place major emphasis on heavy industry at the expense of light industry. Khrushchev wanted more output of consumer goods or light industry, but such production increased only slowly. For example, by 1959 yearly output of shoes had grown to 1.5 pairs per person, compared with one pair several years earlier. But most of the skilled labor force, productive facilities, and raw materials were devoted to industries that did not directly satisfy consumer needs. For many reasons—inefficiency of central planning, a backlog of conservatism from the Stalinist era, the amount of "catching up" that the Soviet Union had to do, an unwillingness to trade freely with the non-Communist world—the Soviet economy was not equipped to meet the demands of both heavy and light industry.

## Farm Production

Except for the war years, hunger and starvation had not afflicted the Soviet Union since the great famine of 1932–1933. But the collective farms barely met the needs of a population that passed 225 million in the early 1960's. The farms were unable to produce enough food to provide surpluses for storage against lean years and for export. Soviet officials now openly admitted that harvest figures given out during Stalin's regime had been exaggerated, and that agriculture was the weakest sector of the economy.

Khrushchev, who had played a key role in agricultural development even before he had become premier, focused attention on the need to increase production. During the Khrushchev years, steps were taken to reduce the bureaucratic red tape involved in collectivized agriculture, and to provide better incentives for the collective farmer. Greater concentration on the production of corn was ordered. A potentially high-yield crop, corn could be used as feed in the critically weak cattle-raising industry.

## The "Virgin Lands" Program

The core of Khrushchev's program, however, was the so-called "virgin lands" venture. Much of the fertile land in southern Siberia and northern Kazakhstan was thinly populated and untilled. Khrushchev decided to gamble on transforming this land into a major food-producing area, even though crop-killing droughts were a threat because of the uneven amount of rainfall from year to year. The youth of the country were urged to volunteer for work on the newly opened collective farms. Tens of thousands of Soviet farm workers were transported to Central Asia.

Despite early hopes, Khrushchev's agricultural program was a failure. After several years of great effort, the food problem of the Soviet Union remained unsolved. The forces of nature, the inefficiency of the bureaucratic Soviet system and of Soviet farm workers, the lack of incentive inherent in collectivization, and the sheer magnitude of transforming Soviet agriculture stood in the way of a major breakthrough in farm production.

**193**

## Check Your Understanding

1. Why was there uncertainty about who would replace Stalin after his death?
2. How was Khrushchev able to gain power?
3. Why was Khrushchev unable to achieve his goals for industrial production?
4. Why did the production of consumer goods continue to lag behind that of heavy industry?
5. How did Khrushchev attempt to solve the problems of agricultural production?
6. *Thinking Critically:* According to the text, "the lack of incentives inherent in collectivization" was one of the reasons Khrushchev's agricultural policy failed. How did collectivization lack incentives? Why would this affect farmers?

## 4. The Soviet Government and the Communist Party

The Khrushchev years witnessed a resurgence of Communist Party power in the Soviet Union. Under Stalin, the Soviet state had become a one-man tyranny, and the Party had become an instrument of Stalin's control. Although Communist Party members occupied all important positions in society, not even the highest officials were safe from Stalin's wrath. On one occasion Stalin allegedly had announced a decision to his colleagues by saying simply, "I vote yes. Who votes no?" No one, of course, opposed him.

When Stalin died in 1953, the Party, the state bureaucracy, the army, and the secret police all vied for political power. In a few short years, the Party had outmaneuvered all rivals and established its political supremacy.

### Principle and Practice

The Soviet political system as it existed under Khrushchev, and before him under Stalin and Lenin, was filled with contradictions. In any government, gaps exist between proclaimed ideals and everyday reality. No political system can always live up to its principles. However, in the Soviet Union, Communist practice and principle seemed in constant conflict.

The Soviet Union was, in theory, a union of independent republics. It was based on a constitution approved in 1918 by the Fifth All-Russian Congress of Soviets for the Russian Soviet Federated Socialist Republic (RSFSR). In 1922 five other independent states dominated by Communist parties joined the RSFSR to form the Union of Soviet Socialist Republics (USSR). Since that time the number of Soviet Socialist Republics had increased to 15. (See map, pages 152–153.)

The individual republics nominally enjoyed certain sovereign rights, including the right of secession. But, in practice, all governments and peoples in the Soviet Union were under the strict control of the government in Moscow. Never would a Soviet citizen hear a speech or read a newspaper article suggesting that a republic should declare its independence.

From the beginning, the RSFSR and its major ethnic group, the Great Russians, dominated the Soviet Union. The RSFSR occupied about three fourths of the land area of the USSR, and Great Russians constituted about half the nation's population. The 14 republics outside the boundaries of the RSFSR were small, and each was populated by a particular minority group. For example, the major ethnic group in the Byelorussian Republic were Byelorussians (White Russians), and in the Georgian Republic, Georgians. Soviet authorities repeatedly insisted that in their country all nationalities were equal. But, in fact, the Great Russians enjoyed a preferred position in the Soviet Union. All citizens were encouraged to learn and to use Russian. Most of the highest levels of power in the country were occupied by ethnic Russians.

### Civil Rights

By the time Khrushchev came to power the Soviet Union was working under its third constitution. All of them were similar, each having been built on the previous one. The first constitution had been approved in 1918 and the second, in 1924. The third constitution, the so-called Stalin Constitution, had been adopted in 1936. It was subsequently revised in 1978. The various Soviet constitutions created two parallel structures of power, the government or state and the Communist Party. The latter was dominant.

The constitutions never described conditions that actually existed. At best these documents were intended for the ideal society toward which the Communists were supposedly building. The difference between constitutional theory and actual practice in the USSR can be inferred from a reading of that part of the Stalin Constitution entitled "Fundamental Rights and Duties of

Citizens." Its 16 articles guaranteed the people a number of civil rights, among them freedom of speech, press, assembly, political activity, religion, and thought. Soviet citizens also had the right to work, to rest, to be educated, and to be supported in old age. Women were pledged equality with men. But all these various constitutional guarantees were subject to the qualification that they were to be enjoyed "in conformity with the interests of the working people." The sole judge in that matter was the state.

As we have seen, Stalin repeatedly violated the rights of the people. He built a police state and tyrannized the people into obedience. Millions were imprisoned and murdered during his years in power. Having witnessed Stalin's excesses, Khrushchev and his colleagues were far less brutal than Stalin. Indeed many of the post-Stalin leaders, Khrushchev included, had participated in Stalin's crimes. Their determination to avoid the violence of the past, however, did not mean that they were willing to give up Communist goals or to relinquish their monopoly of power.

### The Role of the Party

The Communist Party maintained a tight hold over the Soviet people. Nothing important was decided or done without the knowledge and approval of Communist Party officials. To ensure that its policies were carried out, the Party assigned its members to all important posts and offices. Stalin, for example, had been simultaneously head of the Party (First Secretary) and head of the government (Premier). Even at the local level, Communists occupied all strategic positions in government. They also held the most important posts in the armed forces, the police system, the schools and universities, and the trade unions. All factories and mines were managed by Communists, and the steering committees of the collective farms were made up of Communist Party members. Communists determined what was printed in newspapers and magazines and had the power to veto manuscripts submitted to book publishers.

In the Communist Party, power flowed from the top down. A great difference existed between the way the Party functioned in theory and in practice. In theory, the supreme organ of the Party was the All-Union Congress, a body selected by Party members to represent them. The Congress numbered some 5,000 members and convened irregularly. It remained in session just long enough to select a much smaller Central Committee to make all decisions until the next Congress was convened. The Central Committee, in turn, selected a small governing body

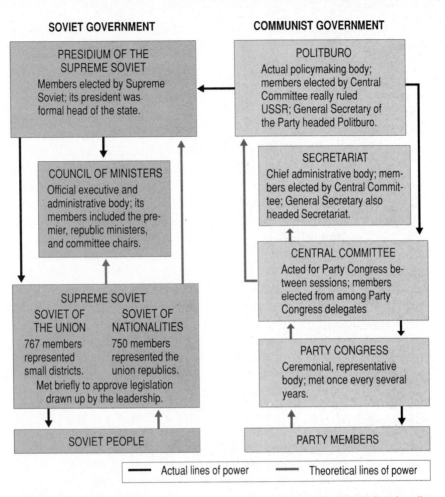

**SOVIET GOVERNMENT**

**COMMUNIST GOVERNMENT**

**PRESIDIUM OF THE SUPREME SOVIET**

Members elected by Supreme Soviet; its president was formal head of the state.

**POLITBURO**

Actual policymaking body; members elected by Central Committee really ruled USSR; General Secretary of the Party headed Politburo.

**COUNCIL OF MINISTERS**

Official executive and administrative body; its members included the premier, republic ministers, and committee chairs.

**SECRETARIAT**

Chief administrative body; members elected by Central Committee; General Secretary also headed Secretariat.

**CENTRAL COMMITTEE**

Acted for Party Congress between sessions; members elected from among Party Congress delegates

**SUPREME SOVIET**

| SOVIET OF THE UNION | SOVIET OF NATIONALITIES |
|---|---|
| 767 members represented small districts. | 750 members represented the union republics. |

Met briefly to approve legislation drawn up by the leadership.

**PARTY CONGRESS**

Ceremonial, representative body; met once every several years.

**SOVIET PEOPLE**

**PARTY MEMBERS**

——— Actual lines of power    ——— Theoretical lines of power

**POWER STRUCTURE.**   With minor changes the above system existed until 1989. Between 1952 and 1966 the Politburo was reorganized and renamed the Presidium. In 1966 the title *First Secretary* was changed to *General Secretary*, the title Stalin had used.

called the Political Bureau or **Politburo**, which in theory was subject to the Central Committee. In practice, however, the Politburo was the real center of power in the Party and manipulated the Central Committee. Politburo members held all the key offices in the **Presidium** of the Supreme Soviet and the Council of Ministers, which were the chief legislative and administrative branches of the government. Thus the same people controlled both the Communist Party and the Soviet Government.

In theory, the Communist Party was run on a democratic basis. On the surface the principle of **democratic centralism** determined Communist Party policy making. This principle implied that all major issues had to be debated at all levels of the

Party before final decisions were reached. But, in practice, all issues were decided by the Politburo, after which they were approved by Party members. A lower party organization never rejected a decision made by Party leaders. Once a decision was made, all Party members had to support the new policy.

### Party Membership

Most Soviet citizens were not members of the Communist Party. In Khrushchev's day only about one in ten adults was a Party member. Membership was open to most people, and the Party actively encouraged citizens to join. Organizations for young people such as the Octobrists (ages 7 to 9), the Pioneers (9 to 15), and the Komsomol (16 to 26) were formed as training grounds for future Party members. Talented young men and women in particular were urged to join the Party. Despite the obvious benefits of Party membership, most citizens shied away from joining. Along with privileges and opportunities, membership in the Party brought unending responsibilities and obligations. Communists would have to serve whenever and wherever the Party demanded. They were also expected to be models of behavior for their fellow citizens. Most people were not willing to make the sacrifices that Party membership necessitated.

### Elections

Since shortly after the Bolshevik Revolution, the Communist Party had been the only political party permitted to exist in the Soviet Union. In the Soviet Union any citizen over the age of 23 had the constitutional right to run for office. But this right was never freely exercised. To ensure election of the "right" people, the government had electoral commissions that supervised both nominations and elections. These commissions decided on a single candidate for each office. Since there were no opposition political parties, there could never be a rival slate of candidates.

Since voters were not offered a choice, there was no need for political campaigns. Instead, for weeks before an election, millions of Party members engaged in a massive "get out the vote" campaign. Partly because of this activity and probably from fear of the consequences of *not* voting, Soviet citizens appeared at the polls in record numbers. At election time no fewer than 99 percent of the eligible voters cast their ballots.

Actually the Soviet government could have dispensed with elections, since the results were known before a single ballot was cast. But the Party considered elections a vital part of the Soviet system. For one thing, they gave an air of legitimacy to the Communist regime, since the people apparently expressed confidence in their government by unanimously approving its choice of officials. Moreover, elections provided an ideal forum for indoctrination, thus strengthening support for the system.

## Check Your Understanding

1. Explain two ways in which practice departed from principle in the way the Soviet Union was organized and governed.
2. Explain the organization of the Communist Party in the USSR.
3. How did the Party control the government of the Soviet Union?
4. Why were so few Soviets willing to join the Party?
5. What was the purpose of elections?
6. *Thinking Critically:* Contrast the "Fundamental Rights and Duties of Citizens" with the United States Constitution's "Bill of Rights." Under Stalin how did principle and practice differ in the two nations with respect to citizens' rights?

## 5. Khrushchev's Role in World Affairs

Khrushchev, bold and unpredictable in dealing with international problems, was ever watchful for opportunities to advance the interests of the Soviet Union. Endowed with boundless energy, he played an active role in Soviet foreign affairs. Alone or in company with other high-ranking Soviet officials, he was a "traveling salesman" for the USSR. At one time or another he visited many of the countries of Europe, the United States, Egypt, India, Indonesia, and China. He also attended sessions of the United Nations. Although at times his blunt speech and aggressive behavior offended those with whom he was dealing, he enhanced the image of the Soviet Union. His efforts to portray his country as a peace-loving nation were less successful, since many of his actions undercut his words.

### Khrushchev's Foreign Policy

Khrushchev made increasing use of economic and technical assistance to further Soviet aims. But he was handicapped because the Soviet economy could not always produce enough goods to satisfy both domestic needs and foreign policy requirements. Nevertheless, Khrushchev managed to step up the flow of goods abroad by drawing on the production of satellite countries. This policy contributed to growing bitterness between the Soviet Union and Communist-bloc governments, who were being exploited to further Soviet goals.

The usual practice of the Soviet government was to extend aid to foreign countries in the form of loans rather than offering outright gifts. Some of the principal recipients of this type of help were Communist China, India, Indonesia, and Egypt. After Castro's rise to power in Cuba in 1959, his Communist regime received extensive aid from the Soviet Union. Khrushchev's critics frequently charged that Soviet aid was more likely to be provided for projects of "high visibility" than for those of great importance. Thus the Soviet regime favored economic assistance for the construction of factories, dams, and hospital buildings, which everyone could see, rather than for less visible improvements in agriculture or education.

### The Hungarian Uprising

Discontent and hostility erupted into violence in Eastern Europe during Khrushchev's regime. One of the Communist governments established in Eastern Europe after World War II was in Hungary. Popular discontent with the Soviet dominated government simmered for many years and finally came to a boil in 1956. On October 23, university students in Budapest staged a demonstration, calling for the introduction of genuine democracy and the end of Soviet control and exploitation. When the crowds got out of hand, Hungarian police and Soviet soldiers opened fire. This action turned the protests into a revolutionary uprising. When Hungary's government denounced the Warsaw Pact and asked the UN to consider the Hungarian situation, Soviet troops moved into that country in overwhelming force. Thus, the Soviet government made clear that there were limits beyond which the satellite countries of Eastern Europe could not go.

The Hungarians resisted bravely, but their defiance was soon crushed. "Freedom fighters" were imprisoned or executed in large numbers. Thousands fled the country and found haven elsewhere in either Europe or the United States.

### A Divided Germany

The question of East and West Germany still remained. Khrushchev was unwilling to negotiate with the United States, Great

Waving the Hungarian flag to protest Soviet occupation of their land, Budapest citizens ride through the streets on a tank. The 1956 uprising was followed by the brutal suppression of dissenting Hungarian patriots.

Britain, and France about divided Germany. While not denying the possibility of a negotiated settlement, the Soviet leader was wary of German unification. He feared that a united Germany, which had cost Russia so dearly in two world wars, might lead sooner or later to the resurgence of German power in central Europe. Such a Germany might threaten not only the Soviet satellite system but the Soviet Union itself. Thus, Khrushchev, like Stalin, refused to budge on the question of German unification. When West Germany became a member of NATO in 1955, the likelihood that the two Germanies could be peacefully united was closed for the foreseeable future.

The German issue was reflected in tensions over divided Berlin. From time to time the Soviet government would touch off a crisis by violating understandings with the West over access to the Allied portion of that city. In 1961, ill feeling between the Soviet government and the West was especially high. After a meeting with Khrushchev, President John F. Kennedy concluded that the Soviets intended to force the Western powers out of Berlin. Khrushchev did not use the ultimate weapon—war—but he did order the erection of a high wall dividing East Berlin from West Berlin. This was the Soviet way of stop-

**201**

This 1962 photo shows East German border police reinforcing weak spots in the Berlin Wall. Explosives had made holes in the masonry. Note the armed guard seated on the completed section.

ping the flow of East Germans into West Germany via Free Berlin, a drain of workers that had greatly hurt the East German economy. The Berlin Wall funneled all traffic through a few checkpoints and slowed the number of East German escapees to a trickle. Thus, the Wall became a symbol of Communist tyranny. Fearful of starting a war, all the West could do was lodge formal protests.

### The Cuban Missile Crisis

In 1962 cold-war tensions touched off a crisis in the Americas. Although Communist parties existed in most countries in the Western Hemisphere, no American nation had a Communist government until Fidel Castro came to power in Cuba. In the early 1960's Cuba began to receive massive economic aid from the Soviet Union, which was eager to establish a foothold in the Western Hemisphere, especially one close to the United States. Although increased Soviet influence in Cuba came as an unpleasant surprise to most Americans, there were few grounds for alarm until 1962. Then, the discovery that the Soviet Union had furnished Castro with nuclear warheads aimed at the United States stunned the American people.

The presence of missiles in Cuba drew a firm reaction from the United States. President Kennedy bluntly warned Khrushchev to remove the deadly missiles or the United States would invade Cuba. The Soviet premier backed down and had the missiles shipped back to the USSR. Although the Soviet Union has continued to aid the Communist regime in Cuba, it has been careful not to provoke the United States again directly in the Caribbean area.

## The Sino-Soviet Split

Following the Bolshevik Revolution, Communists worldwide accepted Soviet leadership. To a considerable extent, the political strategy pursued by Communists anywhere at any time was formulated by the leaders in Moscow. The first serious crack in the seemingly solid front of international communism appeared in 1948 when Tito let it be known that Yugoslavia would determine its own policy in foreign affairs. Although Tito broke away from the Soviet orbit, he did not plunge the Communist bloc into conflict. In the 1950's, however, the unity of the Communist world was seriously threatened by mainland China.

Sino-Soviet relations, at least officially, seemed cordial during the early years of the People's Republic of China. The two Communist giants maintained a united front in international affairs. Much publicity was given to the Soviet Union's programs of economic and technical aid to the Chinese. Following the death of Stalin, however, evidence of tension between the two Communist powers began to build up. Then, after Khrushchev delivered his famous attack against Stalin and his policies in 1956, the rupture came into the open. The differences between Soviet and Chinese Communist leaders soon led to repeated and bitter denunciations of one another.

The break between Soviet Russia and Communist China had been building for years. The Chinese believed that Stalin's successors, particularly Khrushchev, had betrayed Communist ideology by adopting a policy of restraint and caution toward the cause of revolution. Mao Zedong and his comrades suspected the Soviet leaders of dragging their feet when it came to helping oppressed peoples overthrow their governments. The Soviets, on the other hand, were alarmed by China's recklessness in foreign affairs. They were fearful that in the nuclear age such an attitude might spark a Third World War, which would be ruinous to all, including the USSR. Soviet leadership apparently preferred a "cold war" to a "hot" one.

Another point of conflict was foreign aid. Mao's China, desperately poor, resented the Soviet Union's withholding of promised technical and economic assistance. But the Soviet Union

The Sino-Soviet rift was less severe in 1958, when Nikita Khrushchev went to Beijing for secret talks on the Middle East with China's Mao Zedong. Why did the rift worsen?

felt justified in using its limited industrial resources primarily for its own development and for furthering its own foreign policy goals. Soviet leaders were reluctant to sacrifice prospects for a higher standard of living for Soviet citizens by diverting resources to the "bottomless pit" of overpopulated and developing China. Anxious to further its own national interests, the Soviet Union regarded with suspicion the ambitions of its potentially powerful neighbor. Since the Soviet Union had long been acknowledged as leader of the world Communist revolution, the growing Chinese claims of partnership and equal status were especially irritating.

By the early 1960's the differences between the Soviet Union and Communist China had become so sharp that reconciliation seemed unlikely. Only the possibility of a major threat to one or both of these powers from the West seemed likely to restore their friendship. As a result, the Soviet Union found itself locked in tense competition with China for the support of Communist parties throughout the world. Once, the loyalty of these parties to Soviet leadership had seemed beyond question. The case of Albania showed that this was no longer true. Albania's support of Communist China led to a rupture of its relations with the Soviet Union in 1961. Shortly thereafter, Albania withdrew from the Warsaw Pact.

The split with China forced the Soviet leaders to re-examine both the direction of their national development and the aims of their foreign policy. Meanwhile, the rest of the world began to realize that the unity of world communism was a thing of the past.

### Khrushchev's Fall From Power

In October 1964, an amazed world learned that Nikita Khrushchev had been ousted from leadership of the Soviet Union. His sudden forced retirement revealed that Party leaders had had enough of their impulsive chief and his policies. His outspoken behavior in public (on one occasion he had hammered the table with his shoe during a session of the United Nations), his setback in the Cuban missile crisis, and the failure of his agricultural program—all contributed to his downfall. Soviet leaders also were deeply worried by the widening split with the Chinese. In commenting on Khrushchev's removal, *Pravda*, the Communist Party's official newspaper, accused him of "harebrained scheming, immature conclusions and hasty actions . . . bragging. . . ." Obviously Premier Khrushchev had alienated many of the Soviet Union's influential leaders.

## Check Your Understanding

1. What were the goals of Khrushchev's foreign policy in: **a.** Hungary? **b.** Germany? **c.** Cuba?
2. What were the causes of the Sino-Soviet split?
3. Why was Khrushchev removed from power?
4. *Thinking Critically:* Do you think it was inevitable that China would compete with the USSR for world leadership of communism? Why or why not?

## CHAPTER REVIEW

### ■ Chapter Summary

**Section 1.** The USSR had to fight for its very existence when it was invaded by Nazi armies in 1941. Hitler never achieved his goal of controlling and exploiting Soviet resources, due to a combination of fierce Soviet resistance, geographic conditions, and Nazi setbacks in other parts of the world. During the war the Soviet Union and its Western Allies cooperated in an all-out effort to achieve victory. At a series of top-level conferences a spirit of cooperation prevailed. By

Yalta early in 1945, however, the Western Allies were having doubts about Stalin's motives. As the war against Hitler and the Japanese entered its last phase, Stalin's actions made it clear that his underlying purpose in both Europe and Asia was to secure the maximum advantage for the USSR and to ensure his country's security.

**Section 2.** Stalin's policy led to the creation of Communist satellite nations after World War II and to tensions between these Soviet-controlled states and the West. Even after Stalin's death, international relations were dominated by this Cold War.

**Section 3.** In the post-Stalin era the USSR underwent many changes. Under Khrushchev's leadership a program of de-Stalinization was initiated and the autocratic ways of the late dictator were modified. Khrushchev's goal in domestic policy was to make the USSR the world's foremost economic power. Impressive gains were scored in industrial production, but the Soviet economy continued to lag behind that of the United States.

**Section 4.** Under Stalin the Soviet Union had been run as a dictatorship. With his death certain changes took place in the leadership of the Party and the government. The Party gained supreme power. All decisions were made by the Party and then implemented by the government. The same people held positions of power in both the Party and the government. Despite recruiting efforts by the Party, only one in ten Soviets joined the Party. Although elections were held, only Party-approved candidates could run for office. Campaigns were seen as a way to indoctrinate citizens in the Party propaganda.

**Section 5.** The goal of Soviet foreign policy under Khrushchev, as under Stalin, was to extend Soviet power in the world. To that end Khrushchev used foreign aid to influence developing nations and those who had remained neutral in the cold war. Soviet intervention in the Hungarian revolt made clear the USSR's determination to maintain control of its satellites. But in the case of divided Berlin and the Cuban missile crisis, Khrushchev adopted a more flexible policy to avoid the risk of a major war. Many factors contributed to the Sino-Soviet split, and these differences were not easily reconciled.

## ■ Vocabulary Review

*Define:* superpower, satellite, cold war, bloc, containment, Politburo, Presidium, democratic centralism

## ■ Places to Locate

*Locate:* Battle of Stalingrad, Federal Republic of Germany, German Democratic Republic, Berlin Wall

## ■ Thinking Critically

1. Do you think that Stalin was relatively successful in achieving his goals after World War II? Why or why not? Use facts from the chapter to support your opinion.
2. Stalin carried out his policies without regard for the wishes or welfare of the people involved. Did the end ever justify the means? Why or why not?
3. Why was it hypocritical of Khrushchev to condemn Stalin's "cult of personality" and to promote his own de-Stalinization program? How did this policy help Khrushchev?
4. Some authorities believe that Khrushchev's departure from the "hard line" of communism in trying to increase consumer production contributed to his downfall. Why would "hard line" Communists object to this policy?

## ■ Extending and Applying Your Knowledge

1. Read and prepare a book report on *Babi Yar* by Anatoly Kuznetsov. This is an account of the German occupation of Kiev and the Babi Yar executions as seen through the eyes of a young boy.
2. Prepare a timeline of the major battles, invasions, and wartime conferences. Put a check mark next to those that involved the Soviet Union.
3. Prepare a brief oral report on one of the following: Truman Doctrine, Marshall Plan, Berlin Airlift, Warsaw Pact, NATO, Berlin Wall. Include information on when and why it was begun, whether it achieved its goals, and whether it has any continuing effects to the present day.

# 7

# The Brezhnev Years

Leonid Brezhnev succeeded Khrushchev in 1964 as First Secretary of the Communist Party. He would rule the Soviet Union for 18 years.

The Brezhnev years began well enough. Economic growth was steady, although unspectacular. During the first decade of Brezhnev's regime the Soviet people experienced a gradual improvement in their standard of living. Social, religious, and ethnic discontent surfaced, but its extent was downplayed by Soviet authorities. Although the Brezhnev regime encountered some setbacks abroad, Soviet influence continued to expand.

By the time Brezhnev died in 1982, however, the Soviet Union was clearly in a state of economic crisis. Industrial growth was minimal at best. For several years the Soviet standard of living had barely improved. Most embarrassing to the Soviet leadership were its agricultural problems. The country that was once a major grain exporter had now become the world's largest importer. Foreign affairs were almost as bleak. Relations with the United States and China were strained. In Eastern Europe, the Poles were restive under Communist rule. Meanwhile Soviet military forces had become bogged down in a long-term war in Afghanistan.

How and why had the Soviet Union reached such a critical point? Was it simply a case of ineffective leadership? Perhaps some of its foreign policy failures could have been avoided. But what about economic stagnation? Many Western observers argued that the Soviet economic system was beyond repair.

# 1. Problems at Home

Even though Khrushchev was forced out of power, his successors did not break sharply with many of his policies. The men who shared the new "collective leadership," Leonid Brezhnev and Aleksei Kosygin, were committed to economic expansion. During their years in power, however, the economy began to stagnate. The economic planning system, devised by Stalin, was unable to handle the demands of a modern industrial society. In addition to economic problems, the Brezhnev and Kosygin regime had to confront growing ethnic and religious sentiment in the Soviet Union. Complicating matters further, a few individuals, the so-called **dissidents** began to demand an end to oppression.

## A "Collective Leadership"

When Khrushchev was deposed, Kremlin leaders decided not to give one person complete power. Offices in the Communist Party and the Soviet government formerly held by Khrushchev were divided among several top leaders. The two most powerful were Leonid Brezhnev, who assumed the post of Party Secretary, and Aleksei Kosygin, the new Premier. Brezhnev and Kosygin represented a different generation of Communists from that of Lenin, Stalin, and Khrushchev. During a power struggle lasting several years, Brezhnev gradually emerged as the sole head of the Party and the government. But as enormous as his authority was, Brezhnev was always answerable to top Party office holders. In a very real sense Brezhnev exercised less independent power than did many chief executives of democratic governments.

Trained as a metallurgist, Brezhnev had become active in the Communist Party in the late 1930's. Ironically he owed his advancement over the years to the strong backing of Khrushchev. After serving as secretary to various Communist committees, he became a full member of the ruling body in 1957. In 1960 Brezhnev was appointed President of the Soviet Union, an office that carried prestige but little power.

Kosygin, like Brezhnev, was a **technocrat**. For many years before Khrushchev's fall he had ably filled his role as an economist and industrial planner. Although he served in the Red Army during the Civil War, he did not join the Communist Party until 1927. After holding posts in both the Politburo and the Central Committee, Kosygin fell from favor in 1952, coming back to power in 1957. Thereafter, he was a ranking authority on economic matters. Unlike Khrushchev, both Brezhnev and Kosy-

## TIMETABLE

### The Soviet Union Under Brezhnev

1964    Khrushchev removed from power
      Brezhnev elected First Secretary
1965    Liberman reforms introduced
1968    Czechoslovakia invaded
1969    Skirmishes on the Sino-Soviet border
1972    President Nixon in Moscow
      Signing of SALT I
1975    Failure of Ninth Five-Year Plan
1979    Afghanistan invaded
1980    U.S. boycott of Moscow Olympics
      Formation of Solidarity in Poland
1982    Death of Brezhnev

gin were efficient and businesslike, and had no wish to attract attention to themselves in either national or international affairs.

## A New Approach to the Economy

As early as 1962 the Soviet economist Yevsei Liberman had criticized the Soviet Union's economic system as being outmoded and inefficient. He proposed a complete overhaul of the economy to meet the country's needs. Kosygin in particular strongly backed Liberman's plan and, because of Khrushchev's economic failures, was anxious to try a new approach. In 1965 the first steps were taken to put Liberman's ideas into practice, even though they represented a departure from generally accepted interpretations of Marxist-Leninist theory. Liberman wished to modify central planning, the core of the Soviet economic system. He intended to place responsibility for plant management, planning, and production on the shoulders of the local plant managers. For the first time, profit was to be a measure of a plant's efficiency. Before, production beyond established goals was the principal yardstick.

In the late 1960's, Soviet commentators repeatedly stressed that a third major economic shift in the history of the Soviet Union was under way. The first had been in 1921 when Lenin inaugurated the New Economic Policy to rebuild the war–torn

Celebrating the fiftieth anniversary of the Bolshevik Revolution are the following Soviet notables (from left): Party Secretary Leonid Brezhnev; Premier Aleksei Kosygin; Presidium Chairman Nikolai Podgorny. By the 1970's, Brezhnev had emerged as the top official in the government.

nation. Lenin had sought foreign capital, permitted small factories to operate under private control, and allowed farmers to sell their produce for profit. The second shift came in 1928 when Stalin launched the First Five-Year Plan, making all means of production the property of the state. A plant manager's performance was measured chiefly by output. The third economic shift began in 1965 when the Soviet Union introduced Liberman's program. It soon became apparent, however, that the Kosygin reforms were meeting enormous resistance. Conservatives in the Party modified Liberman's proposals and were not cooperative in implementing them. These leaders feared that the reforms would undermine the control over the economy exercised by the Party, the economic bureaucracy, and the military. In addition, many plant managers preferred the existing system, as cumbersome as it was. For all the shortcomings of centralized planning their careers were secure.

During the Brezhnev years the Soviet Union continued to focus on heavy industry. In the Ninth Five-Year Plan, (1971–1975) however, there occurred a slight but important shift in economic emphasis. For the first time in the history of the Five-Year plans consumer goods were scheduled to be expanded at a faster rate than heavy industries. It seemed that the Soviet government was trying at last to respond to its citizen's calls for a more rapid improvement in their standard of living.

Sharp cutbacks were not made in the output of heavy industries. Soviet leaders still regarded this sector of the economy as the key to the nation's growth. They considered heavy industry vital for further economic development and for the production of the weaponry required by both the Soviet armed forces and those of its allies. Indeed, under Brezhnev, the Soviet Union had embarked on a massive military buildup.

## Economic Stagnation

Soviet hopes for a robust economy were not realized. The economy had indeed expanded at a rapid rate during the first several years of Brezhnev's regime. By the early 1970's, however, the economic growth rate had begun to slow. By 1975, the Soviet economy was hardly expanding at all. The Ninth Five-Year Plan failed to meet many of its key goals. The Tenth Five-Year Plan (1976–1980) scaled back production targets for consumer goods and set modest goals for heavy industry.

The Soviet economy had become too large and complex for centralized planning to work effectively. The absence of the profit motive and the use of output quotas for each factory encouraged waste and inefficiency. Moreover, except for those holding important positions, few people saw any point in exerting themselves. The system simply did not reward hard work.

Lazy or incompetent workers were almost never fired, and they were paid just as much as everyone else. Those who were more conscientious could hope at most for a promotion and a small salary increase. But money had limited value since there was little to buy. "They pretend to pay us," Soviet workers sarcastically joked, "and we pretend to work." During the Brezhnev years the size of personal savings accounts soared. What could one do with money except put it in the bank?

Nowhere was the Soviet economy more in trouble than in the agricultural sector. Soviet farmers had 70 percent more farmland than did American farmers, and there were seven times as many farmers in the Soviet Union as in the United States. Still, for much of the period since World War II Soviet farms were unable to meet the nation's needs for foodstuffs and agricultural raw materials.

Part of the problem, of course, was unfavorable weather. But czarist Russia had experienced the very same weather and yet had been one of the world's largest grain exporters. Soviet farms

**COLLECTIVIZED AGRICULTURE.** The state farm below was built in Kazakhstan in 1965 to supply food to industrial areas nearby. This complex includes housing, schools, and other facilities for collective farm workers. Under Brezhnev, many farmers were given personal plots (left), where they could plant and tend their own crops. Production rates were much higher for these plots. Why?

were simply not efficiently managed or worked. Moreover, the Soviet Union's transportation and warehousing system was inadequate. Possibly a third of all agricultural produce was lost, stolen, or spoiled after it left the farm.

The Soviet regime tried to stimulate agricultural production. Managers of collective farms were given more responsibility for planning and for day-to-day operations. Efforts were made to provide greater incentives for workers. Restrictions were eased on the use of personal farm plots and the keeping of livestock. Guaranteed monthly wages were introduced for the first time, and electricity was brought to thousands of rural homes. The government invested vast sums in new equipment, irrigation systems, and fertilizers. All these efforts to improve agricultural production met with little success. Under Khrushchev agricultural production had increased 41 percent. During the first 10 Brezhnev years agricultural production increased only 26 percent.

Beginning in the early 1960's, the USSR periodically had to buy large amounts of wheat and other grains abroad. Because of poor weather conditions, the Soviet Union experienced crop failures in 1963, 1971, 1972, 1975, 1979, and 1980. The inefficiency of the Soviet agricultural system made a difficult situation even worse. In the early 1970's Canada and the United States contracted to make large grain deliveries to Soviet Russia. Following the 1979 crop failure, the Soviet Union signed long-term agricultural import agreements with the United States and Argentina.

Perhaps the failure of collective farms is best illustrated by the success of "private" agriculture. Soviet farmers had the right to till small plots of land, usually no more than one acre, and to raise small numbers of livestock and chickens. What they did not eat themselves, they could sell for profit on the "open market." Khrushchev had tried to restrict the use of private plots, but beginning in 1976 Brezhnev encouraged them. During the later Brezhnev years these small plots, perhaps totaling only 3 percent of all land under cultivation, contributed more than 25 percent of Soviet agricultural output. It is easy to see what part of the farm economy received attention and energy.

### Consumer Dissatisfaction

Because the Soviet economy could not produce adequate amounts of consumer goods and food, the Soviet people did not live well. In fact the Soviet Union had the lowest standard of living of any industrialized country. During the Khrushchev and Brezhnev eras the Soviet people impatiently awaited an upturn in their standard of living. Considering the long years of promises, it was not surprising that grumbling began to mount when consumer expectations were not fulfilled. Basic necessities were not lacking. But products like automobiles, motorcycles, black and white television sets, refrigerators, and vacuum cleaners were not widely available.

The Soviet standard of living had improved considerably during the first several Brezhnev years. By the mid-1970's, however, yearly improvements, if any, were small. The average Soviet citizen obtained enough to eat, but the quality of many types of food was low and variety was limited. Meat, fresh fruits and vegetables were often unavailable or of poor quality. The supply of clothing was adequate, but prices were high and the apparel was often shoddy and styleless. Western visitors to the Soviet Union were frequently approached by Soviet citizens who offered exorbitant prices for their clothing.

The Soviet people, especially those living in urban areas, had to contend with a severe housing shortage. Rents had last been raised in 1928 so rentals were extremely low by Western standards. The trick, however, was getting an apartment in the first place. The best ones were passed from generation to generation. As late as 1960, about 60 percent of all city families had to share their apartments with other people. Over the next 20 years the government built a considerable number of apartment houses. Many were poorly built, and the apartments were still small and cramped. Many people still did not have their own apartments.

In the Khrushchev and early Brezhnev years the Soviets did not generally compare their standard of living with other peoples. Because foreign travel had been tightly controlled for years, few Soviet citizens had had an opportunity to see how other people lived. Consequently most comparisons they made were with their living conditions during earlier decades. Such comparisons did give Soviets some cause for satisfaction. As the 1970's progressed, however, more and more Soviet citizens traveled to the West, talked with those who had, or met foreigners visiting the USSR. The Soviet people were becoming more aware that living standards in many other countries were much higher than theirs.

### The Soviet Elite

The presence of a Soviet elite did not help. Soviet leaders insisted that theirs was a classless society, but in reality Soviet society remained grossly unequal. A small elite lived far better than most. Those few people in the upper rungs of the Party, government, police, and military lived in luxury apartments and spent weekends and vacations at country homes. They drove fine automobiles and shopped at special stores closed to the general public. There they found a wide assortment of high-quality goods sold at subsidized prices. When they were sick, they went to the best hospitals in the country and obtained medication at well-stocked pharmacies. Their children went to the best schools. All schools in the Soviet Union are run by the state, but some are much better than others. The czarist nobility had long since died out. But a new nobility, a new class, had come into being.

## The Rise of Nationalism

Slow economic growth was not the only problem facing the Brezhnev regime. Across the country ethnic and religious sentiment was rising. The Soviet Union was a multi-ethnic society controlled by the Great Russians. Many of the ethnic minorities, particularly those in Soviet Central Asia and the Caucasus, resented this domination. These minorities did not seek political independence, only greater local autonomy. Non-Slavic minorities claimed that they had second-class political and economic status. The Great Russians held most of the important positions within the government and the Party. They had a much higher standard of living than most other national groups. The Muslim peoples of Soviet Central Asia, for example, were among the poorest citizens of the Soviet Union. In Muslim urban areas, Great Russians and other non-Muslims held most of the key jobs in the government and the economy.

Ukrainians, Baltic peoples, and Muslims also resented the soviet policy of Russification and the government's attempt to discourage religious worship. Indeed, throughout the Soviet Union a religious revival was under way. More and more people, including Great Russians, were becoming interested in religion.

Many Great Russians resented the minorities' expressions of dissatisfaction. As they saw it, the Russian Republic was making great economic sacrifices to develop the backward parts of the country. The Great Russians were also alarmed. They feared that one day they would lose their dominant position. As of the 1970's, the Great Russians were slightly more than half of the Soviet population. But other nationalities, especially the Muslim ethnic groups, were growing at a more rapid rate. At some point in the not too distant future, perhaps by the turn of the century, the Great Russians would lose their majority status.

## The Emergence of Dissidents

Ethnic dissatisfaction was not widely publicized in the West during the Brezhnev years. Much more attention was focused on the dissident movement that began to emerge in the late 1960's. The dissidents were private citizens who publicly protested abuses in the Soviet system. The dissidents were not a unified force, and their grievances varied. Many were **human rights** activists who simply insisted that the regime honor its own laws. Some called for greater local autonomy for individual ethnic groups, and others demanded freedom of religious expression.

There were also the *refuseniks*. These were large numbers of people who sought to leave the Soviet Union but had been prohibited from doing so.

Best known in the West were the literary and professional dissidents. Led by Andrei Sakharov, a noted nuclear physicist, they numbered about 2,000. They formed committees to defend human rights and occasionally held peaceful public protests. Some wrote books that were published in the West. Many engaged in *samizdat* or self-publishing. Since Soviet publishing houses would rarely print their work, these writers circulated their manuscripts in carbon copy or mimeographed form.

The Brezhnev regime dealt harshly with the dissidents. From the Party's point of view, these people were seeking to undermine the legitimacy of Communist rule. The dissidents were fired from their jobs, perhaps beaten by state-paid thugs, and otherwise harassed. Some were found guilty of phony charges and sent to jail. Quite a few were declared insane and sent to psychiatric hospitals. Here they were "treated" with mind-altering drugs. The terror of Stalin's day was not repeated in that there were no mass executions. The Party's methods had become more subtle and the victims chosen more selectively.

## Check Your Understanding

1. How did Brezhnev's power differ from that of Stalin?
2. Explain Liberman's program for economic growth.
3. What factors worked against the success of the Liberman program?
4. What were the major causes for the stagnation of the Soviet economy in the 1970's?
5. How did the Soviet government try to encourage agricultural production?
6. List two causes of consumer discontent.
7. *Thinking Critically:* How were the rise of nationalism and the emergence of dissidents connected? What dissatisfactions with Soviet rule were both reacting to?

## 2. Soviet Foreign Policy

The Soviet Union under Brezhnev was faced with the challenge of adjusting to a world vastly different from the one Lenin, Stalin, and even Khrushchev had known. Colonial systems that had once dominated a good part of the world had disappeared. New power blocs had emerged, and many new independent nations had been born. Equally significant, the Soviet Union itself had become a superpower whose strength and influence were felt in all parts of the world. But Brezhnev and Kosygin were as devoted to furthering Soviet national interests as had been Lenin, Stalin, and Khrushchev. The interests of other Communist countries and movements, both East and West, were second to this overriding concern.

## "Peaceful Coexistence"

Soviet leaders were willing to cooperate with the Western democracies whenever such actions furthered Soviet national interests. Khrushchev coined the term **peaceful coexistence** to describe his version of this policy. In the early 1970's, the term **détente** (day-TAHNT) was used to describe the lessening of tension that was then occurring between the Soviet Union and the United States.

Neither peaceful coexistence nor detente meant that Soviet leaders had reconciled themselves to a permanent policy of "live and let live" with the non-Communist world. On the contrary, they had not abandoned their dream of someday bringing all nations under communism. Khrushchev made it quite clear that the policy of peaceful coexistence implied a change in methods, not in goals. Brezhnev, for example, ordered the invasion of Czechoslovakia in 1968 and Afghanistan in 1979. For the most part, however, he recognized that the strong-arm tactics of the past were no longer appropriate. The Brezhnev regime continued to press for every advantage possible in foreign affairs, but it was usually careful not to take unnecessary risks.

## The Widening Split with China

Although Soviet leaders had been deeply upset with Khrushchev's handling of relations with Communist China, his successors did no better. Many of the problems that had started to surface between the Communist giants in the early 1960's grew more troublesome under Brezhnev and Kosygin. Soviet leaders were annoyed by the repeated claims of the Chinese to equality of leadership in the Communist world. China's aggressive and occasionally successful competition in wooing satellite and "friendly" nations away from the Soviet camp was considered even more threatening. Among countries of the so-called "**Third World**" Soviet influence was at times displaced by China's.

Following the skirmishes of 1969, Soviet troops closely guarded the border with China, a continuing trouble spot in Sino-Soviet relations.

One issue that deeply concerned the Soviets was China's attitude towards Third World revolution. To the Soviets, China's aggressive promotion of wars of national liberation was reckless in an age of nuclear weapons. On one occasion, Mao purportedly reassured Khrushchev that the United States was only a "paper tiger." "Yes," Khrushchev replied, "but that paper tiger has nuclear teeth."

A Sino-Soviet border dispute worsened the relationship between the USSR and China. As early as 1954 the Chinese Communists had expressed their determination eventually to regain Soviet-held lands that had once belonged to the Chinese empire. In early 1969 sharp fighting broke out between Soviet and Chinese troops stationed along the border between the two countries. In these local border disputes both sides realized that at stake were several hundred thousand square miles of territory claimed by the Chinese as rightfully theirs.

The 1969 border clashes set the tone for Sino-Soviet relations for the rest of the Brezhnev period. The Soviet Union pursued what might be termed "a carrot and stick" approach towards China. The Soviet Union made it clear that it would use military force if it had to. The number of Soviet troops near the Chinese border was dramatically increased. Great concentrations of artillery and tanks were deployed at strategic points and Soviet air power at east Siberian bases was steadily built up. Moreover, large numbers of missiles were readied for potential use against Chinese military and industrial centers.

The Soviet Union also undertook a number of diplomatic initiatives. Their goal was to strengthen the Soviet military position against the Chinese while isolating the Chinese politically. The Soviet Union signed treaties with Mongolia and Vietnam that permitted the stationing of Soviet forces in these two countries. In addition, the Soviet Union exerted pressure on Japan and Western Europe not to sell military equipment to China. Finally, the Soviet Union sought to ease tension with the United States. This was done in part to lessen the possibility of a Sino-American alliance.

In the long run, Soviet policy toward China failed. The Chinese believed that the Soviets were trying to bully them and, as a result, they refused to compromise. Also, the Chinese proved to be adept at maneuvering themselves out of their diplomatic isolation.

### Soviet-American Relations

For several years after Khrushchev's ouster, the interests and purposes of the USSR and the United States continued to collide in many parts of the world. The sharp differences in policy were underscored in crises that rocked the Middle East, Czechoslovakia, and East and West Germany, as well as wars in Southeast Asia. That these localized crises did not mushroom into world disasters was in some measure due to the mutual restraint of the two leading nuclear powers. Moreover, both the USSR and the United States were inching their way to agreement on arms control. Neither side wished to close the door on that prospect.

In the early 1970's a thaw in Soviet-American relations set in. The key to breaking the long deadlock between the two countries was probably the mutual antagonism between the Soviet Union and China. In 1971 the world was startled to hear that President Richard Nixon would fly to China. Since the United States had refused to recognize Mao Zedong's regime since its establishment in 1949, Nixon's formal state visit in February 1972 was a sensation. But for the Soviet government the visit was a source of worry. During the 1970's, Soviet leaders watched uneasily as the United States and Communist China began to bury their deep differences and move toward a friendlier relationship.

The threat of closer ties between the United States and China compelled Soviet leaders to reappraise their own foreign policy. When Nixon visited Moscow not long after the China visit,

President Nixon's cordial meeting with Brezhnev and other Soviet leaders in Moscow marked a new trend in Soviet-American relations. How was this meeting an outgrowth of detente?

the Soviet leaders were in a conciliatory mood. Various agreements on political, economic, and cultural affairs were quickly reached. Apparently the Soviet Union, like China, consented to modify its support of North Vietnam, which helped make possible a cease-fire agreement in Vietnam not long after.

The Soviet-American detente lasted from the early 1970's to the end of the decade. By 1980 the two superpowers had once again become engaged in heated, although not direct military, confrontation. In 1979, the Soviet Union had suddenly invaded Afghanistan, a poor Muslim country on its southern border. President Jimmy Carter responded by imposing a partial trade embargo on the Soviet Union and by calling for a worldwide boycott of the 1980 Moscow Olympics. The Soviet leaders were also infuriated by Carter's charges of human rights violations against their own citizens. President Carter felt a moral obligation to speak out against the ill treatment of political dissidents. But Soviet leaders regarded such criticisms as foreign interference in Soviet domestic affairs.

## Satellite Countries

The soviets have never forgotten that two massive assaults on their homeland in this century had come from their west. Thus after World War II Stalin constructed a defense belt of satellite states along the Soviet Union's western frontier. (See page map 182.) This protective barrier, extending from the Baltic states in the north to Bulgaria in the south, was and is a vital part of the Soviet security system.

Since the 1950's Soviet practice has been to permit the governments of satellite states to enforce proper Communist behavior and to intervene only when matters threatened to get out of hand. Thus the Hungarian uprising in 1956 resulted in massive Soviet military intervention. (See page 200.)

In the post Khrushchev era, Czechoslovakia was the first satellite to threaten a breach in the Soviet Union's western buffer zone. Czechoslovakia had been dragged into the Communist orbit in 1948. Many Czechs and Slovaks resented the Soviet Union's interference in their country's domestic and foreign affairs. They were angered by the curbs imposed on their lives by local Communist leaders.

Some people looked hopefully to the West for economic and cultural relations that could benefit their economy and improve their standard of living. When Alexander Dubcek (DOOB-check) became premier of Czechoslovakia in 1968, it seemed for a time that these hopes might be realized. Suppression of individual rights was eased, travel restrictions to Western countries were lifted, Western tourism was encouraged, and friendly economic relations between Czechoslovakia and non-Communist countries were initiated. But Dubcek and his supporters had overestimated Soviet tolerance.

In August 1968, the USSR suddenly moved against the Czechoslovakian "renegades." An overwhelming military force, composed of troops from the Soviet Union and other Warsaw Pact nations, crossed the Czechoslovakian borders and quickly occupied the country. Although most Czechs and Slovaks heeded their government's pleas not to resist, they bitterly resented the interference in their lives and affairs. But from the Soviet's point of view too much was at stake. Strategically, Czechoslovakia was a military gateway between Eastern and Western Europe. Equally important, the country's bid for greater independence might have inspired other Eastern European satellites to follow its lead; the entire satellite system might have collapsed.

The Czechoslovakian crisis put to rest any ideas that the Soviet Union was relaxing its foreign policy under Brezhnev and Kosygin. Moscow disregarded the protests raised by non-Communist nations and even the criticisms of Communist parties in Western countries. In what came to be called the Brezhnev Doctrine, Brezhnev declared that "when a threat arises to the

In summer 1980 a victorious Lech Walesa, leader of the Solidarity movement in Poland, announced to his fellow strikers that the government had agreed to their demands. Conditions worsened, however, and Soviet troops were sent into Poland in 1981. Although eventually arrested, Walesa received the Nobel Peace Prize in 1983 for his efforts to ensure workers' rights. He was again active as a negotiator during the labor unrest of 1988.

cause of socialism" in a Communist country it becomes "the legitimate concern of all Communist countries." Thus Brezhnev served notice to the satellite nations that the Soviet Union would correct deviant behavior if the satellites themselves did not.

In summer 1980, a series of labor strikes by Polish workers led to the creation of a trade union movement called Solidarity that was independent of government control. Solidarity demanded higher wages for workers and a greater availability of quality consumer goods. It also insisted on basic political changes: free elections, the ending of censorship, and the independence of the courts and police from Party control.

The Soviet leadership faced a dilemma. To do nothing might encourage resistance to develop in other satellite countries. But if the Soviets sent troops, the Poles might resist. In any case, the Soviet Union did not want the responsibility of trying to rescue Poland from the near economic chaos caused by government mismanagement. Finally, in December 1981, the Polish army with the encouragement of the USSR took power. Order was restored, but dissatisfaction continued to simmer in Poland.

## Relations with Western Europe

Brezhnev assumed, as had Khrushchev before him, that the chief opposition to Soviet plans for Central and Western Europe would come from the countries allied with the United States in NATO. (See page 185.) Moreover, as Sino-Soviet tensions mounted during the 1960's, the Soviet Union had to divert some of its military forces to Asia. For both these reasons, then, a prime objective of Brezhnev's foreign policy was to weaken the NATO alliance. The passage of time and problems within NATO, such as France's withdrawal from active military participation, probably contributed more to its weakening than did Soviet efforts. Both the USSR and the NATO members were increasingly willing to discuss the problems of arms control. In 1970 the Soviet Union and West Germany signed a treaty in which the latter recognized the Soviet Union's special interest in the satellite states of Eastern Europe. Expansion of trade between the Soviet Union and Western Europe also helped to reduce the tense atmosphere in Europe.

## Soviet Influence in the Middle East

The Middle East was and is of major importance to the Soviet Union because the region is near the USSR's southern border and contains enormous oil reserves. In the mid-1950's, Moscow tried to take advantage of the Arab-Israeli conflict to enlarge the Soviet presence and influence in the region. The Soviet Union began supplying Egypt, Syria, and Iraq with modern airplanes, tanks, and other weapons. This military assistance was designed to help the Arab countries challenge the state of Israel. This dangerous game, started by Khrushchev, was continued by his successors.

War finally came in June 1967. The Arab dream of destroying the state of Israel was short-lived. In the Six-Day War an outnumbered Israel quickly defeated Egypt, Syria and Jordan. For the Soviet Union the defeat was humiliating. Arab troops, many of whom had been trained by Soviet advisors, proved to be hopelessly incompetent. They suffered huge casualties and lost large quantities of Soviet-supplied equipment. The Soviets, like the Arabs, refused to accept the outcome of the Six-Day War. The Soviet Union continued to exploit Arab hostility toward Israel. Egypt and Syria were supplied with new Soviet weapons to replace those lost in the war. Meanwhile, the Soviet Union obstructed United Nations' attempts to bring about a lasting peace between Israel and its enemies.

A surprising development in Soviet-Egyptian relations came in mid-1972. Apparently because of discontent among many Egyptians—in the government, army, and the general public—President Anwar Sadat ordered Soviet military personnel to leave Egypt. Attempts were later made to repair the rupture, but Soviet-Egyptian relations have remained cool ever since.

In 1973 Egypt and Syria attacked Israel. The Yom Kippur War ended in a stunning defeat for the two Arab countries. In the wake of that war Egyptian-American relations began to improve. In 1978 President Jimmy Carter helped Egypt and Israel negotiate a peace agreement.

By the end of the 1970's Soviet influence in the Middle East had declined considerably. The USSR continued to be a major arms supplier to several Arab states, especially Syria, Iraq, and Libya. With the defection of Egypt, Syria became the focus of Soviet influence in the region, receiving massive amounts of Soviet military equipment. But with Egypt at peace with Israel, Syria dared not provoke war.

## Asian Policy

Asia always figured prominently in the plans and hopes of the Soviet Union. Over the years Communist parties had been formed in just about every Asian country. Communist revolutionaries, usually with Soviet aid, had won power in several Asian states: Mongolia, North Korea, China, and Vietnam. The record of Soviet involvement in Asia was one of successes, failures, and stand-offs.

One Asian land in which communism had great hopes for expansion was Indonesia. This country of over a hundred million people had the largest Communist party of any non-Communist country, thanks to the sympathy of its dictator-president, Sukarno. In 1965 Sukarno, with Communist cooperation, tried to pull off a coup with the aim of removing high-ranking military officers who opposed him. The army smashed the coup, however, and took control of the country. The army outlawed the Communist Party of Indonesia. In the anti-Communist purge that swept through the country some 300,000 Indonesians were killed.

## Soviet-Indian Relations

For years trouble had been brewing in East Pakistan, which was separated from West Pakistan by a thousand miles. The East Pakistani bitterly resented the domination of the national government and economy by the West Pakistani. Finally, in 1971, the East Pakistani seceded from Pakistan and founded their own nation called Bangladesh. India decided to champion the cause of the rebels and, in a lightning campaign, inflicted a humiliating defeat on Pakistan's national forces. Thus, the independence of Bangladesh was assured.

The Soviet Union, which had been trying to win favor with both India and Pakistan since the British had pulled out in 1948, was forced to choose sides. It quickly expressed support for India. Shortly before hostilities between India and Pakistan began, the Soviet Union and India signed a treaty of friendship and cooperation. In the years following the war, the Soviet Union sent foreign aid in large amounts to India. In addition, trade between the two countries increased. Understandably the Soviet Union's popularity soared among the Indian people.

## The Invasion of Afghanistan

The Soviets were less successful in Afghanistan. In December 1979 Soviet forces invaded Afghanistan to prevent the fall of the Communist government there. It was important to the USSR

In December 1979 Soviet leaders sent combat troops into Afghanistan. Here two Soviet tanks take up position outside an Afghan village. Why did the Soviets fear a change of government in Afghanistan?

that Afghanistan, a country on its southern border, have a friendly and submissive government in power. The Soviets were also concerned that Muslim fundamentalism in Afghanistan might spill over into Soviet Central Asia and encourage rebellion there. A Communist government in Afghanistan might be able to keep the religious zealots under control.

Whatever the motives for intervention, the Soviets soon found themselves mired in a no-win situation. Soviet forces encountered strong opposition from the Afghan people. The Soviet Union, like the United States in Vietnam, had overestimated its capacity to impose a military solution. The resistance fighters soon gained control of much of the countryside. In addition the United States began to channel military aid to the Afghans through neighboring Pakistan. After more than 9 years of fighting, the Soviet Union grimly pulled out its last troops. The number of casualties, the loss of military equipment and the inability to beat back the rebels were humiliating to the Soviets.

### Soviet Role in Southeast Asia

Since the early days of the Comintern, the Soviet Union had carefully watched developments in Southeast Asia. Part of this region, ruled by the French before World War II, was reorganized in the postwar era into the independent nations of Vietnam, Cambodia, and Laos. Vietnam was divided into two parts: a Communist-controlled North and a non–Communist controlled South. Beginning in the mid-1950's, Communist insurgents in the South, with military aid from the North, tried to topple the South Vietnamese government. The United States gradually became more active in efforts to prevent the Communist takeover of South Vietnam. By the early 1960's the United States had several hundred military advisors stationed in Vietnam. By 1968 more than half a million American troops were involved in the fighting.

After many official and unofficial attempts had failed to halt the fighting, North Vietnam agreed in January 1973 to a cease-fire arrangement with the United States and South Vietnam. Apparently both the Soviets and the Chinese had pressured the North Vietnamese to accept the peace terms.

Once the United States had pulled its forces out of South Vietnam, North Vietnam and the Communist insurgents in the South resumed their attacks. South Vietnam fell to the Communists in April 1975.

By the end of the 1970's, Vietnam, now united, had become an important Soviet ally. Vietnam received extensive economic and military aid and in return allowed the Soviet Union to use the naval and airbase facilities at Cam Rahn Bay.

## Check Your Understanding

1. List three factors that caused tensions between the Soviet Union and China.
2. How did the Sino-Soviet split affect Soviet relations with the United States?
3. Using Czechoslovakia and Poland as examples, explain Soviet policy toward its satellites.
4. Explain the USSR's role in: **a.** the Arab-Israeli conflict. **b.** the hostilities between India and Pakistan. **c.** the Vietnam War.
5. Why did the Soviet Union invade Afghanistan?
6. **Thinking Critically:** Based on what you have read about Khrushchev's foreign policy, how did Brezhnev's view of détente differ from Khrushchev's peaceful co-existence? How peaceful was Brezhnev's policy?

## 3. Soviet Military Power

During the Brezhnev period the Soviet Union engaged in a massive military buildup. By the time of his death in 1982, the Soviet Union had equaled or surpassed the United States in many categories of military strength. The Soviets were particularly powerful in ground forces, submarines, and nuclear missiles. By contrast their surface navy and air force lagged behind the United States. Still Brezhnev was the first leader in Russian history who could boast that, overall, his country's military strength was second to none in the world.

### The Soviet Army

As a continental power with the world's longest border, Russia has long relied on its army. In general, Soviet military planners emphasized quantity over quality. The Soviet army was large in numbers but was not especially well equipped with high technology weapons. The army was built primarily as an offensive rather than as a defensive force. The Soviet army, for example, had approximately a two to one advantage over NATO forces in the number of tanks. On the other hand, the Soviet army was not well equipped with gun emplacements—stationary artillery.

Soviet troops were stationed at strategic points near the borders of neighboring countries. The heaviest concentrations were in the east and west. The largest part of the Soviet military forces was stationed in western Russia, and strong army units were maintained in the satellite countries on the Soviet western border. Through the Warsaw Pact, satellite military forces were not only coordinated with, but also controlled by the Soviet high command. As the Sino-Soviet split widened, Soviet forces in Siberia were reinforced.

### The New Soviet Navy

During the 1960's and 1970's, the Soviet Union rapidly expanded and modernized its naval forces. By the final years of the Brezhnev period, the Soviet Union possessed a powerful naval force, second only to that of the United States. The Soviet focus on naval power represented a sharp departure from the country's past. For hundreds of years Russia had been primarily a land power. No Russian leader from Peter the Great to Stalin had much interest in building a large and powerful navy. As they saw it, Russia's military needs were best served by a large standing army. They never envisioned Russia fighting far from its borders.

In the post-World War II period, the Soviet Union developed worldwide interests and commitments. The country required a modern navy to extend its military reach far beyond its borders. Because the Soviet economy was weak, the USSR could not hope to match the United States in surface ships. The Soviet Union built few aircraft carriers because they were very expensive. The Soviet Union did build many heavy and light cruisers and destroyers, which were armed with rocket launchers and equipped with modern electronic devices. A primary goal of the navy was to create a powerful submarine fleet. By midway into the Brezhnev period, the Soviet submarine fleet had become the world's largest.

### A Less Advanced Air Force

Soviet military planners spent large sums of money to increase their country's air power, but their success was minimal. The air force remained the least advanced of the Soviet armed services. The country simply did not possess sufficient advanced technology or engineering skill.

Not long after the close of World War II, the Soviets had unveiled a new jet fighter, the MIG, named after its designers Mikoyan and Gurevich. Over the years the Soviet Union introduced newer and more advanced models of this airplane. The MIG with native pilots flew in combat against American fighters in the Korean and Vietnam wars. MIGs and other Soviet aircraft were supplied to Egypt, Syria, and other Arab states in the 1960's and 1970's. These planes did not perform well in encounters with the American- and French-built jets used by the Israeli Air Force. In 1976 a Soviet defector flew a MIG to Japan, and Western experts who examined the plane found it to be poorly built.

### Nuclear Weaponry

No estimate of a nation's war potential can ignore its arsenal of nuclear weapons. During the 1950's both the Soviet Union and the United States increased their knowledge of the new weapons through frequent testing—on land, in the air, and underground. During these years the Soviet Union made great headway in devising a "delivery system" that depended more on rockets than on planes to carry bombs to targets. At first the United States held superiority in the giant intercontinental ballistic missile (ICBM) class. The Soviets had greater numbers of medium-range types. The Brezhnev regime initiated a massive nuclear missile buildup. By his death, the Soviet Union had equaled or surpassed the United States in most measures of nuclear ballistic missile capacity.

The rapid growth in the nuclear striking power of the Soviet Union and the United States set of a chain reaction of related military developments. Both powers developed sensitive devices to keep track of its rival's progress in the creation of more powerful nuclear weapons. The two superpowers also built elaborate radar networks to give advanced warning of approaching aircraft or missiles. Both countries also developed anti-missile missiles to destroy incoming warheads, and both built defense systems making use of such interceptor missiles.

### The Arms Race

Neither the Soviet Union nor the United States was happy about the expense and potential danger posed by the frantic race to build even more destructive weapons. Successive improvements in military weapons increased the likelihood that wars in which nuclear weapons were used would end with no victors—only survivors. It was little wonder that the two superpowers finally moved, although cautiously, to place brakes on the runaway **arms race**.

Over the years the Soviet Union and the United States reached a number of arms control agreements. The first major step to slowing down nuclear competition was taken in 1963 when the Soviet Union, the United States, and Great Britain agreed to a Test-Ban Treaty. It outlawed nuclear testing in the atmosphere, in outer space, and underwater. The treaty did not, however, ban underground tests. The Test-Ban Treaty was subsequently signed by more than 100 countries.

In 1969 Soviet and American delegates began Strategic Arms Limitation Talks (SALT), and these eventually produced some concrete results. One of the first agreements, reached in 1971, was to improve the so-called "hot line" telephone system between Moscow and Washington. By providing for instant communication between the two capitals, both governments hoped to avoid misunderstandings and accidents that might lead to war. The SALT I treaty in 1972 restricted the deployment of antiballistic missile systems. That same year over 70 nations, including the Soviet Union and the United States, signed a treaty prohibiting the use of biological warfare. The treaty also required each nation to destroy its existing stockpile of such weapons. In 1979 the Soviet Union and the United States signed SALT II. When the Soviet Union invaded Afghanistan, the United States Senate refused to ratify the treaty. The two countries abided by the conditions of the treaty as though it were in force. In 1982 Strategic Arms Reduction Talks (START) began but negotiations dragged on.

## Check Your Understanding

1. What was the major goal of the Soviet army?
2. Why was the creation of a strong navy a sharp departure from Russian history?
3. Why did the Soviet air force lag behind the other armed services?
4. What steps have the two superpowers taken to reduce the risk of nuclear war?
5. *Thinking Critically:* Why did the Soviet Union and the United States continue to build more and more sophisticated nuclear weapons while negotiating to end the nuclear arms race?

## 4. Soviet Culture

Both Marx and Lenin insisted that cultural life and artistic expression in all societies reflected the nature of the prevailing economic system and the dominant social class. They maintained that the tastes, values, and interests of a country's rulers determined the pattern and content of cultural expression in that society. Therefore, literature, painting, drama, dance, and architecture in capitalist society mirrored only the outlook of the dominant class. It followed from their argument that in a classless Communist society, culture would reflect the values and needs of the "people."

When the Bolshevik regime was founded in 1917, the Communist Party faced a dilemma. Since socialism had not sprung into being in the aftermath of a revolution, there was little likelihood of a Socialist culture emerging immediately. During the early and mid-1920's the Soviet government permitted considerable freedom of cultural expression. Much that was produced, however, conflicted with the Party's values, or at least, failed to promote them. Stalin and his successors were determined to enforce a Socialist pattern of culture. In much the same way that the Soviets used dictatorial methods to carry out their economic programs, they stifled individuality and insisted on conformity in cultural matters.

At the center of Soviet policy towards art and literature was the doctrine of **socialist realism.** According to this concept, artists and writers had the responsibility of portraying the world accurately, but this did not mean that they could depict reality as they saw it. There was only one correct reality—Socialist reality. Artistic work must reflect Socialist values and trumpet Socialist successes. If artists and writers deviated from Socialist truths, their work was not art, and they themselves were "enemies of the people."

### Censorship

As literacy became widespread in the Soviet Union, the Soviet people became habitual readers. However, the kinds of written material to which they had access were carefully regulated by the state. This control required the government to maintain an enormous staff to censor books, magazines, and newspapers. Censorship took several forms. Much foreign literature was simply not permitted to circulate in the Soviet Union, either in the original language or in translation. Soviet writing not approved by the censors had no chance of being printed. The Soviet writing that did appear in print had to conform to Party standards. Objectionable passages were changed or deleted.

## Novelists and Poets

Because of censorship, Soviet literature during the Brezhnev years was undistinguished. In fact, few writers of the entire Soviet era compared favorably with the literary giants of czarist times. During the Khrushchev years, Boris Pasternak had won a Nobel Prize in literature for his novel *Dr. Zhivago*. Pasternak's masterful story of the early days of the Russian Revolution was first published in Italy because Soviet authorities refused to allow publication of the novel. The Soviet government would not even permit Pasternak to accept the Nobel Prize.

Early in the Brezhnev era, Michael Sholokov was awarded the Nobel Prize for his trilogy *The Silent Don*. These books were about the Cossacks at the turn of the twentieth century. In 1970, the same literary honor was bestowed on Alexander Solzhenitsyn (sohl-zhuh-NEET-suhn) in recognition of his novels, especially *The First Circle* and *The Cancer Ward*. As in the case of Pasternak, the Soviet government pressured Solzhenitsyn into not accepting his award. He feared that if he went to Sweden, the government would not allow him to return.

Solzhenitsyn had been an artillery officer in World War II and was imprisoned in 1945 for having made an unflattering remark about Stalin. After his release in 1953, he turned to teaching

The novelist Alexander Solzhenitsyn, as he appeared appeared with his family in the Soviet Union in 1972.

# SIDELIGHT TO HISTORY

## Soviet Sports

Just as the Soviet government has exerted control over the fine arts, it has regulated and regimented athletics. The Soviet Union has long emphasized the value of physical fitness for all its citizens. The Soviet educational system has always placed much more emphasis on physical fitness than have American schools. Soviet leaders have been well aware that sports activities heavily influence the behavior and values of both the individual and the group.

Originally sports activities that were likely to foster individualism were not encouraged. The Soviet attitude toward sports was also affected by the traditional policy of central planning. In line with the low priority given to the production of consumer goods, Soviet leaders opposed the use of limited resources for the manufacture of many types of athletic equipment and facilities. As a result, highly individualized and expensive sports such as golf, tennis, and bowling were not popular.

However, as the USSR developed into a superpower, Soviet leaders' attitudes toward sports changed. They came to see that developing world-class athletes had international propaganda value. Success in international sports competition would prove that the Soviet way of life produced "superior" individuals. Beginning in 1952 Soviet athletes have dominated the Olympic games. They particularly excel in ice hockey, gymnastics, weight lifting, and wrestling. Some Soviet athletes, such as gymnast Olga Korbit, have become international celebrities. So successful have the Soviets been that their satellite countries follow a similar athletic policy.

Western critics argue that Soviet and Eastern European amateur athletes are, in fact, professionals. Children with promising talent are quickly identified and urged to attend special schools where they can perfect their skills. As adults, they hold "full-time" jobs but are given all the opportunity they need to train and compete. Successful athletes also enjoy many privileges denied ordinary Soviet citizens, for example, spacious apartments, automobiles, and access to Western consumer goods.

Throughout the Brezhnev period, the Soviet government sponsored tours to other countries by Soviet performers and athletes. Here the Moiseyev Soviet Folk Dance Ensemble performs a dance called "Viva Cuba!" How does this dance reflect the doctrine of socialist realism?

and writing. His first novel, *One Day in the Life of Ivan Denisovich*, was approved by Khrushchev himself. It was a vivid and haunting portrayal of life in one of Stalin's concentration camps and was based on Solzhenitsyn's own experiences. Solzhenitsyn's other works had to be smuggled abroad for publication. In 1974 the Soviet government exiled the author to the West.

During the Stalinist era little great poetry was written. The most notable poets of this period were Vladimir Mayakovsky, a bold composer who committed suicide in 1930, and Boris Pasternak, whose gifts as a novelist were excelled by his talents as a poet. During the Khrushchev and Brezhnev periods, the state allowed poets a freer hand. Their work, especially that of younger men and women became extremely popular, and their compositions were read and discussed the way "best sellers" are in the West. Both established and promising poets had the opportunity to present their works before the mass audiences in huge arenas and meeting halls. Poets' reputations were often made or broken by the reception they received.

Yevgeny Yevtushenko (yef-GEN-ee yef-tuh-SHEN-koh) attracted huge audiences. He published his first book of poems in 1952 at the age of 19. His poetry was translated into many foreign languages, and he visited a number of foreign lands, including

**235**

the United States. Perhaps his best known poem was "Babi Yar", published in 1961. The poem was a moving memorial to the 33,000 Soviet Jews slaughtered by the Nazis in 1941 at Babi Yar near Kiev. Ever courageous, Yevteshenko spoke out in 1968 against the Soviet invasion of Czechoslovakia.

### The Fine Arts

Soviet artists in media other than writing also had to contend with the stern demands of the state. This meant that Soviet artists had to express themselves in guarded terms and forms. Nevertheless, some worthwhile work was produced. Soviet dancers, particularly in ballet, kept alive traditional Russian standards of excellence and sometimes were permitted to perform abroad. A few composers during this period, most notably Dimitry Shostakovich (1906–1975), Sergei Sergeyevich Prokofiev (1891–1953), and Aram I. Khachaturian (1903–1978), won worldwide acclaim for their work as did a number of world-class dancers and other musical performers.

## Check Your Understanding

1. How did Stalin deal with the problem of creating a Socialist culture?
2. How did censorship affect the quality of Soviet writing?
3. How did politics affect the fine arts in the Soviet Union?
4. *Thinking Critically:* The Soviet government uses both its artistic performers and its athletes to further its own goals. Do you think that a government should support and encourage the arts and sports for its own purposes?

## CHAPTER REVIEW

### ■ Chapter Summary

*Section 1.* During the Brezhnev years the Soviet economy began to falter. Industrial production grew slowly, if at all, and the agricultural sector could not produce enough to feed the Soviet people. The Liberman reforms were resisted by the economic bureaucracy. Changes in agricultural policy failed to improve production on the collective farms. All the while, the Soviet people became increasingly impatient for a higher standard of living. They especially resented the few who enjoyed special privileges.

In addition to poor economic performance the Brezhnev regime also had to contend with rising ethnic and religious ferment. A few individuals, the dissidents, began to clamor for human rights.

**Section 2.** In general the Soviet Union pursued a cautious foreign policy under Brezhnev. Although the Sino-Soviet split widened, a full scale war was avoided. The Soviet Union invaded Czechoslovakia in 1968 and considered intervening in Poland in 1981. Only in Afghanistan, however, did the Soviet Union become involved in long, drawn out hostilities.

Soviet foreign policy had mixed results in Asia. Soviet-Indian relations grew closer after the Soviet Union supported India in its war with Pakistan. Soviet policy toward Indonesia was far less successful. In the Middle East the Soviet Union supported the Arab nations in their unsuccessful wars with Israel. By the end of the 1970's, Soviet influence in the region had weakened dramatically.

**Section 3.** Soviet-American relations had its ups and downs. But both superpowers desired to avoid a direct military confrontation with each other. The two countries signed a Test-Ban Treaty in 1963, and in 1972 they agreed to restrict the deployment of antiballistic missile system (SALT I). A later treaty (SALT II) agreed to in 1979 was not ratified by the United States Senate after the Soviet invasion of Afghanistan. After a period with no progress in arms talks, the United States and the Soviet Union began a new series of strategic arms-reduction talks (START).

**Section 4.** After the Russian Revolution, culture was supposed to reflect the Socialist values of the state. When artists continued to use their own themes, Stalin imposed the doctrine of socialist realism. This policy continued under Khrushchev and Brezhnev and as a result, Soviet artists and writers produced little of merit. A few authors produced works critical of the Soviet government.

■ **Vocabulary Review**

**Define:** dissident, technocrat, human rights, peaceful coexistence, détente, Third World, arms race, socialist realism

*Locate:* Czechoslovakia, Poland, Middle East, India, Afghanistan, Vietnam

■ **People to Know**

*Identify:* Brezhnev, Kosygin, Liberman, Pasternak, Solzhenitsyn, Yevtushenko

■ **Thinking Critically**

1. What was the major difference between Stalin's concept of economic planning and the Liberman program? Which seemed to provide the better approach to fulfilling Soviet economic goals? Why?

2. Do you think it was inevitable that ethnic and religious groups would begin to show their resentment of the Soviet government? Why or why not?

3. The production of heavy industry versus consumer goods is known as the "guns versus butter" dilemma. It demonstrates the economic concept of trade-offs. Based on what you have read about the Soviet economy, what do you think the concept of trade-offs is? Give examples from Soviet economic history to support your definition. Which did the USSR choose? Why?

4. How did the Sino-Soviet split work to the advantage of the United States?

■ **Extending and Applying your Knowledge**

1. Research and create a time line showing the progression of the arms race from the dropping of the first atomic bombs on Japan to the latest arms negotiations. Be sure to include the proliferation of nuclear capabilities to nations other than the United States and the Soviet Union.

2. For a look at Soviet artists, read and prepare a book report on *Soviet Emigré Artists: Life and Work in the USSR and the United States* by Marilyn Rueschemeyer, Igor Golomshtok, and Janet Kennedy.

3. Work with several classmates to write the front page of a newspaper describing the problems the government faced in changing people's attitudes toward the Liberman program and collectivization.

4. With several classmates set up a "You Are There" activity in which one of you is a television news reporter and the others are pedestrians being interviewed on a Soviet

street. They should imagine they are office workers, plant managers, farmers, apartment renters, and shoppers, and answer questions about what life is like in the Soviet Union for each person. You can use the information in this chapter or do additional research.

# 8

# The Reform Movement Under Gorbachev

Over the last few centuries, Russia has experienced several brief periods of rapid change. Some of these periods were relatively peaceful. Most were accompanied by violence. The driving force for change has invariably come from leaders at the top rather than from the mass of people below. Peter the Great, Catherine the Great, Alexander II, Lenin, and Stalin all sought to remake Russia. None of these leaders was able to enlist the support of the people for any length of time, and, in each case, coercion was used.

During the mid-1980's, the Soviet Union entered a period of far-reaching reform. As in the past, the movement for change came from the top. The Soviet leader, Mikhail Gorbachev, sought to restructure the Soviet economy in order to increase its growth and to fulfill some of the promises the regime had made to Soviet consumers. This goal, in turn, led him to embark on political reform at home and a quest for improved relations with friends and foes abroad.

Can Gorbachev achieve his goal of economic revitalization? Clearly the current economic system is not working. The basic question is whether Soviet communism has the capacity to allow change. Reform also poses many dangers. "He who rides a tiger," the Chinese say, "dares not dismount." The Soviet people, as you have read, have been oppressed for centuries. As Gorbachev loosens political and economic controls, he may unleash forces that are beyond his power to contain. In an effort to maintain political control, the Communists may try to halt the reform movement. However, Gorbachev and his colleagues may have put into motion forces that are irreversible.

# 1. The Rise of Mikhail Gorbachev

Beginning in 1975 and for the next ten years, the Soviet Union was led by aged and ill men—Brezhnev himself and his successors, Yuri Andropov (an-DROH-pov) and Constantin Chernenko (CHERN-yen-koh). These leaders presided over a Soviet economy that was becoming increasingly stagnant. It was not until 1985, with the selection of Mikhail Gorbachev as General Secretary, that the Soviet Union had the energetic leadership it so badly needed. Under Gorbachev, the USSR entered a period of political and economic reform.

## *Andropov's Attempts at Change*

From the late 1970's on, Brezhnev had relied heavily on Constantin Chernenko for advice and support in Party politics. Nevertheless, on Brezhnev's death in November 1982, the Politburo chose Yuri Andropov to be the new General Secretary. Andropov was 68 years old and suffered from diabetes and kidney disease.

Andropov had been born in the North Caucasus in 1914 to a working-class couple. Over the years he had held many important positions in the Party and in the government. He had been Ambassador to Hungary from 1954 to 1957 and had played an active part in putting down the 1956 revolution in that country. (See page 200.) In 1967 Andropov was chosen to head the KGB, the Soviet secret police. He left the KGB in 1982 for a position in the Communist Party. Several months later he was chosen to be the country's new leader.

Despite his poor health, Andropov moved quickly to consolidate his power. He was determined to weed out the corruption that pervaded Soviet society and to energize the country's stagnating economy. Andropov removed many important but conservative officials and promoted those who shared his insistence on change. But Andropov was essentially a tinkerer, not a reformer. He proposed no overhaul of the Soviet economic or political system. Rather Andropov hoped to make the existing system work more efficiently. He hoped to accomplish this by improving discipline and by eliminating corruption. Andropov attacked absenteeism from work, laziness and irresponsibility on the job, alcoholism, and most of all, corruption. Under Andropov's orders, police stopped people on the street and asked them why they were not at work.

Andropov died in February 1984. During most of his 15 months in power, his poor health had severely limited his capacity to work. It is impossible to say what Andropov would have

## Time of Change

| | |
|---|---|
| 1982 | Death of Brezhnev |
| | Selection of Andropov as General Secretary |
| 1984 | Selection of Chernenko as General Secretary |
| 1985 | Selection of Gorbachev as General Secretary |
| 1987 | Enterprise and Cooperative laws passed |
| | Intermediate-Range Nuclear Forces Treaty |
| 1988 | One thousandth anniversary of Russia's conversion to Christianity |
| | Position of president created and Gorbachev assumes post |
| 1989 | Pullout of Soviet troops from Afghanistan |
| | Opposition candidates allowed to campaign |

done had he been in better health or lived longer. During his brief tenure, he did not try to make any fundamental changes in the Soviet system. He left in place economic centralization and planning. In addition Andropov did not try to reform the agricultural system. Only when contrasted with Brezhnev during the latter's last years did Andropov appear to be a vigorous leader.

### Chernenko's Brief Rule

Constantin Chernenko was chosen to be the General Secretary of the Communist Party in February 1984. Apparently there had been a power struggle between the conservative "old guard" led by Chernenko and the reformist forces led by Mikhail Gorbachev.

At 72, Chernenko was the oldest person ever chosen to lead the Soviet Union. He had been born in the Krasnoyarsk region of Siberia in 1911, the son of a peasant family. His career in the Party spanned 50 years. Chernenko was very much a conservative. He believed that all the Soviet Union's problems could be resolved by Marxist-Leninist teachings and Party discipline.

Chernenko died in March 1985 after only 13 months in office. During much of that time he had been too ill to work. His brief tenure had been a holding action—a return of sorts to

Brezhnev's final year. Chernenko did not undo Andropov's reforms, but he proceeded much more slowly and cautiously.

## The Selection of Gorbachev

When Chernenko died, Mikhail Gorbachev was chosen as the new General Secretary. At 54, he was the youngest person to head the Soviet Union since Joseph Stalin. Gorbachev was born in 1931 in the Stavropol region of the Russian Republic. His parents were peasants. Gorbachev attended the prestigious Moscow State University where he studied law. After holding a series of positions in Stavropol's city and Party organizations, Gorbachev was elected to the Central Committee in 1978, where he was an ally of Andropov.

As General Secretary, Gorbachev moved quickly to strengthen his power. Many conservatives lost their positions. They were retired, transferred, or sometimes simply dismissed. People more supportive of his reformist policies were then brought in as replacements.

From the start Gorbachev built a national and international reputation for enormous self-confidence, energy, and knowledge of matters of state. Compared with previous Soviet leaders, he spoke with a remarkable degree of frankness about his country's shortcomings and in turn offered bold solutions. Most of all Gorbachev proclaimed that the Soviet economy would have to be reformed.

## The Soviet Economy

In the 1980's the USSR faced an economic crisis of enormous complexity. The Soviet economy was simply not working. From the mid-1970's on economic growth had been small and painfully slow. Even production in heavy industry had begun to level off. The Soviet work force suffered from low morale and little discipline. Alcoholism, loafing, and absenteeism were widespread. In most industries, the Soviet Union was falling even further behind Western technology. Agriculture continued to be the most troubled sector of the Soviet economy. Except in Moscow, which received favored treatment, many food products were frequently rationed.

Many Soviet leaders of the 1970's had understood the need for economic change, but only under Gorbachev did the call for reform take on an air of urgency. In part, the times made the leader. Conditions had become so serious that the need for immediate action was hard to ignore. Furthermore delay was no longer possible. The danger was not that a dissatisfied citizenry would overthrow Party rule, but that the USSR would not long remain a superpower. In its present condition, the economy could not continue to support a powerful military force and the country's far-flung international commitments.

## Perestroika

Gorbachev's initial campaign to revitalize the Soviet economy sought to impose greater discipline on the Soviet work force. He angrily criticized drunkenness, a chronic problem in Russia; absenteeism; waste; and corruption. All too often, he argued, Soviet factories turned out shoddy merchandise that no one wanted. Gorbachev directed quality-control inspectors to start rejecting such products.

Gorbachev's economic reform program quickly widened in scope. He soon announced that poor discipline in the workplace was largely a symptom of a broader problem. The Soviet economy needed to be restructured.

Economic reform became Gorbachev's dominant concern. He used the Russian word **perestroika** (payr-uh-STROY-kuh), meaning "restructuring" to describe his program. By the late 1980's little had actually been accomplished. No one, not even Gorbachev, knew exactly where reform was headed, but the general outline of his thinking was clear.

Gorbachev's goal was to increase the productivity of the Soviet economy and to improve the quality of goods, especially in the consumer sector. To accomplish this goal, Gorbachev hoped to decentralize Soviet industry and agriculture. No longer would the bureaucracy make all the important decisions about what and how much to produce. In addition, everyone's pay would be tied to work performance. According to Gorbachev, perestroika held out the promise of a more active and healthier economy and a higher standard of living for those who worked hard.

## Industrial Reform

Gorbachev's first changes were in industry rather than in agriculture. The Enterprise Law of 1987 sought to free factories from government control. Factory managers were to be given a greater role in determining what and how much their enterprises produced. No longer were the managers' functions merely to follow a government production plan. In addition managers were to be given greater control over profits. On the other hand, the factory was now expected to be economically self-sufficient. The government would no longer provide **subsidies** if the factory was not profitable. Instead such factories would be allowed to go bankrupt, and managers and workers alike would have to find other jobs.

Very little actually changed when the Enterprise Law went into effect. Government officials were unwilling to surrender their control over factories and other businesses. Nor were many enterprises allowed to fail. The Communists pride themselves on providing a job for all who want one. Letting factories go bankrupt would result in unemployment—something the Soviets were not yet willing to tolerate.

Many Soviet officials had high hopes for another of Gorbachev's reforms, the 1987 Law on Cooperatives. Under this law and subsequent legislation, citizens were allowed to set up their own private businesses. These cooperatives would be free of state control and could keep any profits they made. In practice, little was achieved. Those who tried to start their own businesses met with enormous resistance. Many government agencies, the laws notwithstanding, refused to grant permission to would-be **entrepreneurs**. Moreover, since the rest of the economy is state-owned and controlled, it was usually quite difficult for individual owners to obtain the needed raw materials or components.

The general public was very hostile to these private enterprises. Most people were furious when cooperative owners made a profit. It made no difference to these people that cooperative owners might have been providing needed products or services or that they might have worked very hard for their money. The Communists are now learning, much to their regret, how successful they have been in teaching the people socialist values. Most Soviet people believe that everyone should receive approximately the same amount of money no matter what they do or how hard they work.

### Agricultural Reform

Gorbachev's first efforts to restructure the Soviet economy were limited to the industrial sector. In agriculture he did little more than reorganize the bureaucracy. These changes caused only chaos and confusion and did nothing to increase productivity. Indeed a cynical Soviet joke proposed that the American Central Intelligence Agency must have been in charge of Gorbachev's agricultural policy. No well-meaning Soviet could have created such a mess!

Mikhail Gorbachev speaks to the 19th All-Union Communist Party Conference in the summer of 1988. Over 5,000 delegates met to discuss their country's future, and Gorbachev came away with almost everything he asked for, including the new title of President of the Soviet Union. This position marks an overhaul of the top-level of power in an effort to loosen the reins of conservative old-line Party bureaucrats.

By 1988 Gorbachev concluded that he had made a mistake in not dealing with agriculture sooner. Had he done so, and assuming that his reforms had been successful, farm productivity would have risen. More food on the table would have demonstrated to the Soviet people that perestroika could bring them tangible benefits. As it was, the availability of food had actually declined in the late 1980's.

In late 1988 Gorbachev announced his intention to pursue fundamental agricultural reform. He proposed that the large state farms and collectives be largely dismantled. In their place Gorbachev intended to establish a private leasehold system. Individual farmers would obtain long-term leases, perhaps for 50

**246**

years, on the land. The profits on agricultural sales would be theirs to keep.

Gorbachev's program represented the most far-reaching change in Soviet agriculture since Stalin's collectivization drive began in 1929. The results remain to be seen. There will likely be continued resistance to the new policy. Less ambitious farmers will not want to give up their secure salaries and undemanding jobs. Farm managers and agricultural bureaucrats will not happily surrender their powerful positions.

## The Social Implications of Perestroika

An unofficial understanding has existed in the Soviet Union for decades. The government has provided the people with economic security and undemanding work. Few Soviets have had to worry about being fired or being unable to afford food and rent. Both are heavily subsidized by the state. In return the people have accepted, although with some grumbling, a relatively low standard of living.

Gorbachev is trying to alter the relationship between the people and the state. He is urging them to work harder and is threatening to penalize them if they do not. If a factory is not profitable, for example, the workers might not receive their bonuses. On the other hand, Gorbachev has promised the people greater rewards if they become more productive. Unfortunately many Soviets seem to prefer the old relationship: little pay, little work, but a lot of security.

The Soviet people are becoming increasingly frustrated with perestroika. Gorbachev has insisted that they work harder but, in return, he has promised them a higher standard of living. He has raised their expectations but failed to deliver on his part of the bargain. Consumer goods are as scarce as ever.

Gorbachev is caught in a vicious circle. Even if perestroika works, it will take years before the average Soviet citizen actually sees results. The problem is that the people will not cooperate with perestroika until there are more consumer goods available, and this will not happen until they cooperate with perestroika.

## Glasnost

Shortly after coming to power, Gorbachev began to urge what he called **glasnost,** a greater openness and candor about Soviet life. In part the Soviet leader was probably trying to remove the veil of secrecy and suspicion that has pervaded Soviet life since the days of Stalin's purges. More important, however, glasnost

**DOMESTIC CHANGES.** Under Gorbachev's direction, the Supreme Soviet voted in 1988 to remove aging President Andrei Gromyko and replace him with Gorbachev (above, right). A devastating earthquake in Armenia in 1988 brought Gorbachev back from a trip to the United States to oversee rescue efforts (above, left). A Soviet edition of a German fashion magazine appeared for the first time in 1987 (below, right). American companies have been invited to do business in the Soviet Union. A pizza company took up the offer and set up shop in Red Square when President Reagan made his historic trip to the Soviet Union (below, left).

was an attempt to enlist the support of the Soviet people behind perestroika. Ironically the economy has not improved, but the Soviet Union has become a much more open society.

At first glasnost merely meant the right to criticize publicly abuses with which everyone was familiar—corruption, incompetence in government and business, and police brutality. Over time the scope of glasnost widened. Today the Soviet people have the opportunity to discuss and write about controversial ideas and previously forbidden topics. The Soviets are now admitting to problems they used to deny existed or claimed were isolated incidents. Soviet newspapers and television programs now have regular reports on such topics as drug addiction, homelessness, inflation, unemployment, and organized crime.

Previously banned books such as Boris Pasternak's *Dr. Zhivago* have appeared in Soviet literary journals. Filmmakers and theater directors have far greater latitude over what they can produce. Historians now deal with embarrassing topics that were once glossed over or totally ignored, such as the Stalin purges or the Berlin Wall. At the end of the school year in 1988 final examinations in history were suspended for graduating high school students. School authorities explained that the history textbooks simply contained too many errors and omissions.

For all the new-found freedom in the Soviet Union, glasnost should not be confused with the American ideas of freedom of speech and freedom of the press. Although there is far less censorship than there once was, it still exists. The Soviet people are still fed slanted reports about the outside world. The Party remains the ultimate judge of what is permissible and what is not. Gorbachev has emphasized that any criticism must be constructive. "It may not undermine socialism," he insists, and in fact it must support the socialist cause.

In addition to glasnost, the scope of personal liberty expanded in a number of ways. Most, although certainly not all, political prisoners were released. The government apparently clamped down on the use of psychiatric hospitals as a way to isolate political prisoners. Emigration and foreign travel became easier. The biggest change is that people are now less fearful of the authorities. Nowhere was this more apparent than in the ethnic demonstrations and disturbances that shook the Soviet Union beginning in 1987.

## The Nationalities Problem

Gorbachev has called the Soviet nationalities problem "a crucially important, vital question of our society." During the late

In 1988 Boris Yeltsin, an opponent of special privileges and critic of perestroika, was ousted from his position as Moscow Communist Party boss and candidate member of the Politburo. In 1989, in the first elections ever in the Soviet Union, he was sent to the Congress of People's Deputies by 89 percent of the voters in his district. Yeltsin's criticisms of the superb Soviet space effort, on the grounds that it diverted resources needed to improve the living standards of ordinary citizens, proved very popular with Moscow voters.

1980's there was widespread ethnic unrest in the Soviet Union. In Lithuania, Latvia, and Estonia large-scale demonstrations demanded greater local autonomy. Ukrainians complained angrily about the second-class status of their language. They insisted that Ukrainian be established as the official language of the Ukraine. In the Caucasus, Armenians and Azerbaijanis clashed in a bitter territorial dispute. In Georgia, the army was used to break up large-scale demonstrations.

Ethnic dissatisfaction had been on the rise during the Brezhnev years, but his regime had kept unrest in check through coercion. The dramatic upsurge of ethnic sentiment and violence was a by-product of Gorbachev's attempt to re-fashion the Soviet economy and society. Many ethnic groups used their new-found freedom to express their nationalism.

Ethnic unrest complicates Gorbachev's economic and political reform program and, in the end, could undermine it. The Soviet Union is a multi-ethnic society. For the country to remain a unified whole, limits must be placed on nationalist demands. But where should Gorbachev draw the line? If he cracks down, he undermines glasnost. If he gives in, he may encourage the ethnic minorities to escalate their demands.

## Church and State

In 1988 the Soviet Union celebrated the one thousandth anniversary of Russia's conversion to Christianity. Unlike previous Soviet leaders, Gorbachev lifted many of the restrictions on the Russian Orthodox Church. This was probably done in an attempt to obtain the support of Church followers for his economic and political programs.

Gorbachev's new church policy was a silent admission of communism's failure to wipe out religious belief. Karl Marx had called religion "the opiate of the masses"—a drug that made them willing to accept exploitation by the capitalists. Beginning with Lenin, Soviet leaders demanded total loyalty to the state and moved against the Russian Orthodox Church and religion in general. Stalin murdered thousands of clergy and closed most of the nation's churches. Although Khrushchev and Brezhnev were less brutal than Stalin, they shut down most of the remaining churches. While Gorbachev has not encouraged religion, he has allowed churches to reopen and made it easier for people to obtain religious materials and books.

## Restructuring of Power

During 1988 and 1989, Gorbachev moved to bolster his personal power while expanding the people's role in the political process. In the summer of 1988, a Party conference endorsed his proposals for a reorganization of the political system. Party control over the government was to be reduced. A popularly elected legislature, the Congress of the People's Deputies, and a new post of president to replace the current ceremonial position were to be created. The new president would have extensive authority over domestic and foreign policy. Gorbachev also announced that members of the new legislature would be chosen on the basis of competitive elections and secret balloting.

In the March 1989 elections, independent candidates challenged the official nominees of the Party in many districts. Many of these non-party candidates favored further "democratization" and more rapid change. They campaigned against the lethargy and conservatism of the Party. When the votes were counted, the Party had won a solid majority, but many independent candidates had also been elected. To the embarrassment of the

## Anti-Semitism

The legacy of anti-Semitism, transmitted from generation to generation under the Romanov czars, persisted under communism. Obstacles were placed in the way of Jews who hoped for careers in the armed forces, the professions, government service, and science. In countless ways the Jewish people were discouraged from preserving their traditional culture and religious beliefs. Only a few newspapers in either Yiddish or Hebrew were permitted. Most synagogues were closed, and the government made it difficult to observe holy days, such as Passover. On one issue, however, the Soviet government became more flexible during the Brezhnev regime. Thousands of Jews were permitted to leave the Soviet Union.

Under Gorbachev opportunities are still denied to Jews, but they can practice their religion without fear. However, emigration has become extremely difficult. The twists and turns of Soviet policy can be illustrated by the experiences of Anatoly and Avital Sharansky.

During the 1970's Anatoly Sharansky had been a spokesman for Jewish refuseniks and human rights activists. The day after Sharansky married in 1974, his wife emigrated to Israel. He had expected to follow her but was denied permission to emigrate. On the basis of trumped-up charges, Anatoly was tried and convicted in 1978 of spying for the United States. He was sentenced to 13 years in prison at hard labor.

Avital spent several years traveling to Western capitals to plead with government leaders to intercede on her husband's behalf. The Western press took up the Sharanskys' cause, and the couple soon became a symbol of Soviet repression. It was not until 1986 that the Soviet government agreed to swap Sharansky for Soviet spies held by the United States.

The couple now lives in Israel and continues to speak out against Soviet anti-Semitism and human rights violations. Many people in the West, the couple argues, have been far too impressed with the changes in the Soviet Union under Gorbachev. There are still more than 400,000 Soviet Jews who would like to leave the Soviet Union.

Party, voters had rejected several prominent Party officials. When the Congress met in June of 1989, it elected a smaller body, the Supreme Soviet, to handle day-to-day legislative business. The Congress also elected Gorbachev to the new post of president.

What were Gorbachev's motives for these changes? The Soviet leader probably believed that opening up the political process was a way to enlist popular support for his economic and social programs. Once again, a Russian leader was trying to engineer far-reaching societal changes. It remains to be seen whether autocratic power, perestroika, glasnost, and democratization can be compatible with one another.

## Check Your Understanding

1. What actions did each of the following take during his short term in office: **a.** Andropov? **b.** Chernenko?
2. What were the goals of perestroika?
3. What were the obstacles to enforcing the Enterprise and Cooperative laws?
4. What was Gorbachev's plan for agricultural change?
5. Why is perestroika unpopular with the Soviet people?
6. How did Gorbachev's idea of glasnost widen?
7. What is the dilemma that the nationalities problem presents to Gorbachev?
8. *Thinking Critically:* Stalin once said that "you cannot make a revolution with silk gloves." What do you think this means? Is Gorbachev trying to do this? Why might he not succeed?

## 2. Soviet Foreign Policy

Under Andropov and Chernenko, Soviet foreign policy drifted. No important initiatives or shifts in direction occurred during their brief regimes. It was as if the policies of the past continued under their own momentum. Soviet forces remained bogged down in a guerrilla war in Afghanistan and in Poland unrest seethed below the surface. Relations with the United States became even more strained.

Once in power Gorbachev engaged in a worldwide peace offensive. He sought to reduce tensions between his country and the Western democracies. In keeping with that policy, Gorbachev vigorously pursued arms control agreements with the United States and the NATO powers. Meanwhile he withdrew Soviet forces from Afghanistan.

## Reasons for Gorbachev's Shift

At the root of the Soviet foreign policy shift is economic necessity. Military expenses have become a severe drain on Soviet resources. In the United States between 6 and 7 percent of **gross national product** is devoted to national defense. Although comparable figures for the Soviet Union are not available, Western experts estimate Soviet military expenditures at about 16 percent of gross national product. Gorbachev wanted to be able to divert some of these resources into economic revitalization.

To modernize its economy, the Soviet Union needs loans and advanced technology from the West. The Soviets would also like to expand trade between their nation and the non-Communist world, but East-West economic relations cannot improve significantly in a cold war atmosphere. Gorbachev hoped that smoother and more peaceful international relations would pave the way for expanded economic ties between his country and the West.

## Improved Soviet-American Relations

Unlike his predecessors, Gorbachev has a warm and friendly personal style. In his public statements he has repeatedly stressed that his country does not have hostile intentions toward other nations. Indeed, most of the Soviet leadership has changed the way it talks about the capitalist world. In the past Soviet leaders routinely described the United States and its Western allies as imperialistic, exploitative, and militarily aggressive. Under Gorbachev, public pronouncements have become much softer. The new Soviet posture may or may not be genuine, but it has certainly convinced many people in the United States and Western Europe.

Gorbachev has backed up his public relations campaign with a number of arms control proposals. More so than previous Soviet leaders, he stressed that a nuclear war is not winnable. Military might, therefore, cannot alone guarantee Soviet national security. Both the USSR and the United States, he argued, would have to agree to arms controls. To reach such agreements, the Soviet Union would have to recognize that the United States and its allies have legitimate strategic interests.

Gorbachev and President Ronald Reagan of the United States met several times to discuss nuclear arms control issues. In late

1987, the two countries agreed to an INF (intermediate-range nuclear forces) treaty. According to this agreement, two classes of nuclear weapons—intermediate-range and shorter-range nuclear missiles—were to be eliminated. The treaty represented an important step towards the reduction of the nuclear arms race. In the past the two powers had been able to reach agreement only on arms limitations. Now, for the first time, the two sides had agreed actually to destroy a part of their nuclear arsenals. Unfortunately, the Soviet Union and the United States were not successful in reaching other arms control agreements, but both sides appear committed to continuing negotiations.

## Afghanistan

Shortly after coming to power, Gorbachev made clear his intention to end the war in Afghanistan, a "bleeding wound" as he called it. More than 100,000 Soviet troops were stationed in Afghanistan. Since fighting began in 1979, several thousand Soviet soldiers had died, and victory still seemed nowhere in sight. American military assistance had enabled the Afghan fighters to take their toll on Soviet forces.

The Afghan invasion seemed to contradict Gorbachev's claims that the Soviet Union was a peace-loving nation. The war was a tragic experience for the Afghan people. Soviet military methods had been particularly brutal and included chemical warfare and the laying of millions of mines, some of them disguised as children's toys. In 1978 the population had been about 15.5 million. By the mid-1980's Afghanistan had become a depopulated country. Hundreds of thousands of people had perished in the war, and about six million Afghans had fled the country.

The Soviet dilemma was how to get out of Afghanistan without appearing weak. Gorbachev and his colleagues had to consider how the Eastern bloc nations would interpret a Soviet withdrawal. Perhaps these nations would conclude that the Soviet Union lacked the determination to maintain its control over them. Then, too, it seemed likely that the Communist regime in Afghanistan would fall without continued Soviet support. However, the war could not go on indefinitely.

In April 1988 the Soviet Union and the United States signed the Geneva Accords, in which the Soviet Union pledged to remove all its troops from Afghanistan by mid-February 1989. The Soviet troops pulled out on schedule. To the surprise of many observers, the Soviet-installed Afghan government did not immediately collapse.

**FOREIGN POLICY.** Gorbachev took the offensive in foreign affairs as well as at home. Here he and his wife Raisa are pictured in the Kremlin with then President Ronald Reagan and his wife Nancy (below, left). Gorbachev also took his message of perestroika to Eastern Europe where he talked with ordinary citizens as well as heads of government. These are Rumanian students (below, right). In 1989, Gorbachev withdrew the last of his forces from Afghanistan (above), ending Russia's involvement in the disastrous eight-year war.

## Unrest in Eastern Europe

Since the end of World War II, Eastern Europe has served as a buffer zone for the Soviet Union, and Moscow is determined to maintain its control over the region. During the late 1980's several Eastern European countries were hit by economic and political unrest. These disturbances were particularly severe in Poland, which experienced a wave of strikes. Although grievances varied somewhat from country to country, Eastern Europeans generally were demanding an improved standard of living and greater political freedom. Poles, Czechs, East Germans, and Hungarians alike were irate over their country's dismal economic performance. Gorbachev had inadvertently contributed to the unrest through his calls for glasnost and perestroika throughout the Communist bloc.

Gorbachev and his colleagues in the Kremlin face another dilemma. If the Eastern European economies are not reformed, continuing poor economic conditions may generate more serious opposition. Yet there is also the danger that reforms will go too far and that the USSR will feel compelled to intervene, either through intimidation or the actual use of military force. Intervention of any kind would threaten reform in the Soviet Union, and perhaps even Gorbachev's position.

## Mixed Results in East Asia

In a speech given at Vladivostok in 1986, Gorbachev announced his determination to improve Soviet relations with the countries of Asia, particularly China and Japan. Sino-Soviet tensions had long been a drain on Soviet military resources. The Soviet Union wanted to expand commercial ties with Japan and perhaps with other countries in East Asia, such as South Korea.

Soviet relations with China had improved slightly during the five or six years before Gorbachev came to power. Apparently leaders in both countries had concluded that they had little to gain from continued hostility towards one another. Chinese leaders maintained that there were three obstacles to improved relations with the Soviet Union. First, Soviet forces had to leave Afghanistan. From the Chinese point of view, the invasion of Afghanistan was part of a Soviet attempt to extend Soviet influence throughout Asia. Second, the Chinese insisted that the Soviets pressure their ally, Vietnam, into withdrawing its forces from neighboring Cambodia. From the Chinese perspective, Vietnam was a stand-in for the Soviet Union. Vietnam's invasion of Cambodia thus represented a Soviet attempt to expand its influence in Asia. Finally, the Chinese demanded that the Soviets decrease their military forces along the Sino-Soviet border.

Under Gorbachev some progress had been made towards reducing Sino-Soviet tensions. The Soviets pulled out of Afghanistan, although not to please the Chinese, and were apparently urging Vietnam to withdraw from Cambodia. Meanwhile trade between the Soviet Union and China was increasing. The Soviets also agreed to modernize some of the factories they had built for China in the early 1950's. In 1989 Gorbachev and Deng Xiaoping, the Chinese head of government, met to discuss their differences.

Although relations will probably continue to improve, it is unlikely that China and the USSR will once again become close allies as they were in the 1950's. China has been working hard to modernize its economy and desperately needs advanced technology. Only the Western democracies can supply this. Certainly the USSR cannot. Furthermore a history of mutual antagonism going back hundreds of years exists between China and the Soviet Union. Time and effort may dim the memory of past suspicions, but slowly at best.

## Check Your Understanding

1. What two reasons are behind Gorbachev's shift in the direction of Soviet foreign policy?
2. What is the importance of the INF treaty?
3. What dilemma did the Afghan war present to Gorbachev?
4. What choices did Gorbachev face in dealing with unrest in Eastern Europe?
5. What three obstacles need to be removed to improve relations between the Soviet Union and China?
6. **Thinking Critically:** The author states that because of hundreds of years of antagonism the bad feeling between China and the Soviet Union may fade slowly at best. In the 1950's the two were strong allies. What occurred to make them allies? Do you think that the break that occurred in the 1960's was more typical of the history of the relations between the two nations? Why are there bad relations between the two?

# 3. Education and Science

In Gorbachev's efforts to restructure the Soviet economy, he has the advantage of an educated population. From the first, Soviet leaders stressed the importance of education and science. Lenin and his successors believed that their "dream" society of the future could not be achieved unless they could transform and uplift the minds and behavior of the Soviet people. They had no illusions about the magnitude of their task. In czarist Russia learning had been a monopoly of the upper classes. At the time of the Bolshevik Revolution the great mass of people, particularly in the rural areas, were illiterate and superstitious. Over the decades Soviet leaders have given high priority to education, and a unique educational system has emerged.

## The Educational System

The Soviet government has made a great effort to wipe out illiteracy. According to the Soviet Constitution, every citizen has the right to a free education. In 1914 perhaps half of the country's children were in primary schools. Today virtually all Soviet children go to school. In part the government's stress on education reflected a determination to eliminate the glaring gaps in privilege that had always existed in Russia. Soviet leaders understood that legal equality alone did not mean equal opportunity. To take advantage of opportunity, an individual had to have good reading, writing, and mathematical skills. The government also recognized that the people had to master a great variety of technological skills if they were going to build a model, modern society.

Although schooling is free, the quality of education in rural areas lags behind that in the cities. Children begin their education in state-operated nursery schools and kindergartens, which they attend for several years. These schools are needed because usually both parents work all day. Children begin their formal education at the age of 7 and end it at age 17. They go either to an 8-year school and then to a technical school or attend a 10-year school. Students in the Soviet Union have a longer school day and school year than is customary in the United States. Whereas American students are in school an average of 180 days, Soviet students attend about 230 days. In addition, Soviet programs of study are more strenuous than those of American schools. Easy courses are rare, and homework assignments are generally heavy. Concentrated study of mathematics, science, and foreign languages is started earlier than in the

United States. Education is the main route to success in life, and as a result, many students study very hard.

Most Soviet students, particularly those who are not academically inclined, do not continue formal schooling beyond the eighth grade. Many of these youngsters enter technical or trade schools. The better students who are in a ten-year school have a two-year college preparatory course in grades nine and ten. A talented student or one with "influence" may hope to enter one of the country's universities or institutes, but there are far more applicants than places.

University graduates are in great demand. Those who receive degrees from the better known schools are eagerly sought by the state factories and government organizations, just as large American corporations recruit promising graduates of American universities. In the Soviet Union prospective employers compete fiercely for outstanding graduates. Since it is impossible for most Soviet citizens to get ahead without an education, students who stopped their formal schooling often continue studying on a less formal basis. Evening and correspondence courses are very popular in the Soviet Union.

The Soviet Union like many other modern societies has discovered that the actual results of the educational system often fall short of expectations. Studies are constantly being made to determine why some children have not learned how to read, have become juvenile delinquents or social dropouts, or have not acquired adequate vocational skills. Under the spirit of glasnost some educators have been calling for less rote learning as one cure.

## The Importance of Science

Because Soviet leaders have been determined to modernize their society, they have glorified the value of science. They have counted on it to help them in their efforts to expand the economy, and have relied on the contribution of scientists to strengthen the Soviet military establishment. Soviet scientists have made vital contributions to their country, but these accomplishments have fallen short of the government's expectations.

Soviet science has undoubtedly come a long way since the Bolshevik Revolution. Although scientists had long enjoyed an honored place in czarist Russia, their achievements had scarcely touched the lives of the great mass of people. The Imperial Academy of Science, founded by Peter the Great in 1725, had encouraged many areas of scientific research. It was one of the oldest institutions of its kind in the world and included among its members brilliant mathematicians, chemists, biologists, and geographers. Many of Russia's scientists fled the country during and just after the Revolution. This exodus created a serious scientific gap that took the new Soviet regime years to fill.

In the 1920's and 1930's, the Soviet government hired foreigners to fill many scientific and engineering positions. Meanwhile, the regime began developing facilities for the education and training of Russian scientists and engineers. The old Imperial Academy was reorganized as the Academy of Sciences of the USSR, and ultimately acquired tremendous authority and responsibility. Today it oversees research in literature, language, economics, law, history, and philosophy, as well as science and engineering. The Academy also controls much of the work done in the country's research institutes and laboratories.

## The Direction of Scientific Research

Marxist-Leninism, often referred to as "scientific socialism", has influenced research and teaching in the USSR just as it has shaped political and social developments. This was especially true during Stalin's time. When scientific theories and discoveries seemed to conflict with Stalin's political "truth," they were denounced. The scientists involved were exiled or demoted to unimportant posts. For a long time Einstein's theory of relativity was rejected in the Soviet Union. Similarly, Norbert Wiener's science of cybernetics, on which modern computer-contolled systems are based, was in disfavor in the Soviet Union for years.

Probably the most sensational example of science reshaped to conform to political ideology was the case of the biologist Trofim Lysenko. He insisted that characteristics acquired after birth were genetically passed on to the next generation—a theory rejected by reputable scientists. Lysenko managed to convince Stalin that the theory was correct because it supposedly conformed to Marxist-Leninism. Stalin prohibited research that conflicted with Lysenko's theory and had biology textbooks rewritten to include it. In consequence, Soviet biology was out of step with the rest of the world for many years.

During the Khrushchev era, biologists who rejected Lysenko's views were allowed to resume research in genetics and biology. Then, in 1964, after Khrushchev fell from power, the Academy of Sciences denounced Lysenko and his theories. Since then, Soviet biology has begun to catch up.

As is the case in social and economic matters, the Soviet government has long accepted the value of centralized planning in scientific research. Planning had doubtlessly helped to eliminate duplication of effort. Moreover, Soviet authorities can channel large-scale efforts into a few chosen projects. This means that Soviet science can accomplish enormous feats, for example, in space exploration. But research projects not chosen for special attention remain ignored, and there is only one source for funds and personnel—the State.

Soviet government agencies have been attracted to scientific endeavors that are eye-catching or have military purposes. The end result is a mania for gigantic projects as well as political and bureaucratic interference in scientific research. Centralized direction and control of scientific research has stifled individual initiative and discouraged any experimentation not directly related to officially approved projects. Soviet scientists have achieved most of their greatest successes in scientific areas having military applications. For example, the Soviet Union was able to develop an atomic bomb in only six years.

Since the death of Stalin and the removal of Khrushchev, Communist Party bureaucrats have meddled less and less in scientific affairs. But there still remains much government interference and centralized control. In keeping with Gorbachev's policy of glasnost, a number of Soviet scientists have begun to criticize the scientific establishment and have called for reforms.

### Space Research

In 1957 the USSR became the first country to rocket a satellite into orbit around the earth. Four years later a Soviet cosmonaut, Yuri Gagarin, became the first man to orbit the earth in a space vehicle. In 1963 Valentina Tereshkova became the first woman to fly in space.

Soviet achievements in space exploration far outweigh those of the United States. The Soviets have led the way in lunar exploration. In contrast to the United States, Soviet lunar probes have used only unmanned rockets. By means of instruments landed on the moon by these rockets, Soviet scientists on Earth ingeniously analyzed lunar conditions. The Soviet Union has also landed unmanned spacecrafts on Mars and Venus and has investigated Halley's Comet. The Soviets have placed a space laboratory in orbit around the Earth and have completed manned space flights of long duration.

### The Disaster at Chernobyl

Like many other industrialized nations, the Soviet Union has built a number of nuclear power plants. On April 26, 1986, a nuclear reactor at the Chernobyl power station in Kiev in the

On April 26, 1986 a nuclear reactor at the Chernobyl power plant near Kiev exploded. A large area of the Soviet Union and Europe was showered with radioactive debris. Workers buried the reactor in concrete, but 31 plant workers were killed and over 100,000 people in the immediate area were evacuated. In this photo, a Soviet technician checks one of those evacuated for radiation exposure.

Ukraine exploded. Several days passed before the reactor was brought under control. Meanwhile, radiation spread into the air. Glasnost notwithstanding, the Soviet government was slow to warn its own people and neighboring countries of the danger. When Soviet leaders finally announced the disaster, they were remarkably candid.

Chernobyl was the world's worst nuclear disaster. Soviet scientists subsequently estimated that there would be 40,000 extra cancer deaths among the 75 million people living in the western region of the USSR. American nuclear advocates were quick to argue that a Chernobyl-like catastrophe could never occur in the United States, or in any Western country. Still, the explosion of Chernobyl served to reshape the nuclear power debate in the United States and in many other countries. Understandably there has been growing public resistance in the Soviet Union to the building of nuclear power plants, and plans for several have been canceled.

### Environmental Pollution

In the late 1980's the Soviet government finally awakened to the need to protect the country's environment. Soviet leaders discovered that pollution is not a monopoly of the "capitalist-imperialist" powers. For more than 70 years, the Soviet Union has been preoccupied with promoting industrial growth. Clean air and water were readily sacrificed for greater productivity. In many parts of the Soviet Union, the air, streams, lakes and seas, forests, and the very earth itself have been spoiled. Siberia's Lake Baikal is being polluted by a local factory. Parts of the Caspian Sea are covered by oil slicks. Hazardous wastes have washed ashore at Black Sea beaches. Air pollution in the USSR's industrial centers consistently exceeds the Soviet Union's air quality standards.

In the past, environmental problems were ignored or "swept under the table." Now, however, reports of pollution fill the media. The policy of glasnost has played a major role in encouraging journalists and citizens alike to complain about environmental hazards. But clearly, too, public attitudes are changing. So far there has been mainly talk but little action. It remains to be seen whether providing antipollution measures will get as much attention from the economic planners as meeting production goals.

## Check Your Understanding

1. Why was education so important to early Soviet leaders?
2. Why do Soviet students work so hard?
3. What effect has the use of central planning had on scientific research in the Soviet Union?
4. What is the importance of the disaster at Chernobyl?
5. **Thinking Critically:** Soviet economic planners may not agree to anti-pollution measures. What arguments would you use to try to convince them that pollution is not cost effective?

## CHAPTER REVIEW

■ **Chapter Summary**

**Section 1.** The regimes of Yuri Andropov and Constantin Chernenko were only caretaker governments. The Soviet Union continued to drift in both domestic and foreign affairs as it had in the last years of Brezhnev's rule. When Mikhail Gorbachev came to power in 1985, he began by calling for changes in the way workers behaved and in the shoddy goods they produced. Quickly the scope of his demands widened and he called for a restructuring of the Soviet economy. He called this restructuring perestroika. His goal was to revitalize the economy, increase production, and improve the quality of goods. Perestroika began in the industrial sector, but by 1988 Gorbachev realized that the agricultural sector also needed to be changed.

The Soviet people were unhappy and frustrated by perestroika. Gorbachev promised that their standard of living would improve. When little or nothing happened, they became disillusioned. In an effort to enlist their support for perestroika, Gorbachev proclaimed glasnost, or an openness in society. Today the Soviet Union is a much freer and open society than before Gorbachev.

Because of glasnost the Soviet people can read books, see movies and plays, and hear about events and situations that had previously been banned from the Soviet press, theaters, and television. Censorship still exists but the Soviet people are now aware of problems such as homelessness that the authorities never admitted before. A by-product of glasnost has been a resurgence of ethnic unrest.

In order to further consolidate his position, Gorbachev in 1988 assumed the position of president of the Soviet Union. This new post had extensive authority over domestic and foreign affairs. Gorbachev now had about as much power as Stalin had in 1929.

**Section 2.** In foreign affairs Gorbachev attempted to improve relations with Western nations. This shift in policy resulted from his recognition that the Soviet Union needed some of the money it spent on national defense to improve its economy. It also needed loans and advanced technology from the West. Gorbachev took the initiative and negotiated an INF treaty with the United States, pulled Soviet troops out of Afghanistan, and attempted to smooth relations with China. In Eastern Europe he faced the dilemma of dealing with opposition without undermining perestroika and glasnost.

**Section 3.** The Soviet educational system was seen by early Soviet leaders as a way to close the social and economic gap that existed during czarist times by providing education for every Soviet citizen. In addition education would ensure that the skills would be available for building a modern nation. Virtually all Soviet children go to school, although rural education lags behind that in the cities.

Soviet leaders have used science to support Marxist-Leninist teachings and to promote military and industrial projects. Central planning is used to decide what projects should be supported, and these receive the only research money available. The Soviet Union has scored remarkable achievements in space, putting the first man and later the first woman into space as well as studying various planets by rocket.

After the disaster at Chernobyl, public reaction in the Soviet Union as well as elsewhere resulted in the cancellation of several planned nuclear power plants. Soviet citizenry is also calling for an end to industrial pollution.

■ **Vocabulary to Review**

*Define:* perestroika, subsidy, entrepreneur, glasnost, gross national product

■ **Places to Locate**

*Locate:* Latvia, Lithuania, Estonia, Ukraine, Armenia, Georgia, Chernobyl

■ **People to Know**

*Identify:* Yuri Andropov, Constantin Chernenko, Mikhail Gorbachev, Anatoly Sharansky, Avital Sharansky

■ **Thinking Critically**

1. In reference to Gorbachev's policies, the author states that the "times made the leader." What do you think this means? What conditions in the Soviet Union seemed to make it necessary for Gorbachev to act?
2. The Sharanskys claim that Westerners are too impressed with the changes in the USSR under Gorbachev. Why do you think Westerners are so impressed? Based on your study of Russian history, what elements of Gorbachev's policies impress you the most? Why? What things do not impress you? Why?
3. Many Soviet citizens are disappointed and frustrated at the slowness of perestroika and the uncertainty it introduces into their lives. What is this uncertainty? Are these feelings understandable considering Soviet history? Why or why not? How was glasnost an attempt to win support for perestroika?

## ■ Applying and Extending Your Knowledge

1. Read one of the current biographies of Gorbachev such as Zhores Medvedev's *Gorbachev* and report on his career up to his selection as General Secretary.

2. Raisa Gorbachev is a personality in her own right, unlike the wives of earlier General Secretaries. Do research and prepare a report on the status of women in the Soviet Union today. Report on their educational status, choice of occupations, wages, and legal rights.

3. Prepare a bulletin board display of photographs from current newspapers and magazines showing life in the Soviet Union under Gorbachev. If possible, find photos of life under Brezhnev for comparison and contrast.

# APPENDIX

# BIBLIOGRAPHY

## General Works

Clarkson, Jesse. *A History of Russia (2nd ed.).* Random House, 1969. A comprehensive survey of Russian history from earliest times to Brezhnev era.

Cole, J. P. *Geography of the Soviet Union.* Butterworth, 1984. A survey of major features of Soviet geography.

Dmytryshyn, Basil. *U.S.S.R.: A Concise History (4th ed.).* Macmillan, 1984. A widely used college history text; includes primary source material.

Florinsky, Michael. *Russia, a Short History (2nd ed.).* Macmillan, 1969. A history of Russia from the ninth to the twentieth century, by an expert.

Kochan, Lionel and Richard Abraham. *The Making of Modern Russia (2nd ed.).* St. Martin, 1983. A general history. Particularly good on cultural, social, and economic developments.

Lydolph, Paul. *The Geography of the USSR.* Wiley, 1964. An excellent text for reading and reference.

Paxton, John. *A Companion to Russian History.* Facts on File, 1983. A reference work of about 2,500 entries, describing the basic facts of Russian and Soviet history.

Riasonovsky, Nicholas V. *A History of Russia (4th ed.).* Oxford University Press, 1984. A readable survey of Russian history.

Smith, Hedrick. *The Russians.* Ballantine, 1984. A fascinating account of Soviet society in the early 1980's.

Tolstoy, Leo. *Russian Stories and Legends.* Pantheon, 1967. A collection of Russian tales on the theme of friendship and cooperation.

Van der Post, Laurens. *A Portrait of All the Russias.* Morrow, 1967. Vivid photographs bring to life the varied peoples of the Soviet Union.

Vernadsky, George. *History of Russia (rev. ed.).* Yale University Press, 1961. A scholarly and readable work, long regarded as a standard on Russian history.

Wheeler, Geoffrey. *The Peoples of Soviet Central Asia.* Dufour, 1966. An introduction to the history and culture of the peoples of Central Asia.

## Early Russia   *(Chapters 1–2)*

Benz, Ernst. *The Eastern Orthodox Church.* Doubleday, 1963. An excellent survey of the traditions and beliefs of the Eastern Church.

Fairservis, Walter A. Jr. *Horsemen of the Steppes.* World, 1962. Sketches life on the steppes through famous leaders such as Ghengis Khan and Tamerlane.

Grey, Ian. *Ivan the Terrible.* Lippincott, 1964. An interesting biography, maintaining that Ivan was no more "terrible" than other rulers of his day.

Voyce, Arthur. *Moscow and the Roots of Russian Culture.* University of Oklahoma Press, 1980. The author traces Russian cultural heritage back to the Moscow of Ivan III and Ivan IV, presenting the art, traditions, and life of that period as the basis for later cultural developments.

Zenkovsky, Serge, ed. *Medieval Russia's Epics, Chronicles, and Tales (rev. ed.).* Dutton, 1974. Writings and folktales of the 11th to the 17th century; some translated for the first time.

## Czarist Russia   *(Chapters 3–4)*

Chekhov, Anton. *Four Plays.* Hill & Wang, 1969. Four of the best-known plays of the Russian playwright—"The Sea Gull," "Uncle Vanya," "The Three Sisters," and "The Cherry Orchard."

Gogol, Nicholai. *Dead Souls.* Norton, 1986. Gogol's classic work on the evils of 19th-century serfdom.

Gorky, Maxim. *Childhood.* Beekman, 1975. Originally published in 1913, this story gives a striking picture of life in czarist Russia.

Klyuchevsky, Vasili. *Peter the Great.* Beacon, 1984. The most satisfactory biography of Peter.

Lermontov, Mikhail. *A Hero of Our Time.* Ardis, 1988. A haunting portrait of a disillusioned young noble.

Massie, Robert K. *Nicholas & Alexandra.* Dell, 1985. This popular biography of the last czar and his wife offers an intriguing view of how their personal lives affected Russian history.

Rice, Tamara (Abelson) Talbot. *A Concise History of Russian Art.* Praeger, 1963. A study of Russian art before 1917; many good illustrations.

Seton-Watson, Hugh. *Decline of Imperial Russia, 1855–1914.* Praeger, 1952. A careful analysis of the last years of czarist Russia.

Tolstoy, Leo. *War and Peace.* Norton, 1966. This great classic is a panorama of Russian life during the Napoleonic Wars.

Troyat, Henri. *Catherine the Great.* Dutton, 1980. An entertaining and thoughtful biography of the great empress.

Tupper, Harmon. *To the Great Ocean: Siberia and the Trans–Siberian Railway.* Little, Brown, 1965. This book makes the building of the railroad an adventure as well as a lesson in Russian history and geography.

Turgenev, Ivan. *Fathers and Sons.* Bantam, 1982. The familiar struggle between generations is the theme of this powerful novel.

## The Soviet Union   *(Chapters 5–8)*

Bialer, Seweryn. *The Soviet Paradox: External Expansion, & Internal Decline.* Knopf, 1986. The author argues that the Soviet Union of the 1980's has entered a period of economic decline while maintaining enormous influence abroad.

Conquest, Robert. *The Harvest of Sorrow: Soviet Collectivization and the Terror–Famine.* Oxford University Press, 1986. Describes Stalin's forced collectivization of agriculture and his deliberate creation of a famine.

Fischer, Louis. *The Life of Lenin.* Harper, 1964. A noted biography of the central figure in the Bolshevik Revolution.

Gelb, Norman. *The Berlin Wall: Kennedy, Khrushchev, and a Showdown in the Heart of Europe.* Times Books, 1987. A well-written history of the Berlin Wall and the conflict it created between East and West.

Goldman, Marshall I. *Gorbachev's Challenge: Economic Reform in the Age of High Technology.* Norton, 1987. A penetrating study of the economic dilemmas facing Gorbachev.

Kuznetsov, Anatoly. *Babi Yar.* Washington Square Press, 1982. The author recalls his youth during the German occupation of Kiev in World War II.

Mandelstam, Nadezhda. *Hope Against Hope: A Memoir.* Atheneum, 1976. Recollections of the life, work, and thought of a gifted Soviet poet by his widow.

Marples, David R. *Chernobyl and Nuclear Power in the U.S.S.R.* St. Martin's Press, 1986. An account of the Chernobyl nuclear plant accident and its aftermath.

Medvedev, Zhores A. *Gorbachev.* Norton, 1986. A biography of Gorbachev by a Soviet dissident.

Pasternak, Boris. *Doctor Zhivago.* Ballantine, 1981. The epic novel of the Revolution, which earned Pasternak the Nobel Prize.

Payne, Robert. *The Rise and Fall of Stalin.* Simon and Schuster, 1965. A sound biography of the Soviet leader.

Rueschemeyer, Marilyn, Igor Golomshtok, and Janet Kennedy. *Soviet Emigré Artist: Life and Work in the U.S.S.R. and the United States.* M. E. Sharp, 1985. A look at Soviet artists and their work.

Rybakov, Anatoly Naumovich. *Children of the Arbat.* Little, Brown, 1988. A moving autobiographical novel of Soviet life during Stalin's purges.

Schroeter, Leonard. *The Last Exodus (rev. ed.).* University of Washington Press, 1979. A study of Jewish self-awareness and emigration.

Sholokhov, Mikhail. *The Silent Don.* Knopf, 1959. A novel of the Cossacks of the Don River; won a Nobel Prize.

Solzhenitsyn, Alexandor. *One Day in the Life of Ivan Denisovich.* Bantam Books, 1984. A sensitive story of life in a slave-labor camp during the Stalinist era.

Treadgold, Donald W. *Twentieth Century Russia (6th ed.).* Westview Press, 1987. A fact-filled history of the Soviet Union in this century.

Walesa, Lech. *A Way of Hope: An Autobiography.* Henry Holt, 1987. An autobiography of the leader of Poland's Solidarity movement.

Willis, David K. *Klass: How Russians Really Live.* Avon, 1987. Describes the pervasive inequality in the Soviet Union.

Yevtushenko, Yevgeny. *Yevtushenko: Selected Poems.* Penguin, 1967. Poems by one of Russia's foremost poets.

# GLOSSARY

This Glossary contains definitions for the social studies terms used in this volume about Russian history. These terms are printed in bold type the first time they appear in the text. The page number following each definition tells you the page on which the word is first used. Often words have more than one meaning. The definitions given below are the ones that will be most helpful to you in reading this book.

**absolutism**  form of government under which the ruler has un-limited power (112)

**alliance**  association among nations based upon mutual pur-pose, interest, or advantage (48)

**anarchy**  absence of government (59)

**annexation**  process of adding territory to an existing country (76)

**appanage**  land given by the czar to a member of a ruling family as a source of income (52)

**appeasement**  policy of giving in to demands to maintain peace (165)

**aristocracy**  privileged upper class (39)

**arms race**  competition among nations to develop more and bet-ter weapons (231)

**autocracy**  form of government headed by a ruler with absolute power (1)

**autonomy**  self-government or self-rule (26)

**bloc**  group united for a common purpose or action (185)

**Bolshevik**  member of the Communist group that overthrew the existing government during the Russian Revolution (116)

**bourgeois**  from the French word for "town dweller"; term that has come to mean middle class (141)

**boyar**  member of the Russian aristocracy; a landowner (39)

**buffer**  region or territory located between unfriendly powers that acts as a deterrent to war (14)

**bureaucracy**  system of government administration by bureaus or departments (74)

**capital**  resources used to produce goods and services (111)

**capitalism** economic system in which businesses are privately owned and in which there is open competition in a free market (139)

**censorship** policy of stopping publication and distribution of literature, art, or any creative material found objectionable by the government or other authorities (97)

**central planning** process by which the government sets economic goals and oversees their implementation (156)

**coalition** union that is convenient and often temporary between parties with a common interest or goal (86)

**cold war** non-military political, economic, and diplomatic conflicts between Communist and non-Communist countries in the post-World War II era (184)

**collective farm** land organized as a unit under government supervision and cultivated by using the resources of a number of farms (113)

**Comintern** Bolshevik organization designed to promote international Communist revolution (162)

**commune** community of households who own property jointly and whose affairs are supervised by an assembly of household representatives (109)

**communism** system of government in which the state owns all land and controls production of goods and services; one political party maintains power, with the goal of distributing all goods equally to the people (22)

**conservative** person who prefers the existing social and political order (78)

**constitutional government** government guided in its basic operation by either a written or an unwritten constitution (125)

**consumer goods** materials such as food and clothing purchased by people for their own use (158)

**containment** post-World War II policy adopted by the United States under President Truman that was designed to limit the spread of communism beyond those countries where it already existed (185)

**coup** sudden overthrow of a government (70)

**cultural diffusion** spread of cultural characteristics from one group to another (33)

**culture** all the tools and objects people make and use, their language, religious beliefs, customs, traditions, foods, clothes, and activities (21)

**czar** emperor of Russia; considered the successor to the Byzantine emperors (54)

**275**

**democratic centralism**  underlying principle of Communist Party policy in which all major issues must be discussed at all levels of the party before final decisions are reached; in practice, decisions are made by the Politburo  (197)

**democratization**  loosening of political controls  (8)

**détente**  relaxing of tensions among nations  (218)

**dictator**  ruler exercising absolute authority over the government  (151)

**dissident**  Soviet opponent of the government's policies  (209)

**Duma**  parliament established under the October Manifesto of Czar Nicholas II in 1905  (94)

**dynasty**  line of families that transfers its right to rule by inheritance  (59)

**emancipation**  liberation  (109)

**entrepreneur**  person who starts up and operates his or her own business  (245)

**ethnic group**  group of people sharing a common culture and often a common geographical location  (21)

**Ex Com**  Executive Committee of the Petrograd Soviet  (138)

**fascism**  system of government in which the state is supreme and under which a dictator exercises total social, political, and economic control through a single political party  (164)

**federation**  league or association of states  (39)

**free enterprise**  economic system in which individuals choose and operate businesses and sell goods and services with a minimum of government involvement  (159)

*glasnost*  Soviet policy of "openness" instituted under the administration of Mikhail Gorbachev  (247)

**gross national product**  total value of goods and services produced in a country  (254)

**heavy industry**  manufacture of steel, machines, transportation equipment and the machinery to make these goods  (156)

**human rights**  basic freedoms that every person is entitled to  (216)

**icon**  religious representation of a Christian personage, such as a saint; considered sacred  (45)

**imperialism**  policy by which a nation extends its control over other lands to gain an economic or political advantage  (116)

**indemnity**  compensation for damages suffered by a nation during war  (78)

**industrialization**  movement of an economy away from agriculture and trade and toward industry and technological advancement  (16)

**inflation**  rising prices caused by a scarcity of goods and an abundance of money and credit  (155)

**intellectual**  person who values knowledge, the arts, and rational thought  (97)

**kulak**  prosperous Russian peasant  (159)

**liberal**  supporter of moderate political change and social and economic reform  (95)

**light industry**  manufacture of food, textiles, and other goods that do not require large machines  (156)

**Menshevik**  faction of the Social Democratic party opposed to the Bolsheviks  (116)

**moderate**  person opposed to extreme views in politics  (113)

**national identity**  sense of unity of a people who share the same land, language, and culture  (33)

**nationalism**  devotion to and pride in one's country  (99)

**neutral**  not supporting or assisting either side in a war or dispute  (122)

**oral tradition**  cultural heritage (stories, folktales, poetry, songs) passed from one generation to the next by word of mouth  (37)

**peaceful coexistence**  Soviet policy of cooperation with Western democracies whenever such action furthers Soviet national interests  (218)

**perestroika**  Soviet attempts under the administration of Mikhail Gorbachev to reform internal economic systems  (244)

**permafrost**  layer of permanently frozen ground hundreds of feet thick  (11)

**Politburo**  chief political committee of the Communist Party of the Soviet Union  (197)

**popular front policy**  practice adopted by the Comintern in 1934 of joining with Socialist and Radical parties to oppose fascism  (164)

**Presidium**  highest policy-making body in the government of the Soviet Union  (197)

**proletariat**   industrial workers who work for wages (112)

**protectorate**   nation, state, or people that depend on a stronger country for defense and foreign affairs (119)

**provisional government**   temporary administration of a country or area (138)

**purge**   persecution and execution of leading Communists by Stalin in 1935–1936 to eliminate all opposition to Stalinist rule (151)

**radical**   person who demands revolutionary changes in government (99)

**reparations**   payment required from a defeated nation for damages inflicted during a war (146)

**republicanism**   belief in representation by elected officials (86)

**romanticism**   artistic movement stressing rebellion against social conventions (104)

**rota**   seniority system of military rule designed to strengthen the Kievan federation (39)

**Russian Orthodox Church**   state church of Czarist Russia; its power was drastically reduced by the Communist Party (22)

**Russification**   policy of the czars and, later, Stalin to impose on the ethnic groups within Russia the language and culture of the Great Russians (26)

**satellites**   Eastern European countries subordinate to the Soviet Union in matters of national policy (181)

**scorched-earth policy**   military tactic of burning one's own food and supplies and destroying livestock so that invaders cannot use them (87)

**serf**   peasant who worked under slavelike conditions for a landowner (75)

**service nobility**   those who obtained membership in the nobility in return for service to the state (56)

**socialism**   political and economic system under which the government owns and controls the means of production and operates them for the welfare of its citizens (109)

**socialist realism**   Marxist doctrine of promoting development of social consciousness by ensuring that art, literature, and music glorify the state and promote its interests (232)

**soviet**   in the USSR, one of the legislative assemblies that exist at the local, regional, and national levels (138)

**sphere of influence**   region in which another nation claims the right to exercise economic and political control (166)

**status**   position of a person within a social system (73)

**steppe**  fertile area  (10)

**subsidy**  grant or gift of money by the government for financial aid  (245)

**strategic location**  site of a nation or area having political, geographic, or economic importance  (43)

**subsistence**  maintenance by minimum standards of economic survival or physical existence  (115)

**superpower**  term often used since the 1950's in reference to the United States and to the Soviet Union  (170)

**surplus**  amount in excess of what is needed  (115)

**taiga**  forest land  (10)

**technocrat**  technician trained specifically for government service; a scientist or engineer making policy in areas that appear too difficult for the ordinary person to judge  (209)

**Third World**  developing nations, usually nonaligned with either the United States or the Soviet Union  (218)

**totalitarianism**  form of government in which one person or party exercises complete control over all aspects of life and excludes all opposition to its policies  (134)

**tribute**  payment by a conquered region to a conqueror in exchange for protection or peace  (37)

**tundra**  treeless region  (10)

**zemsky sobor**  council of nobles set up by Ivan II to advise the czar  (59)

**zemstvo**  local self-governing bodies set up by Alexander II  (99)

# ACKNOWLEDGMENTS

## Text Credits

George Kennan, *Siberia and the Exile System,* 2 vols. (New York: Century, 1891), Vol. 2, p. 365. Samuel H. Cross and Olgord P. Sherbowitz-Wetzer, trans. and eds., *The Russian Primary Chronicle: Laurentian Text* (Cambridge, Mass.: Medieval Academy of America, 1953), p. 59. Manuel Komroff, editor, *Contemporaries of Marco Polo* (New York: Boni and Liveright, 1928), p. 22. From *Russia: A History* by Sidney Harcave, p.50. Copyright © 1964 by J.B. Lippincott. Copyright © 1987 by Sidney Harcave. Reprinted by permission of Sidney Harcave. From *Russia: A History* by Sidney Harcave, p. 232. Copyright © 1964 by J.B. Lippincott. Copyright © 1987 by Sidney Harcave. Reprinted by permission of Sidney Harcave. Alexander N. Radishchev (Leo Wiener, translator), *A Journey from St. Petersburg to Moscow* (Cambridge: Harvard University Press, 1958), pp.139-149, passim. Bertram D. Wolfe, *Three Who Made a Revolution* (New York: Dell Publishing Company, 1964), pp. 322–323. Quoted in N. N. Sukhanov,Joel Carmichael, trans., *The Russian Revolution, 1917: Eyewitness Account,* 2 vols. Copyright © 1955 by Joel Carmichael, Vol. 2, p. 623. Reprinted by permission of Joel Carmichael. Louis Fischer, *The Life of Lenin* (New York: Harper and Row, 1965), p. 674.

## Art Credits

Book designed by George McLean.
Cover concept and design by Hannus Design Associates.
Cover photograph: Grant V. Faint/The Image Bank.
Maps: Precision Graphics.
Title Page and Chapter Opener art: Leslie Evans.

**Photographs**  9 Sovfoto; 12 *(top left)* Sovfoto, *(top right)* Wide World Photos, *(right)* Burt Glinn/Magnum, *(bottom)* PIX/Camera Press/TS/RSO; 19 *(top)* PIX/Camera Press/TS/RBO, *(left)* Sovfoto, *(top right)* Harrison Forman, *(bottom)* Sovfoto; 25 *(top left)* United Nations, *(top right)* Wide World Photos, *(bottom)* Sovfoto; 34 Historical Pictures Service, Chicago; 45 *(left)* American Russian Institute, *(right)* PIX/Camera Press/TS/RBO; 46 Sovfoto; 53 Historical Pictures Service, Chicago; 55 *(all)* Sovfoto; 58 Historical Pictures Service, Chicago; 66 The British Museum; 68 *(left)* The Bettmann Archive, *(right)* Sovfoto; 71 *(top left)* Rijksmuseum, Amsterdam, *(top right)* Brown Brothers, *(bottom)* RON/Popperfoto, London; 78 The Granger Collection; 81 Sovfoto; 88 Bibliotèque Nationale, Paris; 100 *(top left)* Erich Lessing/Magnum, *(top right)* Burt Glinn/Magnum, *(bottom)* Sovfoto; 106 *(top left)* The Bettmann Archive, *(top right)* Charles Phelps Cushing/H. Armstrong Roberts, *(bottom left)* The Bettman Archive, *(bottom right)* Sovfoto; 110 *(top)* from an original in the Free Library of Philadelphia, *(center)* Culver Pictures, Inc., *(bottom)* The American Museum of Natural History; 118 Historical Pictures Service, Chicago; 123 Wide World Photos; 125 Sovfoto; 130 *(top)* Charles Phelps Cushing/H. Armstrong Roberts, *(bottom* ENA/Popperfoto, London; 136 Sovfoto; 137 Culver Pictures, Inc; 144,146 Keystone Press Agency; 148, 151 Sovfoto; 155 Culver Pictures, Inc; 159,160 Sovfoto; 166 Wide World Photos; 173 Photoworld/FPG; 176 *(both)* Sovfoto; 178 Charles Phelps Cushing/H. Armstrong Roberts; 186 Richard Q. Yardley, "The Unintentional Cupid" *The Baltimore Sun,* April 7, 1949. Used with permission of Susan Yardley Wheltle. 191 Burt Glinn/Magnum; 201 Keystone Press Agency; 202 Wide World Photos; 204 Keystone Press Agency; 211 Wide World Photos; 213 *(top)* Burt Glinn/ Magnum, *(bottom)* Sovfoto; 219 Keystone Press Agency; 221 Sovfoto; 223 A. Keler/ Sygma; 226, 233, 235 Wide World Photos; 246 Novosti/Sygma; 248 *(top left)* Sovfoto, *(top right, bottom left)* Wide World Photos, *(bottom right)* Frederique Hibon/Sygma; 250 Wide World Photos; 256 *(top)* Patrick Roberts/Sygma, *(bottom left, bottom right)* Wide World Photos; 263 Elisabeth Hedborg/Sygma.

# INDEX

This index includes references not only to the text of the book but also to charts, maps, and pictures. These may be identified as follows: c refers to a chart; m refers to a map; p refers to a picture.

Kazakh, *c*23, 27, *m*152–153. *See also* Great Russians
Kazars, 43
Kennan, George, 8–9
Kennedy, John F., and Berlin blockade, 201–202; and Cuban missile crisis, 202–203
Kerensky, Alexander, 143–144
Khachaturian, Aram I., 236
Khazars, 13, 35, 40, *m*41, 42
Khiva, *m*83, 119
Khrushchev, Nikita, *p*191, *p*204; succeeds Stalin, 190, *p*191; de-Stalinization program of, 192; economic policy of, 192–193; industrial policy of, 192; agricultural policy of, 193; "virgin lands" program, 193; and Communist Party, 194–199; deposed, 205
Kiev, *m*6–7, 36, 38, *m*41, 54, *m*58, *m*152–153; Chernobyl disaster, 262–263, *p*263
Kievan period, *c*35, 38–47, *m*41; and Mongol invasions, 47–52
Kirghiz, *m*83, *m*152–153
Komsomol, 198
Korbit, Olga, 234
Korea, *m*83, 122, 123, *m*152–153, 186; war in, 187–188
Kornilov, Lavr, 143
Kosygin, Aleksei, *p*211; and collective leadership, 209–210; economic policy of, 210–216; foreign policy of, 218
Kremlin, 47, *p*58, *p*66, *p*100
Kremlin Museum, 35
Kulaks, 159–160
Kurile Islands, 5, *m*6–7, 82, *m*83, 178, 180, 186–187

L
Lake Baikal, *m*6–7, 20, *m*83, *m*152–153
Lake Ladoga, *m*6–7, 20, *m*41
Land reform, 128, 139
Languages, 21–29, *c*23, *m*23
Laos, 227
Latvia, *m*58, *m*152–153, 171, *m*179, 181, *m*182, 250; annexed, 5; people of, *c*23, 24
Law on Cooperatives (1987), 245
League of Nations, 165, 177
Leipzig, Battle of, 88
Lena River, *m*6–7, 18, 80, *m*83, *m*152–153
Leningrad, 2, *m*6–7, 17, 18, 38, 69, *m*152–153; climate of, 8; in World War II, 173; siege of, 174. *See also* St. Petersburg
Lenin, 114–116, *p*146; as leader of Bolsheviks, 116, 134, 139–142, 143–148, *p*148; returns to Russia, 140; death of, 148–149, *p*148; eco-

nomic policy of, 156–157; and Comintern, 162–163
Lermontov, Michael, 104
Liaodong, 122
Liberals, 95, 113
Liberman, Yevsei, 210–211
Literature, of Kievan period, 46; in czarist Russia, 101–107, *p*106; contemporary, 232–233, 235–236
Lithuania, *m*58, *m*152–153, 171, *m*179, 181, *m*182, 250; annexed, 5; people of, *c*23, 24
Louis XVI (king of France), 86
Lutheranism, 24, 77
Lvov (prince), 138, 139, 142, 143
Lysenko, Trofim, 261

M
Magyars, 13
Malenkov, Georgy, 190
Manchu Dynasty, 163
Manchuria, 84, 122, 123, 178, 180, 186
Mao Zedong, 164, 165, 187, 203–204, *p*204, 219, 220
Marie Antoinette, 86
Maritime Province, 120
Marshall, George, 184
Marshall Plan, 184–185
Marx, Karl, 94, 114, 115, 140, 154
Mayakovsky, Vladimir, 235
Mensheviks, 116, 135, 146, 142, 143; and First Duma, 127; oppose Lenin, 140
Methodists, 77
Methodius, 44
Metropolitan, The, 54
Metternich, Klemens von, 90–91, 117
Michael (czar), 59, 64–65, 73
Middle East, Soviet influence in, 224–225
MIGs, 230
Mikoyan, 230
Military power, under Brezhnev, 228–231. *See also* Air force; Army; Navy
Military Revolutionary Committee, 143–145
Minority groups, *m*23, 216; and nationalism, 249–251. *See also* Ethnic groups
Moderates, 113
Moldavia, *m*91, *m*152–153, 171
Molotov, Vyacheslav, 190
Mongolia, *m*6–7, 51, *m*83, 123, *m*152–153, 220, 225
Mongols, 13, 14, *m*23, *p*25, *c*35; invasion by, 5, 18, 47–54
Montenegro, 120, 121
Moscow, *m*6–7, 22, *m*23, *m*72, *m*83, *m*88, *m*152–153; Duchy of Muscovy, 2; invasion of by Napoleon, 5;

climate of, 8, 10; subway system, 18, *p*19; named seat of Russian Orthodox Church, *c*35; center of Muscovy, 53–56, *m*58; as third Rome, 54, 56; in World War II, 173

**Mt. Ararat,** 28

**Mousorgski, Modest,** 107

**Murmansk,** 2, *m*6–7, *m*152–153

**Muscovy,** Duchy of, 2; expansion of, 52–59, *m*58

**Music,** in czarist Russia, 101–102, 107–108; contemporary, 236

**Muslims,** 40, *m*41, 51, 77, 98, 216, 227. *See also* Islam

**Mussolini, Benito,** 164

# N

**Nagasaki,** 180

**Napoleon Bonaparte,** 5, 63, 86–91, *m*88, *p*89

**Narodnik movement,** 111, 113

**NATO** (North Atlantic Treaty Organization), 185, 201; and Soviet foreign policy, 224

**Navarino Bay,** 117

**Navy,** 229

**Nazism,** 5, 164, 165–166, 170, 171–173, 175, 177. *See also* Hitler, Adolf

**Nazi–Soviet Non-Aggression Pact,** 165–167, 171

**NEP.** *See* New Economic Policy

**Nerchinsk,** *m*83, *m*152–153; Treaty of, 84

**Neva River,** 20

**New Economic Policy** (NEP), 156–157, 159, 210–211

**Nicholas I,** 95–97, 98, 104; foreign policy of, 116; and Russo–Turkish War, 117–118, *p*118; and Crimean War, 118–119

**Nicholas II,** 99, 101, 108, 135, 137–138, *p*137, 139–140; foreign policy of, 116; and October Manifesto, 126–127; and First Duma, 127; and Rasputin, 129

**Nikon, Patriarch,** 67

**Nixon, Richard M.,** 220–221, *p*221

**Nomadic people,** 34, 35–36

**North Africa,** 175

**North America,** Russian expansion into, 82

**North Korea,** 225. *See also* Korea; South Korea

**North Vietnam,** 221, 227. *See also* South Vietnam; Vietnam

**Novgorod,** *c*35, 36, 38, *m*41, 49, 50, *m*58, *m*72

**Nuclear weapons,** 180, 184, 202–203, 220, 230–231, 254–255, 262

**Nuclear power,** 262–263, *p*263

# O

**Ob River,** *m*6–7, 18, *m*83, *m*152–153

**October Manifesto,** 126–127

**Octobrists,** 198

**Odessa,** 2, *m*6–7, *m*152–153

**Okhotsk,** *m*6–7, 81, *m*83, *m*152–153

**Old Believers,** 67, 76, 77, 79

**Olympics** (1980), 221

**Oral traditions,** 37

**Orel,** 80, *m*152–153

**Ottoman Empire,** 13, 28, *m*58, 70, *m*72, *m*88, *m*91, 117–119

# P

**Pacific Ocean,** 2, 81

**Pakistan,** *m*6–7, 225–226

**Palace Guard,** 69

**Paris, Treaty of** (1856), 119

**Pasternak, Boris,** 233, 235, 249

**Paul I** (czar), 86, 95, 102

**Peaceful coexistence,** 218

**Peasants,** in Kievan period, 39–40; and serfdom, 63, 75, *p*78, 109, *p*110, 111; freedom of migration abolished, 75, 111; revolts by, 78–79; and land reform, 128; as landowners, 139, 141; and NEP, 156

**Pechenegs,** *m*41, 42

**"People's Will,"** 99

*Perestroika,* 244–247

**Permafrost,** 11

**Persia,** *m*82

**Pescadores,** 122

**Peterhof,** *p*71

**Peter III,** 69–70

**Peter the Great,** 66, 68–69, *p*68, *p*71, *m*72, 74–75, 109; revision of calendar, 141

**Petrograd,** *p*155; revolts in, 136–138, 143, *p*144; food shortages, *p*136. *See also* St. Petersburg

**Philaret** (Feodor Romanov), 64

**Pioneers,** 198

**Plekhanov, George,** 114, 116

**Podgorn, Nikolai,** *p*211

**Poland,** *m*6–7, *m*58, *m*91, *m*179, *m*182; annexed, 5, 8; Slavs of, 22; Alexis' war with, 66; Partitions of, 70, *m*72; as part of Russia, 87, 89–90; revolt of 1863, 99; divided between Russia and Germany (1939), 166–167; after World War II, 178, 181; Solidarity in, 223, *p*223; strikes by workers, 257

**Politburo,** 197–198, c197

**Political parties,** 113–116. *See also* Name of particular party

**Pollution,** 263–264

**Polovtsy people,** *m*41, 42

**Popular front policy,** 164–165